RIDERS TOWARDS THE DAWN

ALBERT H. FRIEDLANDER

# RIDERS TOWARDS THE DAWN

From Holocaust to Hope

CONTINUUM · NEW YORK

1994

The Continuum Publishing Company
370 Lexington Avenue, New York, NY 10017

Printed in Great Britain

*Library of Congress Cataloging-in-Publication Data*

Friedlander, Albert H.
    Riders towards the dawn : from Holocaust to hope / Albert
Friedlander.
    p cm.
    Includes bibliographical references and index.
    ISBN 0-8264-0635-1
    1. Holocaust, Jewish (1939 - 1945) – Influence. 2. Holocaust (Jewish
theology) 3. Holocaust (Christian Theology) I. Title.
    D804.3.F74 1994
    940.53' 18 – dc20                                              93-29851
                                                                        CIP

In loving memory
of my twin brother
CHARLES H. FRIEDLANDER
(1927–1992)

And with hope for the future
to our daughters
NOAM, ARIEL and MICHAL FRIEDLANDER

# CONTENTS

# ACKNOWLEDGEMENTS

The world of scholarly discourse is vast and stretches across the globe; and I have been influenced and helped by so many friends and colleagues that it is impossible to present a list which would exclude more than it could ever include. I would have to begin with Leo Baeck and conclude with Elie Wiesel and, between them, the remaining letters of the alphabet would each yield scores of names. I must, however, mention my editors Robin Baird-Smith and Sarah Baird-Smith without whose encouragement, ruthless cutting of the manuscript, enthusiasm and kindness this book would not have seen the light of day. And I must thank my wife and partner Evelyn, 'a woman of valour' who supports me in everything I do and whose own work with The Hidden Legacy Foundation is a constant inspiration to her sometimes lazy husband. Finally, the Westminster Synagogue and the Leo Baeck College have always shared in my search and have given me support and forbearance throughout the work which unites us and is part of the tradition which we convey to the future.

AHF, June 1993

# INTRODUCTION

O
N 3 August 1914, Lord Grey of Fallodon wrote: 'The lamps are going out all over Europe; we shall not see them again in our lifetime'. Perhaps we should have said: '. . . in our century'. There have been fitful illuminations, off and on, between the two world wars. Once in a while, we have thought that the age of brutality which started in the trenches of that first world war was drawing to a close. And then, in the Balkans, in the Far East, or even in the city streets, explosions take place which leave the world darker than before. Trying our best to reach the twenty-first century, we wonder how much of the human endeavour can be saved from destruction, when even the planet on which we live is damaged by the rapacity of humankind. Is there a way into the future?

This book cannot begin to chart such a course. At first, I thought that we might be able to celebrate the return of faith, to look to the traditional enthusiasm which is awakening in the Western world and its religions. Yet most of this re-awakening, in Judaism, Christianity, and Islam, is the stirring of a fundamentalism which wants to escape from the past and from the present, into a closed citadel of dogma and ritual where the bruised ego of the believer might be healed. It is a formula which has had some success in the past: the Church in its ivory tower, and Judaism in its ghetto, have been able to survive the massive disturbances of the past, have come out from the walls and given assent to the new world for which they have been preserved. Yet I cannot believe that this formula will work today – the realities of our time challenge this type of survival.

First of all, we have not begun to deal with the problems of the past. The Holocaust can never be fully understood; but we must open ourselves to the questions it asks of us. And religion cannot be the same after Auschwitz. This does not mean that we must have an 'Auschwitz theology'.

I want to use the word as little as possible in this exploration of post-Holocaust thinking, even though I explore the thinking of many theologians. But our world is also in a post-religious time; and many of the answers we seek are found outside religion. Each age, we are told, develops its own paradigms: ways of thought which draw from current philosophy, language, experiences, and even the patterns of church, mosque and synagogue. Nevertheless, past insights cannot be excluded from contemporary thought. Yehuda Halevi, St Francis of Assisi, or Al Halladsch share experiences of the human soul with us which are timeless. But then – are these to be our teachers after Auschwitz? And are we only to turn to the religious establishment in a time when we know that religion has failed in countless ways? Who else should instruct us?

Today, people flee across a darkened landscape and have no time to give or to receive instruction. Nevertheless, one may begin to discern a group that I have called the *Riders Towards the Dawn*: those who come out of darkness and have not forgotten it, but who also know that dawn lies ahead, and that they must journey towards it.

I am interested in these individuals, far more than in the finished products of religion handed out in the tracts of fanatical believers. Of course there will be religious women and men to help us in our quest; but there will be others, non-religious, as well. At one time, I divided them into 'hares and tortoises'. The hares streak along at blinding speed, in new directions, and we tend to lose them, although they are going the right way. The tortoise, like the turtle, carries its carapace along with it. It has its own home, its tradition, to support it or at least to protect it. Sometimes it is a traditional faith, sometimes a convoluted philosophy. Many cannot get under the shell. Some of us can accept a particular philosophy, a system, a pattern of religious dogma and action, which either solves the problems of the past for us or at least permits us to say: 'this is all too difficult for me. My teacher will solve everything; all I have to do is to believe in my teacher'.

I report on my own journey as one who has found a teacher, or rather, many teachers. They come out of many disciplines. There is my intellectual mentor and friend, George Steiner. There is my rabbi, Leo Baeck. My *rebbe*, Elie Wiesel. And then there are many colleagues with whom I journeyed for a while along this road, ranging from Eugene Borowitz and Stephen Schwarzschild to the doubters and sceptics who continue to instruct me. I am a continuing disappointment to them in that I do not choose one of them, slip on the shell of his or her system, and conclude that I have found my haven. I find I cannot do it, or even recommend it.

I hope many will join this group of *Dawn-Riders*, because I feel they are travelling in the right direction. They began in the past, did not abandon it, but have moved forward into new life. In a very real way, they have addressed themselves to the problems of philosophic anthropology as set by Kant: What can I know? What shall I do? To what can my hope aspire? What is the human being? The first question is answered by metaphysics, the second by ethics, the third by religion, and the fourth by anthropology. But the Dawn-Riders are not strict followers of philosophic injunctions. Most of them deal with these questions in their own way. They can turn to poetry. A scientist like Primo Levi is also a poet. And it is not surprising that a historian, Eugen Taeubler, turns to poetry in order to move across the narrow borders of his discipline.

In some ways, this is what this book wants to do, as well. I want to transcend boundaries and preserve something of the unbalanced, inchoate mass of reality. It is not good to organize our perceptions into an orderly procession of word-pictures which can be substituted for reality. If we can accept the shock of recognition as we listen to Elie Wiesel or Piotr Rawicz, or catch one stanza of a Paul Celan poem, we will have achieved a great deal. Nevertheless, there is at least some organization in the chapters that follow. An introductory meditation begins with the Holocaust and the maimed reality which was left in its shadows. Then, at a way-station of the road, at a Passover meal, we sit down with some of those who escaped from the darkness, even if only temporarily. They ask questions of one another, and begin to explore the nature of evil, to which I respond within my limitations.

Unavoidably, we turn to the responses to the darkness which rise out of religion in our time. Jewish traditionalists of great profundity and compassion are presented. Progressive Jewish thinkers give their own approach to the challenges of life after the Holocaust – and some are surprisingly traditional. The Christian Riders Towards the Dawn follow, with particular attention to Dietrich Bonhoeffer and Martin Niemoeller who represented the best of German Christianity in an evil time. I have spent more time with Bonhoeffer and his sometimes difficult doctrine – perhaps because he did die in one of the camps. Pastor Niemoeller's life is also inspiring, but his doctrine is less difficult to expound. He was a traditional Christian, and it is important to see how this could lead to a first half-century of service to country and opposition to Hitler – and to a second half-century (almost) of service to his reborn country, where he got into trouble with its leaders by fighting rearmament.

And then, in order to provide a background to the new paradigms of contemporary thought, we turn to the countries themselves: the United

States, France and Great Britain, Italy, Germany, and Israel. Somewhere in there is another country – the land of the poets. Here we must not be lulled into a sense of security. This land was safest, since it could not undergo the variety of changes which have turned Europe upside down. That, of course, is one of the most frightening aspects of living after the Holocaust; and suddenly, we see its seeds sprout again, a harvest of dragon's teeth. Violent nationalism returns, and with it the need to attack neighbours with whom one has lived in amity.

The murders of our time were born in the Holocaust, when human beings were expendable. But viewing humans as expendable preceded Auschwitz; the land enclosure laws of an earlier time, the use of famine in Ireland, the discovery that economic problems are solved if you value land or products more than the human being, all of these preceded Auschwitz but became part of it.

Towards the end of our journey, we meet again to discuss the various issues that may have become clearer with our study: can Jews and Christians and Muslims pray together? Does the concept of a suffering God bring us closer to God, or further away? But this already brings into the heart of the matter, into our opening meditation and into our journeys with the Dawn-Riders. At the end, we can meet again. There is much to do before the dawn rises and we come to the end of the road. But, as always, the journey matters even more than the destination.

PART 1

# [ 1 ]

# JOURNEY INTO DARKNESS

Some will say the world will end by fire,
Some say by ice.
I hold with those who favour fire –
But ice is also nice
And would suffice

Robert Frost

THE destruction of the world is always imminent, and awareness of personal and communal death lies at the edge of every human experience. Protective devices exist in the minds of the individual and for the community: no one wants to get close to the edge and look death in the face.

Can we trust the politicians to keep us alive? Can we be confident that scientists, working for the sake of 'pure science', will stop at the brink of an enterprise of research where the results may be suborned for the destruction of an enemy – biological warfare? Looking at human beings in our time, in the age after the Holocaust, is there a way which leads from darkness towards light, from despair to hope, from the images of destruction to the time of rebuilding?

The Jewish experience contains the contention that in every age and area of human experience there are those Riders Towards the Dawn who do not surrender to the darkness of the night, but who continue their journey towards the East in the firm expectation that the light will come again. 'Watchmen, what of the night?' Night comes, and also the day! They are the prophets and the rabbis, the poets and the psychiatrists, the independent thinkers, who can point the way for us. This contention too, is based on structure of faith, built upon Biblical texts in which so many encounters of humanity fighting darkness are recorded, from the first page in Genesis where the formless and void, the 'nothingness' confronting Creation was overcome. Humanity was realistic about its chances of survival in the Biblical world. The philosopher Kohelet (Ecclesiastes) recorded this clearly:

17

*Dor holech, v'dor ba* ... one generation goes, another generation comes, but the earth abides forever ...

or even the reverse, as Leo Baeck once reinterpreted the text: 'One world goes, another world comes, but the generations – humanity – abide forever'. *Adam* and *Adamah*, humanity and the earth are joined together. Their lives are interdependent, and God's promise not to destroy the world by water (an early memory of the Ice Age? the 'heavy-water' of atomic research?) is a rainbow of faith standing as a bridge between the threatened world and its Creator. Again, in our time, the statement has been reversed: humankind destroys and contaminates the water, and thus creates another possibility of destroying the world.

How will the world end this time? Two professors of Jewish thought at Columbia University and at the Jewish Theological Seminary, Jacob Taubes and Joshuah Heschel, were walking together, when Taubes expressed his deep fears about the future to Heschel. Heschel tried to reassure him: 'Remember the many prophecies of the past – the many times in which the destruction of the world was forecast?' They walked on quietly for a while. Then, Taubes said: 'But you know – every time the destruction was forecast – it came true'.

The Holocaust came true in our time; and the next three generations have been maimed by it. It was a unique fire which consumed the landscape of Europe. Faith and reason were maimed within the Jewish and Christian houses of worship. Apathy overtook those of other faiths, the onlookers, and the conscience of the world was destroyed. The arguments of Buddhist philosophy, the stoicism of the Far East where individual life is as a drop flung up by the waves of the ocean, returning to the whole, cannot be submitted as a proof that consciences differ between civilizations. Hiroshima and Nagasaki have their own complexities, but they too make moral demands upon the perpetrators and victims which unite humanity in its sufferings and demand responses which cannot separate themselves from the evils of the twentieth century. Every minority has to be dealt with in terms of a new understanding of the responsibility we have towards our neighbour. When we discover the rationalizations within ourselves we realize how much the Holocaust has maimed our consciences, how much we have become the children of an age of brutality.

Jews – and the world – have to move out of the shadow of the Holocaust. Self-centred, we can make Auschwitz an unending catastrophe which blinds us to the new holocausts of our time. But our emphasis upon the Holocaust is not a plea for sympathy, a demand that the world mourn for us. What we want the world to remember is the evil that caused the deaths and which is still endemic, that the world was destroyed and that it can be destroyed again.

Jews live with the awareness of that destruction, but they know that they are not unique in possessing such knowledge. Noah represented all of humanity confronting the destruction of the world. Job witnessed the destruction of the good person not as a Jew, but as the representative of every just person who endures unmerited suffering. Written into our own history, we encounter the times of destruction and of survival which are more than private celebrations of the human spirit. For the Jews, destruction was announced, and destruction came: Jeremiah saw the approaching Babylonians, and the destruction of Jerusalem in 586 BC; and Ezekiel saw Israel reborn in the Valley of Dry Bones. Rabbi Jochanan ben Zakkai saw the Romans burning Jerusalem and the Temple in 70 CE, and hoped for the Messiah. And long before Yehuda Halevi had built houses of faith which would secure Jewish life, the communities themselves went up in flames. In every generation living in darkness, there were those Riders moving towards the dawn. Each one followed a road which was obscured for those who only saw the night and the fire. There were those who moved along a special path and left a message for the next generation. But in that generation, the time after the Holocaust, entering the twenty-first century, it is no longer possible to live in the ice-age of faith, paralysed by doubts and fears, unable to move beyond the trauma of a suppressed past. Christians as well must undertake this, for sometimes they substitute apathy for painful awareness. Much can be subsumed by faith, which is so highly sensitive to the truths of its mythology that it can move away from the keen razor-edge of the connections between the events of history.

But the messengers who come out of the darkness are their own message when they are silent. They are Christian as well as Jewish, victims, observers, historians. We listen to them, and their answers are not always our answers. Twentieth-century humanity cannot be healed fully; we remain flawed and maimed as we enter the new century. But they do not bring instant healing. Our own mythologies help us to understand something of our own nature; something of the nature of *tikkun*, of rebuilding the world, which is within human capacity while dawn still succeeds the night.

Israel has to remain as a special challenge and problem to Jews as well as non-Jews. The problem of right and wrong, of survival and annihilation take on a greater intensity there. Israel, it must be remembered, is sacred soil: for Jews, Christians, Muslims and the Bahai. The shaken identity of the Jew, the individual and society there cannot be healed until there is a return to the Torah and its principles, and a life lived by all in accordance with the ancient vision and its development through the centuries. The vision can be respected, but the progressive Jew and the secularist are just as much part of the people of Israel as the Jew living in the fastness of Mea Sh'arim. Sometimes the new walls surrounding the religious Jew become barriers which not only exclude other Jews but also the Messiah and the age of redemption.

The curiosity of the fractured identity lives in religious Jews as much as the secularist. And there are times when we catch a vision of the Jew at his best in his or her secularity. The border-areas of Jewish life are often the most exciting and hopeful lands. The secularity and the ethical strains which are woven into a Jewish communal life, often outside the synagogue, can be seen as the source for a contemporary view of life which can challenge evil through the structure of law or by religious faith.

We can begin to move towards a concept of humanity which includes evil as a component part of our make-up; which sees the glory of human existence in winning partial victories against darkness; and which celebrates the hope that even a journey moving into darkness has dimensions of hope within itself.

# 2

# THE NIGHT

I N the spring-time of the year, during the Passover season, Jews open their homes to family and friends for their Passover Seder. One year, on the second night of Passover, a number of friends came to us from different lands and areas of concern: a sub-editor of *The Times*; writers who had recorded their experience of the Holocaust in novels, plays, and radio scripts; and friends out of the worlds of music and religion. The Passover Seder is a socio-drama and psycho-drama through which we come to experience the events of our history which took place over three thousand years ago. These come to be seen as our own experience: '*b'chol dor va-dor* . . . in every generation we are obliged to see ourselves as having been personally redeemed from Egypt . . . to say to our children: this is what God did for *me* when I came out of Egypt . . .' Each year we recognize ourselves in the past.

One of our guests was Jakov Lind, whose *Soul of wood* is one of the most profound delineations of the evil done in the time of the Nazis. Jakov entered totally into the Seder, reading parts of the Haggadah, the text used at the Seder table, as did the others with us on that evening. Now, according to the rabbis, one should prolong the observance of the Seder as much as possible, finding new answers, exploring every text. According to the tradition, one group of rabbis at Benai Brak became so absorbed with the text that their students had to come to them in the morning to remind them that it was time to recite the morning prayers. At one point, we became very much like them. We had come to that part of the text which deals with the four children who ask the key questions of the ceremony: the wise one, the wicked one, the simple one, and the one who does not know what to ask. Tradition, of course, extols the wise one who is generally featured in the illustrations of the Haggadah as a rabbi. He wants to know everything!

And he is lauded for this. Yet on that night Jakov Lind demanded the role of the wicked one who asks cynically: 'Why do you observe these rituals?' and who thus excludes himself from the community of Israel. 'The wicked one,' said Jakov Lind, 'is the true representative of the Jew of today. He is the most profound person there, and I identify myself with him!' Others at the table that night agreed with him – and a long argument ensued, just as in the days of Benai Brak.

In effect, we were discussing the Holocaust. The question was of survival at an evil time, when the Jews were persecuted and the enemy tried to destroy us. There were different approaches.

Jakov Lind is a great bear of a man with a joyous zest for life and an unquenchable sense of humour. When it came to the confrontation with absolute evil, these qualities were merged with his courage and strength as an individual. Nevertheless, as he recalled the events of that time for us, he grew sombre and dark. 'You cannot encounter evil without being touched by it,' he told us. When the Nazis had invaded Holland, different responses were available to an embattled Jewish community. Some – the Frank family, for example – went into hiding. Bruno Bettelheim's writings excoriated the Franks for what Bettelheim felt was a defeatist, negative reaction: and Anne, Margot and her mother, and the others in hiding, did die in the concentration camp. Otto Frank survived, and I have talked to him many times in the course of the years. Otto Frank had taught his children – and Anne's diary confirms this – to keep believing in human goodness. They were betrayed by a Dutch thief trying to bargain for himself by offering a Jewish hiding place to the Nazis.

Jakov Lind, in a similar situation, started from the other premise, from the belief that absolute evil was at work. He felt certain that this evil would seek out every hiding place, and Jakov did not trust neighbours who would be living under such tremendous pressure. But then – how to survive? He decided to jump from the frying pan into the fire. *He would volunteer for slave work in Germany!* No one would suspect that as he was working in the heart of the Nazi establishment, as he was travelling up and down the Rhine as a 'stupid Dutchman', that he was a Jew in hiding. And he talked about some of the events of that life at our Seder. He survived; but he was damaged and flawed. Can one live as 'the wicked one' of the Haggadah, denying membership in the Jewish community, on occasion cursing his own people in order to fit into the scene? His writings record the dark passages of his life as he moved through the darkness and returned to the light of day. The 'wickedness' was not in him but in his surroundings. And all of it is mirrored in Jakov Lind's novels and short stories.

Another year, another Seder. And Piotr Rawicz sat at our table and we talked again about the wicked son. Piotr's great book *Blood from the sky* is another one of those letters written out of the Holocaust kingdom. On that journey into the centre of hell, Piotr once found himself in a Ukrainian prison, where he tried to pass himself off as a native; this was not easy for a circumcised Jew. How *can* one be something that one is not, and be so convincing that the enemy is deceived?

A quisling Ukrainian was sent into the cell to quiz him: could he prove he was really a Ukrainian? 'Who is our greatest national author?' asked the traitor. Now: if someone would attempt to assume a British identity, in the same situation, one would be tempted to give the normal answer: 'William Shakespeare!' But what would that prove? Rawicz writes:

Humeniuk did not even glance up at Boris. Clenching his teeth, he flung out a question like a sour village schoolteacher, displeased with his pupil's answer even before he hears it: 'Who is the greatest Ukrainian poet?' It was then that the game began to amuse Boris. His brain was working as it hadn't worked for a long time. He thought: If a man wishes to prove he is an Englishman, and a well-educated Englishman, he will prove nothing by answering 'Shakespeare' or 'Byron' to such a question. Of course not, for everyone has heard of Shakespeare and Byron, whether English or not. On the contrary, what he must do is imply, and get his interrogator to acknowledge the implication, that it is unthinkable he should be asked such a question. He must immediately mention some such figure as Eliot or Sitwell. Well now, in asking who is the greatest Ukrainian poet, our friend is expecting me to voice one name and one name only: that of the bard, Tara Shevchenko ... but everybody here – not just the Ukrainians, but the Russians, the Poles, and Jews living in the Ukraine – knows that this singer of the serfs' hardships and of Cossack pride is the glory of your nation. That's stale. If I were to cite Shevchenko, I'd please you, my good Humeniuk, but I wouldn't appeal to your imagination and, most important of all, I wouldn't prove anything to you. I need, or rather *you* need, something quite different.

And Boris named an avant-garde poet who had died not long before, at the age of twenty-nine, an old friend of his, known and loved by perhaps 200 readers.

Humeniuk leapt up in protest: 'What else could I have expected from a gallows-bird like you! You have the nerve to say that Hranich, poor twisted devil, is our greatest poet! That he is a poet at all! Why, you're joking! I knew friend Hranich, he used to make me feel sorry for him. To be frank, I've never understood a word he wrote, and I don't think there is anything to understand . . . His work is a crazy quilt of gibberish just about on the level of a child of four . . .'

'That may be your opinion,' said Boris, 'but it isn't mine. You asked me a question, and I answered it as honestly as I could.'

'Honestly, honestly . . .' Humeniuk was entering more and more fully into his role as a schoolmaster called upon to examine a pupil, who might be brilliant but who was also alarming and eccentric.

'Well, we don't see eye to eye on that score. Not by a long shot. We'd better forget about poets and turn to more down-to-earth matters . . .'

Humeniuk looked up. He shouted hoarsely at the sentries: 'Get this heap of dung out of here, and be quick about it!'

And turning to Lesch: 'That's no Jew. Take my word for it, he couldn't be. He's trash, of course. Politically, I wouldn't trust him an inch. But as for being a Ukrainian – alas, he is . . .'

*Blood from the sky* is one of the most remarkable novels written about the *Shoah*, a report out of the darkness which testifies to the greatness of human beings confronting absolute evil; and Rawicz also records the human flaws. No one escaped out of that hell without being injured. Like Jakov Lind, Piotr could laugh and be a good companion at the Seder table. But he had eaten with the devil – where there was food. And he came to remind us that the 'bad son' cannot be driven away from the Seder table: *kol dichfin, yete v'yechol* – let all who are hungry come and eat with us, says the Haggadah. There were those in the camps who broke and submitted. They either became robots, automatons called *muselmen* who lost the will to live and died first; or compliant slaves who did dreadful things, and also died. At all times, one has to remind oneself that their sins were the sins of their captors and that they, too, deserve compassion on a certain level. More than that they establish a background enabling us to see the nobility of those who kept their integrity. Piotr Rawicz, like Paul Celan, Jean Amery, Primo Levi and others who had been wounded too deeply in the encounter with absolute evil eventually moved out of a life that had become all darkness: suicide seemed the only way out. We are left with the anguish of friends who did too little to prevent that exit, and with the responsibility of the listener who knows that the testimony, at least, must endure and remain alive. Darkened images sit at every Seder table, and the door is not only opened to Elijah to come and to proclaim the coming of the Messiah. The open door reveals evil looming outside, the persecution of the past and of the future.

Elie Wiesel's recreation of the Elijah as one who has escaped from Auschwitz, the events of Passover and of the *Shoah* intermingle. There is always readiness and room to welcome a stranger to the Seder table. In the story, the man who comes interrupts the Seder celebration, tells them that he has escaped from the death camp, warns them, implores them to be aware of the danger – and is rejected. Celebrating the escape from death in an earlier time, confident of the divine protection which is proclaimed in the prayers of Passover, the group assembled greet the warnings with anger. They cannot, will not see that destruction is waiting outside the front door. But the little boy at the Seder knows that this was Elijah entering their home, sitting in Elijah's seat, drinking his wine. Afterwards, he sees the stranger freely getting on one of the freight trains heading East, towards the death camps. And then he knows that this was Elijah; for, three days later, did not this Elijah, as in the Bible, ascend to heaven in a fiery chariot so that all that remained was ashes, and memory, and the knowledge of the fiery chariot?

The many teachings of Wiesel, the greatest of the messengers in our time, must be covered at length to do some justice to a rich and varied presentation which is of the greatest importance because it *does* go from darkness to light and reaches the dawn of our own days – and because, ultimately, it is more than a 'theology of the Holocaust', it is the teaching *beyond* the night. One point must be stressed from the very beginning: his fiction is not fiction; it is reality in its ultimate form. Too much interpretation, too many allegorical discoveries, and attempts to create a Christian or Jewish Holocaust theology have taken place in our time. Elie Wiesel, Nobel Peace Prize laureate and fighter for human rights, must be understood through his actions more than through his fiction. The fiction matters, of course – it is the attempt to say what cannot be said in any other way; but it is not the totality of his message.

Most readers of Elie Wiesel begin with one image which appeared in his first book *Night* and which has haunted the world ever since. It is the image of the tree of death. A child and two adults are hung on gallows in the presence of the assembled concentration camp prisoners. The adults cry out their defiance, but the child remains silent:

'Where is God? Where is he?' someone behind me asked. At a sign of the head of the camp, the three chairs tipped over.

Total silence throughout the camp. On the horizon, the sun was setting ... the two adults were no longer alive ... the third rope was still moving; being so light, the child was still alive ...

25

Behind me I heard the same man asking: 'Where is God now?' And I heard a voice within me answer him: 'Where is He? Here He is. He is hanging here on the gallows . . .'

That night, the soup tasted of corpses.[1]

The philosophers and theologians of our time surround this text. They search each sentence for symbolic meaning, for the theological message, and for all levels of the parable without pausing to consider that it was, first of all, an eye-witness account of an event that had actually taken place. The text is testimony; and there have been times when Wiesel has cried out against the many commentaries which tend to obscure the reality of what had taken place: a child died; and it wanted to live. A million other children also died in the concentration camps – but perhaps one has to concentrate on one of these children in order to understand the enormity of what took place.

Many Christians see this story as an allegory of Golgotha, and one can understand the reasoning and the emotions which bring them to that conclusion: three stark gallows reaching up to the sky, torturers and onlookers, and the middle figure of innocence. Some Christians see it as parody and assert, quite properly, that Christians do not think of the Cross without thinking of the empty tomb. Yet they are reminded, by this story and the structure surrounding it, of human and divine suffering; and a Holocaust story is then linked to all suffering victims of history.

One important Christian scholar whom we must not ignore here is Dorothee Soelle, one of the great radical theologians of our time. Her 'death of God' theology shocked the Christian community, as did her 'Political Night Prayers' in Cologne Cathedral, where she brought radical politics into the house of prayer. However, the clear understanding she brought to Elie Wiesel's work was also pioneer work among the Christians; and her 'interpretation' of the gallows in Wiesel's *Night* is also part of the new dialogue between Christianity and Judaism where each side has made an attempt to study the other tradition. She stresses:

That God in the form of *Shechina* hangs upon the gallows of Auschwitz and waits so that 'the beginning movement towards redemption commences from the direction of the world'. Redemption does not come to man from without or from above. God wants to use man to work upon the completion of his Creation. Precisely for that reason, God also has to suffer with man.[2]

It is important to recognize here that Dorothee Soelle places this basic Jewish teaching into the Christian tradition, acknowledging an inheritance which was still being ignored by many Christians. She related Christ to Auschwitz in her writings, as well as to Vietnam. This was a political theology which could confront the events of the Holocaust and of the new terrible conflicts of her time in a manner calculated to awake the Christian conscience. She taught that humanity had to respond to all suffering. But in her emphasis upon the human response, she also came to a statement regarding God and suffering which rose above the dogmas of different theologies:

> The decisive sentence that God 'hangs here, on the gallows' has two meanings. First, it is a statement about God. God is no hangman – nor an all powerful spectator (which would be the same thing). God is not the powerful tyrant. As between those who suffer and those who cause suffering, between victims and executors, 'God' – whatever humanity makes of this term – is on the side of the suffering. God takes the part of the sacrifice. He is hanged.
>
> Second, it is a statement about the boy. If it is not at the same time a statement about the boy, then the story remains untrue, and we can renounce the first statement . . . we must learn to hear the Roman captain's 'Truly, this was the Son of God' in the sentence 'Here he is – He is hanging here on the gallows.' Everyone, every single one of the six million was God's beloved son, God . . . is not in heaven. He hangs there . . .[3]

We would multiply quotation from Christian scholars here, for many give their own interpretation of this Wiesel text. As in the passage above, they say more about Christianity than about Wiesel; but this, too, is important. Wiesel has created a breakthrough in Christian thinking, and precisely those Christian scholars most concerned with the dialogue between Jews and Christians (Eckhardt and Lyttel) have built on Wiesel's writings to the point where we say that the novels and public statements of Wiesel are the bridge between Jews and Christians concerned with the Holocaust and its aftermath. And, as in the case of Dorothee Soelle, this stance tends to make them outsiders within the community of Christian academics and clergy. They are the Christian conscience responding to the voice of the prophet – and they admit more guilt than the average Christian is prepared to accept. Wiesel does not speak as a theologian. He is a witness, someone who reports back to the world what happened in that other dark world we are not prepared to enter. But we must not ignore the impact he has had upon the thinking, honest searchers after truth within the Christian tradition. In the end, Wiesel received the Nobel Peace Prize (1986) because he went beyond the boundaries of Jewish life and thought and challenged the cruelties and evil which took place *after* Auschwitz and which made him cry out against the murderers in Bosnia and Serbia, whom he wants to see tried as war criminals by a world which seems to be forgetting the lessons from the Nazi time.

This does not mean that we may ignore the Biblical dimensions in the work of Elie Wiesel. His experiences are not only those of the Holocaust kingdom. As a child in the *Yeshiva*, instructed in Jewish lore, he came very close to the Biblical roots of Jewish life, and many of his latest books deal with the figures of the Bible. Quite simply, Wiesel speaks to us as a Jew; he is not an objective scholar looking at Hasidic life or at the nature of ancient prophecy. He is a firmly believing Jew.

When we have walked this far with Elie Wiesel, exploring both the Biblical dimensions, Talmudic thought, the Hasidic community, and his commitment to social justice in the world, we can accept that he will accompany us, often visible, through our other explorations. More than anyone else, he is the Rider leading us to the dawn of new awareness and of new understanding.

But ultimately, we also have to learn that we have a lonely journey to make where we make our own decisions and tremble when the darkness does not open up before us. Then, we must simply continue upon the way and hope.

The messages which came to us out of the innermost circle of hell were unequivocal and short: absolute evil does exist in our world and in our time. It did not end in the death camps, and even those who carried the word were maimed in ways which came to personify humanity itself; we cannot encounter such evil without being changed. Some of the messengers, like Elie Wiesel's Elijah figure, only stayed a short time in our midst after they had delivered their teachings, and then turned back into the darkness. All of them, whether they left us or elected to stay, despite their private anguish, in a world which still needed their word, gave far more than that word: they gave themselves to us. In a way, this is the first answer to this first question about evil and corruption:

*Total evil will maim the individual without necessarily destroying the essence of his or her humanity.*

Something strange takes place within our thinking here. When we turn to the theologians, we will hear much about the 'death of God' – a school of theology, an attempt to answer the problem of total evil by destroying humanity's myth concerning God or by denying God reality in the world after the *Shoah* (the two concepts strive towards the same result: an absence of God-thinking in our lives). This answer basically derives its vitality out of a Christian environment where the 'death of God' becomes a necessary part of the belief in Resurrection, atonement, and salvation in a world where evil rules human beings flawed by original sin. The contradiction of life is only resolved in the paradox where God dies to live again. But here, in the report from the poets and writers, something else emerges:

*Humanity died in Auschwitz.*

It is almost a truism to say that it was not God who was silent at Auschwitz, but that man was silent. There was no outcry; only a few scattered voices protested against the kingdom of night. Looking out of the camps, the inmates could only despair. Where the 'righteous of the nations' gave their help, often by sacrificing themselves, they also gave evidence that help was not impossible, that there *could* have been an outpouring of the human spirit which would have negated some of the evil. That there were so few of them does not mean that they can be forgotten or deemed insignificant – but they cannot become an excuse for the guilty onlookers. What our witnesses do convey, of course, and that is far more important, is that there exists a spark within human beings that can evidence itself even in the death camps. To some extent, where the person had not been crushed by the total environment of evil, they found this human spark among the other victims; and one cannot deny this totally to the guards who surrounded them. Evil moves through human beings who are at times imperfect tools even for the devil. The whole structure of the camps was geared to depersonalize the inmates, so that those in charge would no longer think of prisoners as humans. This was the bureaucracy of death. Those who administered its assistants had also been depersonalized.

*Absolute evil exists in the world.*

Our guides into darkness moved from different premises, even if they were united by their common humanity. Elie Wiesel has been seen as a member of the 'death of God' school. Certainly, in the camps and beyond the camps, moving into a world where his testimony was unwanted, Wiesel gives voice to the doubts and challenges against faith which must be part of all life after Auschwitz. Then as now he had to remind the world of the reality of evil, a vision which led him through the award of the Nobel Peace Prize in his fight against evil. It does not mean that an awareness of God did not come to manifest itself in his writings and in his life as Hasidic thought and community life become interwoven into his work and his daily life. In his emphasis upon the reality of evil Wiesel took a necessary stance against those who would relativize it, a lesser evil to match a lesser God.

It is true that evil comes to us through human beings and is weakened by the flaws and virtues of these tools. Nevertheless, one cannot use this truth to place evil into a compartment where the human mind can cope with it adequately. Hannah Arendt was the first to put forward the concept of 'the banality of evil'. It was and is a brilliant insight into the way ordinary people and the bureaucracy managed to become the purveyors of death, to manipulate the machinery of death which has made impersonal killings an accepted part of our civilization. Yet acceptance of the 'banality of evil' becomes a danger to the human spirit as we try to establish a realm where evil is not accepted as a natural concomitant to life. The brilliant rational thinking of Hannah Arendt helps us to recognize evil in the everyday experiences of our life; in the non-thinking and apathy of those who almost unknowingly become tools for evil; almost, it makes us understand the Holocaust. And *that* is the great danger for those of us who do not want to forget what has happened and who see its seeds in the world of today. We cannot relativize evil. We cannot just equate it with the inadequacy and weakness of human beings. We have to see its reality, face it as the *tremendum* which cannot be dismissed. Absolute evil existed, and still exists. We cannot become convinced that we can end it by explaining it.

This is a religious position, of course; and dangers also lurk here. Some religions hypostasize evil into an absolute Force, a Satan standing against God and sharing the rule of the world. In Judaism, Satan was always a small figure in the Bible, a functionary in the divine Court, or the demythologized figure of the serpent in the Garden of Eden. But there is a breadth in the Jewish tradition which accommodates many approaches, and which does not insist upon one solution. Next to Elie Wiesel stands the figure of Primo Levi. A Jewish humanism is here reinforced by a scientific thinking which takes its logic and clarity – and its ability to encounter absolute evil – from the periodic table as much as from the half remembered liturgies and ceremonies of the Jewish past. It was not only the task of a scientist which gave Levi the chance to survive: scientific thinking and the thought of the purity of the elements also supplied inner strength.

In order to survive, one had to bring something into the kingdom of night which did not belong to the night; and, in order to save the world, one had to bring out something which could awaken the frozen souls of the onlookers. We cannot, must not suggest what that special, Promethean fire should be. I stand with deep reverence before the traditionalists whose pure and simple faith sustained them; who died in that faith, and who lived by it. And yet, in my own life as a rabbi, I sometimes feel closer to the open, doubting stance of Primo Levi or Paul Celan than to the narrow perfection of Hasidic faith. The 'Hasidic tales from the Holocaust' frighten me: they are so exclusive, so geared to the salvation of the righteous. The *rebbe* makes his leap of faith across the chasm of death and his salvation is a matter of course. Doubters and unbelievers are left behind. I cannot argue with those who moved from death to life, who are survivors of faith. I respect them. And I know that there must be enclaves of faith, surrounded by the walls of tradition, where those who have seen absolute evil can live in the quiet serenity of the enclosed community of tradition.

But I live in the outside world, where faith and doubt commingle. Those Riders Towards the Dawn who instruct me live in a broken world; and the spark of the divine which they brought with them out of hell, their humanity, is a reassurance even when it challenges my belief – particularly when it challenges my belief. The rationalist and sceptic may well resent this approach, for it deprives the rebel of rebellion. And it is of course too easy for the religionist to avoid problems of faith by positing a world where the unknowing or the doubting are still carried by the arms of the eternal and secure their salvation by God's grace. That is more a Christian than a Jewish approach. Judaism lives in the realm of secularity, in this world; the boundaries are indistinct, weave back and forth. We have no straight path to heaven; nor do we yearn for it; nor do we abandon the world for it. In Buddhist teaching, there is the Bodhisattva who moves through the world, upward and upward, until he comes to the wall of paradise/nirvana – and leaps over it. But there is another type of Bodhisattva who comes to the wall, turns back to suffering humanity, and tries to lead others to that place; he chooses the 'greater vessel' – the Mahayana faith – which accommodates the group rather than the individual. Perhaps this is still more the religious, saintly type – and it worries more rabbis to be seen this way. Rabbis are teachers, and our kinship is with all those who instruct within the community.

I think of Manes Sperber at this point, one of the great teachers and writers of the European tradition – his way led from Zablotov in Galicia through the *Shoah* and into the literary life of Paris. Again he was the secularist, the doubter who instructs out of the humanism he shared with so many of his Jewish contemporaries (he was born in the same year as his friend Arthur Koestler). Like Elie Wiesel, Sperber was befriended by André Malraux who said in his introduction to a Manes Sperber text: 'Truths, passion, and fate whose ragings are to call up are here transformed in the spirit of the author into that which has to take their place: neither scepticism nor faith, but *human experience transformed into lucidity*.'[4]

We see this lucidity in Primo Levi as in Manes Sperber. It is not valid to deny the total believer such clarity of thought: but the doubter who shares our world of half light is more accessible than the believer in the palace of faith. Sperber was very much part of Jewish life: he translated the prophets out of the Hebrew text, and his death cut short his own translation of the Book of Psalms. One of his disciples and friends records a story which Sperber was fond of telling:

Zalman and Scholem are walking together on a Sabbath afternoon. When they are out of reach of anyone who might hear them, Zalman asks: 'In the *shtetl*, people are going around and telling everyone that you have become an unbeliever. Tell me, quite simply: do you still believe in God?' Scholem doesn't answer him. Zalman repeats and repeats the question. Finally, Scholem says: 'Come to me tomorrow, and I'll give you an answer.' The next day, Zalman returns with his question: 'Scholem, do you still believe in God?' And Scholem replies: 'No. I no longer believe in God!' Zalman then says: 'But why couldn't you tell me this yesterday?' 'Are you crazy?' says Scholem. 'How could I say such a word on *Shabbat*?'

There has always been room within Jewish life for the doubter and sceptic, the Socratic gadfly who challenges and strengthens religious thinking confronted by absolute evil. The *apikoros* (from 'Epicurean') had a recognized place in the *shtetl*. Another story, out of the folk tradition:

Moshe comes to the rabbi and reports to him: 'I have become an *apikoros*!' 'Really?' says the rabbi. 'The *Tenach* (Bible) no longer convinces you?' 'Who reads those ancient legends!' responds Moshe. 'But what about the proofs for faith given by Saadia and Maimonides?' asks his teacher. 'Rabbi', says Moshe, 'one doesn't have to bother with such nonsense when one has decided to be an *apikoros*.' 'Moshe, Moshe,' replies the rabbi, 'you don't know enough to be an *apikoros*. You are simply an ignoramus!'

In contrast, Sperber could write: 'I learned to translate the prophets, particularly Isaiah whose message still concerns me, the unbeliever, and

Jeremiah whose suffering with his own people made me discover that love can be an ever-flowing well of misfortune.'[5] Sperber once replied to the question, 'What is truth?' with the answer 'That which does not resemble a lie!' In trying to come to terms with the darkness through which we have travelled, this insight is as important as any teaching of faith.

What happens to us when we have listened to the messengers and heard the tale? Are we the wedding guest of Coleridge's *Ancient Mariner* who continues as 'a sadder and a wiser man'? We have listened. We have shared the anguish. We have come to see what we can know and what we cannot know: we can never enter the innermost circle of hell. There is still the danger that this insight will make us exclude Auschwitz from the present realities of existence. It was the past. It must never happen again. And, therefore, it becomes easier to dismiss it, particularly if we earnestly and ethically concern ourselves with present ills. But Auschwitz continues to live in the world of today, even if that world is not Auschwitz. We live in a world built upon Auschwitz, which cannot be understood without this knowledge. Again, a Hasidic tale (Rabbi Nachman's) illumines this:

> Once, there was a kingdom, high in the mountains, which was not accessible through the blocked-up passes to the outside. Yet there was enough in that land to suffice: a rich harvest, a benign ruler. 'The harvest has gone bad and poisonous. If we eat it, we will become mad! What can we do?' The king pondered the matter, and then replied: 'We have no option. We must eat it, or we will die. But you, our wisest counsellor, must eat less than all of us. You must preserve a spark of sanity so that, regularly, you can pass through our midst, shouting at us, reminding us: "We are mad! We are mad!"'

This is what messengers tell us as we enter a new century. They remind us of evil endemic within us, of evil which is endemic within the society in which we live. We can begin by recognizing our own flaws, by reminding ourselves of the *yetzer ha-ra*, the evil inclination which often breaks out in our thoughts and our actions. We can then turn to our own resources, can try to rediscover our inner strength: they may lie in our faith, or be part of our doubt. We can then turn to our outer resources: the community of faith, of friends who sustain us; or we find strength in the company of the outsiders who walk a more lonely path but move towards the same goal.

It is not enough. Human beings are sustained by the societies in which they live. Despite the criticisms levied against the democratic countries who, in the West, belong more to the 'haves' than to the 'have-nots', we can accept the positive values of these lands and we can recognize that freedom of the individual and concern for the others is part of the tradition in which we live. Religious communities also grow stronger in these lands, even when we recognize that it is often persecution which brings out the best in faith communities. If Jews only persisted within a strong Jewish life because they were persecuted, this would be a denial of the roots of our tradition. Again, it becomes too easy to let others make the choice for us. In the 1930s, Jews coming to Palestine were sometimes asked ironically: 'Do you come out of Germany, or do you come out of conviction?' Yet the refugees who did not come because they were convinced Zionists ultimately contributed as much to the development of Jewish life in that new land. Alongside the ideologues, teachers like Samuel (Akiva) Bergmann, Fritz (Yitchak) Baer, Gerhard (Gershom) Scholem, and the more-than-Zionist Martin Buber deepened the dimensions of Jewish thought as much as the arrivals from Eastern Europe and the United States. Nor can one overlook the dimensions of the land itself. Israel is the land of the Bible, and the past has its impact upon the present. The early pioneer song which runs *'anu banu artza* . . . We've come to the land to redeem it and to be redeemed by it' contains a fundamental truth in which feelings of pantheism are joined by an awareness of teachings grown old in Jerusalem when the world was younger. Somehow, someway, the land will also help make peace between the Israelis and the Palestinians, both children of Abraham who was covenanted to the land. The anguish of a land where siblings hate one another will not be cured in this century; but the land is waiting to bring its slow and caring healing.

Can one say the same about Europe? Amidst the turmoil of fading boundaries, newly awakened and virulent nationalism, and the confrontation of various ideologies, we come to see that the messengers out of the kingdom of darkness give more than advice to the individual. It is an illusion to think that one can create a new society, a new pattern upon the ruins of Europe which will not contain within itself some of the evil of Auschwitz. Just as the deeply pious Carmelite nuns, who wanted to remove the poison from the place that was Auschwitz, tried to establish a house of prayer there, and failed abysmally, so one cannot build a new society upon the ruins of the old. The clearest example for this is the story of the GDR, of East Germany, which becomes a cautionary tale for our times.

The story does not begin with the fall of the Berlin wall although the complications of the new 'united' Germany since then tell their own story. One has to start with the end of the Nazi state, and the establishment of the GDR. It was a genuine attempt to create something new and better – but it did so by attempting to hide the past, by blaming the 'other' Germany for the sins of the Nazi period, and by wiping out the memories of what had been committed in that land, in that place. But Auschwitz thinking still lived in that land. How? Quite simply – and this was deemed to be a positive approach – by removing individual responsibility and placing moral thought and action into the collective state. The Germans had become accustomed to this: it enabled them to survive in some fashion under Nazi dictatorship. Their highest duty was to the state, which would and did make all decisions for them. 'One Volk, one Reich, one Fuehrer!' One must not generalize about a German character which demands order, which wants to submit to authority, which turns over responsibility to its leader. Yet something of this pattern is perceptible in a society which tries to redeem itself by appealing to past tradition or by importing an immediate, new tradition which is to be equated with law. West Germany was so shattered by the victory of the Allies that even the hasty withdrawal of total authority and the handing over of the government to the 'new' Germans, i.e. Adenauer, did not make it retreat to former patterns. They, too, wanted to ignore the past. And so they imported cosmopolitan thinking, Western approaches, and became a free and open society – even if they did take on some of the worst characteristics of a materialistic society. In the GDR, on the other hand, stripped of its economic assets by the Soviets, there was an attempt to blend new masters and an old German tradition.

The new German democratic state was a dictatorship which conceived of itself as benign. Buchenwald and Sachsenhausen continued to be places of 'correction' for the torture and execution of anti-communists, but the state sincerely strove to care for the individuals who had surrendered themselves to their loving parent. Anti-social elements were suppressed, and we can begin to understand why anti-Semitism, suppressed by the state, now springs up again in those areas where no central government exercises an iron rule. But 'Papa State' also rebuilt the old system. Comparing the development of Poland and Germany these days, Andrej Szceypiorski points out:

The old, right, conservative Prussian model re-established itself: the dominance of the man in the life of the family and in society; a strong disciplining of children, forcing obedience on the part of the younger for the older generation. This was a Protestant peasant model, taken from the nineteenth century ... which incorporated within itself the most extreme German right in its Wilhelminian form.[6]

It is odd how often pornography is suppressed by dictator-ruled countries where obscenities are committed against the bodies of dissidents. Perhaps it gives the illusion of being a moral state in a land where so much is suppressed and where the moral decision is taken away from the citizens. The flaws of West Germany are clearly evident in the postwar period. Yet West Germans were given the opportunity to make moral decisions as individuals, while East Germans relied on the state to deal with the past and with the present ethical problems. The unredeemed responsibilities of Auschwitz tainted both lands; but the problems of that unconfronted past are much more present in the Five New Lands of the East, now part of the one Germany – and one must not let the past history of the GDR destroy the slow advances towards the redemption of the West. Whether or not this will come to instruct us is another matter. Yet the fact remains that the new European community will, to some extent at least, be dominated by Germany. And Auschwitz is in Germany, no matter what its geographic location. We do not persecute children for the sins of the parents. We do not talk of guilt here, but of responsibility for history. This is valid for all of Europe, East and West, and to those areas of the Middle East or the Far East affected by the Holocaust.

The teachers to whom I have listened affect me both as an individual and as a member of society. The poison still lives in the world, just as radioactive clouds still move across the face of the earth. The final adviser whom I would draw into this segment of our reflections is therefore Arthur Koestler, another agnostic, who was also one of the great teachers of our time. Koestler doubted the survival of humanity:

[Humanity is doomed to destruction] – that is an undeniable fact for me. Particularly, because nuclear weapons are now part of human existence. This is not true for just the next ten or twenty years or for the next century, but forever. What has been fashioned can no longer be unmade.

It is also true because the human being, *homo sapiens*, never ceased to live out his delusions of killing and destroying – and then there is also the ever clearer contradiction between science, technology and morality.[7]

His fears of a nuclear catastrophe are linked with the 'Holocaust' itself. We cannot live in the time after Auschwitz without thinking of Hiroshima and Nagasaki, though the events are distinct from one another. But Koestler is also important because he had a clear understanding of the way in which the individual surrenders to the state (*Darkness at noon* is one example of his vision). Koestler understood how humans submit themselves to structures which have shaped language into a flag, a vision, to which they can submit themselves without working the problems out for themselves. He saw the danger of language. The fact that religion often fulfils this fatal function is reason enough to listen to Koestler's warnings. His own view of that God who failed (just as the secular vision of communism failed) is touched on in his interview:

> You call me an agnostic – that is not totally incorrect. Let us understand each other properly: I claim it is very difficult to believe in a God who could have prevented Auschwitz and did not do so.
>
> Auschwitz and numberless other horrors. To assume the existence of an omniscient, omnipotent God who works on the basic principle of love contradicts the whole history of humanity. It then does become natural to look for an explanation which could take the place (of the God idea).[8]

Koestler, in fact, posits a higher reality which can be entered through mystic experiences. What he does give us for this world, after the prediction of destruction, is his assertion that, in the end, no prediction is possible, because a new alternative may always arise, no matter what logic has to say. 'A hope may be irrational, illogical, but it is necessary'. If others could give us only a fraction of what he gave to the questing mind in darkness and in need, there would be far more light in the world, even in the world after Auschwitz.

NOTES

1. E. Wiesel, *Night* (London, Fontana Collins), p. 76.
2. D. Soelle, *Lieden* (Kreuz Verlag), p. 179.
3. Ibid., pp. 181–2.
4. H. Sperber, *As a tear in the ocean* (1952).

5. L. Reinish, 'Manes Sperber in Memoriam', *Europaische Ideen*, no. 58 (1984).
6. In 'Bilder und Zeiten', *Faz*, No. 184 (10 August 1991).
7. A. Koestler, *Europaische Ideen*, no. 58 (1984) p. 15.
8. Ibid., p. 16.

PART 2

# [1]

# THE SEARCH FOR THE ANSWERS

## TRADITIONAL JUDAISM AFTER AUSCHWITZ

THERE are not sufficient answers for Auschwitz in traditional Jewish thought for our time. This is a minority opinion: more Jews today adhere to Orthodox Judaism, and the leaders of that community defend the traditional answers strongly. I cannot rid myself of the suspicion that the average Orthodox Jew does not concern himself too much with the issue of the Holocaust – it is seen as a matter for the rabbis to decide. The issue of evil in the world today is not always linked to the past; and when a mother cries out in anguish at the death of her child she does not connect this with the enigma of Auschwitz. She will ask: 'Why?' with great bitterness, and much depends upon her relationship to the rabbi and her faith, and upon the rabbi who has to speak to her need rather than defend dogma. In a way, it is possible to cope with life after Auschwitz by ignoring the *tremendum* of the Holocaust and assimilating to the thinking of the general community, those who simply do not want to face it any more. But the cloud remains; the poison is still in the atmosphere, and we have to turn to the thinkers of our time who can face the past. Yet we must not overlook the tradition, both in terms of what it says now and what it said then. In this chapter, then, we will briefly review five of the outstanding traditionalists, exponents of Jewish law, the Halachah, and then turn back to the time of darkness in order to see what Halachah said then, and whether this answer, debated in Israel as much as in Europe and America, still has a validity which one can respect even when one cannot accept it.

*Yitzchok Hutner*

Rav Hutner was born in Warsaw, in 1907, and studied at the famous seminary of Slobodka, the 'crown' of traditional Jewish learning in Eastern Europe. He was an *illui* – a wunderkind, child prodigy, surrounded by admirers from the time of his early youth. For a while, he had studied in Palestine, in Hebron, where Rav Kook had some influence upon him. He returned to Warsaw, but also studied in Berlin. In 1932 he studied in Jerusalem, and he returned to Europe in 1935, but was able to emigrate to the United States in 1935. There, he became the head of the Rabbi Chaim Berlin Yeshiva, and later created a special school, the Kollel Gur Arye, an 'Advanced Institute' of higher Jewish learning. Combining great Talmudic learning and acuity, filled also with some of the mysticism of the Hasidic movement, he became the teacher to whom many turned to ask the questions after darkness had fallen upon Jewish life. Some of these are relevant for us:

1. Is the concept '*Shoah*/Holocaust' applicable to what tradition called the *Churban*, the destruction of Jewish life during World War II?
2. Should the Holocaust be taught as a special subject, as many schools do or plan to do, or should it be included into the normal curriculum of Jewish history and seen as part of the instruction for that special epoch?
3. If the latter, what then is the connection between the Holocaust and the rest of Jewish history?

These questions were put to Rav Hutner by the directors of *Yeshivot* and of many Jewish schools. He replied by giving a lecture at his *Yeshiva*, attended by leading teachers of the traditional community. What follows is a paraphrase of much of that lecture which is highly representative of what concerned Orthodox scholars, loyal to the traditions, would say.

Rav Hutner saw the need for a clear definition of what he termed 'Holocaust' only for the purpose of presenting the destruction of the Jews, without admitting that this term was a correct one. After all, it came out of secularity; and any approach to Jewish history had to be aware that 'Israel and the Torah are one' – that there is a sacred dimension present in any study of history.

The term *Shoah*, as an alternative to 'Holocaust', was coined by Yad Vashem, the Holocaust Research Institute in Israel, who saw this total destruction as something unique in the world. There is something to this; but, by stressing the quantitative aspects of this destruction which made it unique, they overlooked 'the new, significant, meaningful pattern of Jewish history created here'. When one places this persecution of the Jews into the flow of history, one notes that two new developments come to be expressed here. There was always massive and brutal persecution of the Jews which differed solely in terms of intensity, of different types of brutality. But two new areas have opened up in the persecution of the Holocaust.

The first change relates to modern times when Jews were at least promised equality. During the French Revolution, the Jews were given equality as citizens, but not as Jews. Later, after World War I, at Versailles, the Jews and other minorities were given specific rights which were then taken back. This happened in Russia, too; but what Lenin gave, Stalin took away. In England, the Balfour Declaration of 1917 gave Jews their rights to a homeland in Palestine; but Churchill, in 1922, weakened it considerably. Rav Hutner points out that anti-Semitism is not only a situation of pogroms and violence, but the erosion of civil rights which perverts the structure of law in a society: in the developments within Germany under Hitler, the legal system in fact became a method of genocide. The Jews were fooled into believing they could trust their neighbours who promised so much; these promises were only way-stations on the road towards the Holocaust. At this point, the Jews woke up and realized they could no longer respond to the outside world with trust.

How does the Torah relate to this world? In Torah, God's plan is seen. In Deuteronomy 31, 16–18, God warns Moses that his people will worship the foreign gods around them '. . . and I will conceal My face from them. They will be consumed, much evil and suffering will come to them . . .'

Hutner translates the worship of foreign gods as 'the enticement by the foreign people' to which the *yetzer ha-ra*, the 'evil inclination' within human beings, responds. Hutner goes through a chain of rabbinic arguments to show that it is worse to say 'I have sinned' than to admit guilt. Israel has been 'enticed' by the nations surrounding it, and repentance with a movement towards the Messianic time cannot take place until guilt is admitted. The so-called *baale teshuvah* (repentant returnees to the Jewish tradition), as individuals show that *teshuvah* (repentance) is in the air. David Ben Gurion attempted to call an armistice between the religious and non-religious in Israel. Hutner argued that this stance leads to postponements in time which favour the secularists. The traditionalists work with eschatological, not chronological time! The Jewish people cannot surrender to a secular view of history when one lives within a Torah-view of history.

Hutner also came to believe that where, previously, East and West had separate developments in their treatment of the Jews, this ended when

Amin el-Hosseini, the Grand Mufti of Jerusalem (an Islamic leader), made common cause with Hitler, visiting Nazi leaders who included Eichmann. The Grand Mufti even inspected Auschwitz and Maidanek! This was shortly before the Wannsee Conference which brought the 'Final Solution' into its active phase. The continuous support given to Yasser Arafat at the United Nations was another phase of development. Again secular history does not explain this development in the Torah story of Esau and Jacob. For Hutner, any aspect of the patriarchal story is a prefiguration of what will befall the People Israel. This, of course, is a pattern of thought which is also found in fundamental Christian approaches to the Bible.

How does all this relate to the term *Shoah*? *Shoah*, quite simply, describes a unique catastrophe unrelated to past or future events. It is like an earthquake. *Churban*, on the other hand, the *Churban* of the European Jewish community, is an essential aspect of Jewish history which cannot be denied the meaning it receives from our Torah-view of history. Yet even traditional Jews close their eyes to its meaning, since they share a 'fair weather' approach to Jewish life in which the punishments and hardships foreseen in the text of the Torah are disregarded and discounted. We have to teach them and our children the 'admonitions' as well as the promises. The *Shoah* may point to a new, unique concept but this ignores the ancient wisdom, and empties the term *Churban* of its deeper meaning. In the Torah-view, there is a sequence which runs: *Churban – galut – ge'ula*: destruction – exile – redemption. When we understand this, the questions asked become irrelevant.

The important question here lies in the positing of *tochacha* (admonition) as unrelated to specific sins of Israel, but as a component part of Israel as 'the chosen people' upon whom God places special tasks which involve suffering. The reasons behind this Jewish suffering are only known to God. Any attempt to explain the suffering in terms of secular history tramples upon the memory of the sacred martyrs who have died as members of the Jewish community. And the only way in which one can begin to understand what happened is to turn back to the Torah, which is to be the guide for all of life.

One may want to disagree with Rav Hutner. Yet can we, after the Holocaust, deny the right of any Jew to withdraw to the comfort of an observant, praying, and closed community, from an outer world which has moved from false promises of equality to acts of extermination? This may in some ways be the most understandable approach to life. Nor, when Rav Hutner speaks, is this just a 'withdrawal'. Hutner is one of those moving towards the dawn, the true, final dawn – the Messianic age. Rav Hutner has not abandoned the world of humanity. Rather, he calls the Jewish community back to its task as a priest-people, as the 'Suffering Servant' of so many Biblical passages who must learn to accept their role, their suffering, and their hope for the coming of the Messiah. He rejects the secularist approach to history and to life, and calls his people to return to the ways of the Torah. In the end, this way it extended to all of humanity: the time of the Messiah does not belong to any group exclusively. His religious thinking is part of a closed system which rejects other approaches, but it does not reject humanity.

One can disagree with his interpretation of history, and with his view of the secular and the non-Orthodox Jew who walks upon a different road. Rav Hutner would never agree with Rav Kook, who was prepared to work with Jews who did not share his own approach. And Rav Hutner's rejection of David Ben Gurion involves the making of ultimate demands which can lead to the destruction of Jewish life in a State where there are so many dangers from the outside. This type of insistence upon an absolute tradition will, at the very least, weaken the defences against enemies. (The violent expansionist views of traditionalists who by now link hatred against the Arabs with their demands for all of the occupied territories is a case in point.) Yet one should also compare Rav Hutner with the great Talmudists and Halachists in the death camps who showed how open a traditionalist approach can be when confronting impossible conflicts of religious faith in an untenable situation. At the end of this section, we turn to the 'Halachah of the concentration camps' and a variety of religious approaches in Israel and the Diaspora in which Rav Hutner's views come to be seen again in an often curiously transformed manner. First, though, we can look at another traditionalist: a profoundly observant Jew whose life is established in that secular community. He is a university professor rather than the rabbi and centre of community and we will try to see whether there is the same movement towards eventual redemption after the night, or whether there is a new understanding and at least a parallel road which traditonalism can walk without the separation and the anguish demanded by Rav Hutner.


*Michael Wyschogrod*


Michael Wyschogrod was born in Berlin in 1928, and came to the United States where he became an Orthodox rabbi. He established himself early within academic life. He first taught at the City College of New York (1956–1963) and came to Baruch College, founded by the Orthodox Jewish community in New York for traditional education in 1968. In the course of his work, he also became professor for the Philosophy of Religion at the City University of New York, and wrote a book entitled *Kierkegaard and Heidegger, faith and the Holocaust* and, recently, a work on the theology of Karl Barth. His openness to dialogue can be seen in the teaching assignments he has undertaken in Germany, and his participation in the *Kirchentage* (the bi-annual assemblies of the Protestant Church in Germany). There is a warmness and a liberal spirit in Michael Wyschogrod which permits him to work alongside Reform rabbis and secularists – something which the traditionalist often finds harder to do than to work with Christians, where the boundaries are much more clearly defined. Nevertheless, Professor Wyschogrod is very clear in his own possession of the tradition, and in his rejection of Progressive thinking in almost all areas of Jewish life.

Michael Wyschogrod continues to be a valued and open partner in the dialogue between Jews and Christians and between Jews and Jews because of his position within the community. Unlike Rav Hutner, he is not the representative spokesman of a recognized group. He does not enter into the political arena; unlike Rav Hutner, he does not feel the need to challenge Ben Gurion and the secular Jewish establishment. Professor Wyschogrod is a scholar and a philosopher; but he makes a distinction between faith assertions and the proof procedures of analytical philosophy. He feels secure enough to let his religious statements speak for themselves. He can make his faith statements without analytical verification or the approval of any religious authorities – or rebels. His faith is based upon revelation. His language is that of Jewish thought, and he can understand the Progressives who make different assertions in the same language. Wyschogrod can look upon Progressives with whom he works benignly, perhaps in the hope that they are on the way towards his position, in faith and in ritual, but have 'not yet' arrived there.

In order to understand his approach to the anguish of the Holocaust, it is helpful to see how he defines himself against a similar thinker, Irving 'Yitz' Greenberg, the most imaginative and challenging Orthodox rabbi in his approach to a problem which he does not see solved by standard traditional thinkers like Rav Hutner.

Michael Wyschogrod, in many ways, is much closer to Rav Hutner's arguments, taken as they are out of the Torah tradition. Nevertheless, he goes beyond the closed world which has rejected the thoughts of the outer world. Wyschogrod begins his analysis of Greenberg by acknowledging the basic insight that 'both Judaism and Christianity are religions of salvation'.

In Judaism, this is seen in the Torah structure where God is the creator who has entered history and plans to save Israel and humanity. Judaism's central prayer, the *amida*, concerns itself mainly with the forms that salvation will take. God is the 'shield of Abraham' who 'awakens the dead', 'gives knowledge', 'heals the sick', 'will rebuild Jerusalem', etc. As Greenberg sees this, Judaism gives humanity the happy tidings that they will be saved by God. But what does the Holocaust do to such an assertion? God was silent and did not speak out. Jewish thinkers can respond to this in various ways. For any existential approach to Judaism, where one builds upon historical events, cannot confront the Holocaust without becoming silent (unless it defines itself simply as an abstract philosophy). If the Exodus was a salvation experience, the Holocaust is the experience of destruction.

Another way, generally followed by traditionalists, is that 'nothing happened' – or, at least, no more than what has happened in every century of Jewish existence where catastrophe has come upon Israel which Israel ultimately survived. For that reason, one must continue to believe in God as the giver of salvation. Greenberg, according to Wyschogrod, rejects both approaches, for a belief in the absence of God, a falling into atheism, gives authority to precisely the way of thinking which produced a Hitler. At the same time, how can Greenberg recognize an Orthodox position which relativizes the Holocaust? Any Jewish or Christian thinking which falls into a 'Pollyanna' pattern of God and the happy ending is irrelevant today. And the Holocaust as a punishment of the Jews turns faith into demonism. For Rabbi Greenberg, 'there should be no theological or general statement which could not be believable when confronted with the death of the children who went into the fire'. 'Yitz' Greenberg believes that such a statement can be made, when one turns to dialectic theology. This tension between opposing truths is developed by Rabbi Greenberg in some detail, and we will return to it. Here, we are more concerned with Michael Wyschogrod's reply to this dialectical structure.

He feels that the kind of dialectical thinking demanded by Greenberg can only lead to a self-torture, insanity. Greenberg is not insane: but he does not understand dialectical thinking. Here, Wyschogrod, expert philosopher and theologian, calls upon the Christian thinker Karl Barth in order to challenge the Judaism of Rabbi Greenberg. Barth rejects a dialectic theology which tries to deal with the faith structure of a relationship between God and man where a free act of grace unites the two. This kind of thinking does, of course, fit into the philosophy of Hegel where, in the world of ideas, thesis and antithesis can find a synthesis where the conflict is resolved – until the next move in the dialectic. The anguish of personal existence can only confront this great scheme with Kirkegaard's outcry of 'either/or' where the human being demands the right to make decisions. The dialectics of history can be assigned to forces which can tear us apart, but cannot be a theology for those who refuse to submit, who want to be the captains of their soul. The simple faith of the believer? Unbelief of Rubenstein? Or a new statement within this dialectic which Greenberg would propose?

Irving Greenberg, in Wyschogrod's appraisal, accepts the challenge to faith which will no longer be satisfied by traditional thinking. He compromises by an approach which recognizes doubt but still searches for 'moments of faith' in which one finds salvation and saviour between the burning children and unbelief. We move back and forth, then, between faith and doubt. But, says Wyschogrod, while this can describe our psychological situation, it cannot be the foundation for a faith where one must occupy a theological position. Truth is truth. If you move back and forth between the believer and the unbeliever, you only gain the disadvantages of either position. And faith is faith. Wyschogrod cannot live with the concept of the doubting Jew who is only to be judged by his righteous actions, who moves in and out of phase. The rituals are too important for Wyschogrod: can one keep the dietary laws one day and not the next? Observe one *Shabbat* out of two?

Michael Wyschogrod has to challenge Greenberg, as he has to challenge the Progressive rabbis he encounters in the work he shared with them in Germany. We work together in Germany, and the constant kindness and decency with which he reaches out to me rests in his conviction that I – or for that matter Irving Greenberg – live our lives in accordance with inner principles which are more clearly expressed in our actions than in our theology.

Our love for God was not destroyed by the Holocaust. When we pray the traditional prayers, we express a Jewish response which is stronger than our challenge to it. And Michael Wyschogrod finds belief in God's salvation within the radically different Orthodox rabbi Irving Greenberg as much as in the Reform rabbi who can at times be found in a traditional Jewish service. In a way, he becomes a gentle dictator who will simply ignore the different theological positions and practice in his conviction that we are all part of the 'body of Israel' in which God reveals himself. 'Abraham believed in the Lord, and the Lord accounted it to him as righteousness'. No matter how Irving Greenberg may express the dialectics of his faith and doubt, Wyschogrod is convinced that the 'moment of faith' in a Jew is one which affirms the promises of Torah, the vision of 'God Who Saves'. The repetitions of the liturgy in the Jewish prayerbook through the millennia are stronger than the questions asked in times of suffering. Wyschogrod here refers to a conversation he had with Karl Barth who had said to him that Jews only had the promise; Christians had both the promise and fulfilment. Influenced by the 'money atmosphere of Basel', Wyschogrod pointed out that among humans a promise can always be broken, but that God's promise contained the fulfilment as well. 'His promise is as good as money in the bank! When we Jews have the promise, we have the fulfilment, and if we do not have the fulfilment, we do not have the promise!' Barth, says Wyschogrod, thought about this for a moment, and then said: 'You know, I've never considered it from that side!'

Faith must always be linked to confidence in God. Wyschogrod feels that a rabbi with doubts might not tell a family whose child is suffering from cancer that God watches over that child. He, Wyschogrod, would feel compelled to say this, to bring the good tidings even if this moment of sorrow will not let them hear this immediately. As a working rabbi in a congregation where I encounter similar situations on a regular basis, I cannot accept Wyschogrod (or the traditionalists of all religions who feel that they must testify to God's healing power on such an occasion). It is no more than an extension of their approach to the Holocaust where they would give the same testimony and witness to the whole community and to the world – but I must then posit a difference between their theology and the human situation. I mourn with the grieving parents who have lost their young daughter; and my grief can be part of their comfort. Perhaps we deal with psychology here, but we also address faith in a time of doubt, and one cannot win a theological argument in a house of grief.

Wyschogrod rejects Greenberg's anger, particularly the suggestion that one should spit on God if the millions who died in the Holocaust were punished for their sins. But the punishment for sins is either true or false. In the same way, the belief that God will save the victims of the Holocaust is either true or false. Some truths are uncomfortable and it *is* psychologically unsound to speak them on certain occasions – but that does not make them untrue. Greenberg wants to flee into a dialectic theology which might enable him to blend his belief with his doubt; but Wyschogrod will not permit this to him. He might permit it to Greenberg's inspiration, Elie Wiesel, since Wiesel as a fiction writer is not bound to the rules of theological logic. But Greenberg also makes the claim that there is a sense in which the Holocaust is a revelation. Greenberg knows that this will be resented by Jews and

Christians, and tries to answer them in advance by reminding them that belief in Sinai is the belief in God's revealing Himself to History. History must have meaning, and the Exodus and Sinai cannot be divorced from history – but neither can the Holocaust! Either the Holocaust is a revelation experience – or history has to be surrendered as a place where meaning shows itself.

Wyschogrod suggests this as a meaningless, unnecessary dilemma. There are other ways of understanding history. The Sinai revelation brought a specific message; and the prophets, speaking to God, continue to bring messages from God to the people. No event has a single meaning: there are many interpretations. The Exodus, for example, has been explained by the tradition in ways which we do not centre upon the power of God, but deal with various social and even economic causes of a society inimical to Jewish life. The only way we know that God saved is the revelation – there are no events which are in themselves 'revelation experiences'; revelation only comes to us through the prophetic word and God's address to us. If I miss a plane which is destroyed by a disaster, I might say that God saved me – but the event is not a revelational one. Revelational acts are designated as such by the word of God: Abraham's selection, the Exodus, etc. – but not those acts where God's anger strikes out at us. For that reason, no one should dare declare the Holocaust a revelation – particularly, since acts of revelation are also acts of salvation. They reveal the loving God who saves us, who redeems us (as in choosing Abraham) and who gives us promises for the future. Religious thinking is inductive, but does not draw punishing acts by God into this system. God is always redeemer; His anger is a passing phase. That is why the 9th of Av, when Jews fast as they recall the destruction of Jerusalem, is insignificant when compared to the Passover redemption.

How can the Holocaust be considered a revelation? Does it reveal that God is angry? That he doesn't care for His people any more? That the devil has more power than God? We don't want to hear this. Wyschogrod feels that Greenberg plays a dangerous game with his 'moments of faith'. It does not become a basic principle of his faith, since Greenberg remains a 'Torah-true' Jew. It is merely a protective device – but it makes for a damaged theology. Holocaust as part of Jewish faith? Such a way of thinking lies at the borders of a Judaism and Jewish people whose instinctive reaction to the word 'Hitler' is *yemach sh'mo* – may his name be blotted out. Redemptive relevations are there to be remembered; the Holocaust is there to be forgotten. To have the Holocaust teach us that there are only 'moments of faith' may be Greenberg's teaching of a dialectic theology – but it will not serve us. Greenberg wants the Holocaust to teach us that 'no one should be powerless today' and that 'everyone must have a place to which one can flee'. The Holocaust speaks for the support of the weak and the underprivileged. He thus tries to draw moral lessons out of the Holocaust event. But the Holocaust was total evil, and to draw these lessons from that evil is a suicidal pacifism. Lessons from the Holocaust? More negative than positive lessons come out of that horror. And Wyschogrod wants to rely more upon contemporary forces against evil – the police – rather than create new power structures. What worries Wyschogrod – and shames him – is that the Holocaust has not driven him to insanity. He acknowledges that neither he nor Greenberg are, in fact, insane: and that is as it should be. We will still go to weddings, recite the ancient prayers of joy, see children born and play in the streets of Jerusalem – and it all rises out of our faith in God. God is there. God guards His people, even if this does not appear to be so. That is Wyschogrod's faith: always and at all times – not just in certain 'moments of faith'.

Nevertheless, it appears to me that this faith is also flawed. Wyschogrod's 'Torah-true' faith surrounds him with an environment in which he sustains his beliefs with traditional observances into which faith stances have been built through the millennia. He can therefore view the non-traditionalists with a compassion that still sees a grain of the ancient faith in them and waits for it to come to fruition. When he confronts Rabbi Greenberg, whose traditional observances are accompanied by a radical theology, he can point out flaws within the thinking; but he compares thoughts with ritual acts and concludes that the latter will in time shake off the former flawed thinking. He is, I believe, right in pointing out that the dialectic does not exist between equal polarities of belief and unbelief. That unbelief exists within belief itself, in the questioning attitudes towards God which have been part of Jewish life since Abraham stood before Sodom, since Job confronted God and challenged the standard faith. Wyschogrod insists that the interpretations by tradition are the core of Jewish faith; that tradition (Halachah) is the sole determinant of how to interpret the past. But Progressive Judaism stresses individual autonomy to the point where he will deny it any authority. And when an Orthodox rabbi like Greenberg gives new interpretations and makes them a 'contemporary revelation', Wyschogrod simply denies this.

He is right in rejecting the Holocaust as a source of revelation. He is wrong in assuming that tradition and Halachah is the only way to understand God – particularly in the time after the Holocaust. Wyschogrod himself exercises a considerable amount of personal freedom in his interpretation of the text and in setting standards for life. He challenges Progressive Judaism in his contention that it is too much oriented to the outside, and particularly rejects the Progressive nineteenth-century heritage of Kantian ethics. In *The body of faith: God in the People Israel*, Wyschogrod sees the Jewish people in a manner reminiscent of *Yehuda Halevi* (a people with a specific religious insight, chosen, gifted) whose ethics must be derived out of the tradition and not the outside world. Kantian universal ethics are opposed by the insights given by revelation and placed into the body of Israel itself. In a way, Wyschogrod here resembles the person most unlike him: Leo Baeck, the Progressive, in some aspects neo-Kantian thinker, who saw the People Israel as being a revelation of God. For Wyschogrod, ethics become based in the family, is not autonomous, is based on the human vision of the order to whom it is bound by family obligation. God is personal, precedes being (an interesting challenge to Anselm's ontological proof that the state of being belongs to what is the highest – but that, says Wyschogrod, places 'Being' above God). The Jew is fulfilled in his relationship to the living God and within the Jewish people. Indeed, Wyschogrod says: '. . . if anything, it is the Jewish people that is Judaism.' It is that faith, one could argue, which makes Michael Wyschogrod so irenic a person. In his phenomenology of Jewish life, he accords the Progressives and dissenters enough space to treat them with respect even when he disagrees with them. And yet, after the Holocaust, to cling to the tenets of traditional thought and of Torah to the point where he would argue for the rebuilding of the Temple in Jerusalem, places him upon a pathway to the dawn, the Messianic age, which few can follow. Again, he feels that it is the prophet who must validate the Messiah. But the prophets we need will have to consider the world after the Holocaust with the awareness that we are not just dealing with a past event that has ceased to have influence, a dark star gone nova a long time ago. The black holes in space still baffle physicists and need explanation. And the Holocaust, which is *not* revelation, has torn apart much of the traditional structure of thought which Michael Wyschogrod can affirm for himself – but not for us. Whether or not we return to the ritual observances he demands, he cannot expect us to return to his 'Bible way' of thinking. The Bible, approached through the 'science of Judaism', modern scholarship, can be interpreted in different ways, and it may speak to us about the Holocaust in a way which does not demand the surrender of our rational faculties. Whichever way we turn, it is still a comfort to find independent traditional thinkers like Professor Wyschogrod along the way.

*Immanuel Jakobovits*

Lord Jakobovits, previously the Chief Rabbi of the United Synagogues of Great Britain, can be viewed as a representative of tradition in a way which an independent thinker like Professor Wyschogrod could never achieve. Always, in Jewish life, the authority of the Jewish scholar has been directly related to his knowledge and wisdom. The Chief Rabbi of Great Britain has always had a special role, even though Israel and its various Chief Rabbis would now claim the centre of the stage. In a curious way, the non-Jewish community has given the Chief Rabbi of Great Britain a special role. He is the person consulted by them on the attitudes of the Jewish community, and becomes both ambassador to that world and the spokesperson for Jewish thought. He has far less to say on internal Jewish matters, where the *dayanim* (the Judges of the Rabbinical Courts) have jealously safeguarded their own prerogatives.

Immanuel Jakobovits was born in Germany (Koenigsberg) and came to Great Britain as a refugee. In the course of time, he acquired a great deal of experience: as Chief Rabbi of Ireland (the title is more imposing than the actuality), as the rabbi of an important traditional congregation in New York City (The Fifth Avenue Synagogue) and, finally, as the Chief Rabbi in the British Commonwealth. He also became an expert on 'Judaism and medicine', and was knowledgeable, scholarly, and in some ways, charismatic as the dedicated leader of the traditionalists.

Lord Jakobovits' attitude to the Holocaust may be said to be in the process of development. In some ways, it is harsh – he has not set foot in Germany since he left it. In Israel, he is considered a 'dove' because of his outspoken criticisms of many Israeli government policies. A number of his children have settled in Israel, and he visits often. Yet he speaks his mind in ways that often cause him problems. He is now independent of the religious 'establishment' which dominates Israel.

Some years ago, Rabbi Jakobovits wrote a preface for a book of prayers and meditations – a Holocaust liturgy I had prepared together with Elie Wiesel for *Yom Ha-Shoah* (Holocaust Memorial Day). Much of this preface was really more of a challenge to the book than in support of it.

In it, Lord Jakobovits places the Holocaust firmly into a historical framework where the destruction of the Temple, the *Churban*, is still a part of the liturgy of mourning kept by Jews to this very day. But the sages would not have considered 'Churban Studies' in their academies, would not have centred a curriculum of Jewish studies upon that theme. The Jewish spirit is not secured by the memory of destruction, but by reliving experiences of salvation: 'in every generation one is duty bound to consider oneself as though one has come up out of Egypt!' The Seder is embellished; memorial celebrations of the Holocaust should be kept low, even though Lord Jakobovits believes that the State of Israel would not have emerged if it had not been made possible by 'the desperate pressures and superhuman Jewish energies generated by the Holocaust'. He does not urge us to brood on this theme, and he stresses positive rather than negative factors as the reasons for Jewish survival. He concludes the preface by saying:

> To me, the meaning of being a Jew has not changed with Auschwitz. What has changed is that millions of Jews are now being threatened by self-liquidation even more than by oppression, and it is this threat which the legacy of the Holocaust summons us to counter with unprecedented urgency and vigour.

In the proceedings of a conference on nuclear arms, Lord Jakobovits outlined the position taken by 'Jewish Law'. He did not refer to the Holocaust, preferring a straightforward exposition of the problems of war and peace in the Halachah. He did refer to the historical situation of the destruction of Jerusalem in 70 AD, and praised Rabbi Johanan ben Zakkai's decision to leave the doomed city and surrender to the Romans:

> It is absurd to defend Judaism by risking the liquidation of the last Jew to uphold it . . . It would likewise be utter folly to fight for the preservation of our Western ideals at the expense of the human element able to transmit them to future generations.
>
> The attempt to resolve our problem by direct reference to whatever Jewish sources could be found thus proved inconclusive, if not altogether questionable.[1]

This is the approach with which he has so often challenged the Israeli 'hawks'.

On the issue of the Holocaust, Lord Jakobovits' views have varied very little over the years. His personal anguish at the loss of a large family, his reluctance to visit Germany, and his opposition to Holocaust liturgies have all been recorded. In terms of theology, he has noted that the anguishing problem has not changed from the time of Job or the outcry when a single child is killed by any of the pogroms through history. 'Infinite pain cannot be enlarged by multiplication. This size of suffering can hardly affect its justice or meaning'.[2]

I find the need within myself to take issue here. What Lord Jakobovits says has some justification in the language of theology – but is totally divorced from the reality of life. A million dead children – or even two – are different from the case of one child, since the mourning of their families, as well as the mourning of the world, surround those deaths and extend to an uncountable number of other lives. Jakobovits is at pains to emphasize that he is only speaking *theologically*:

> A single baby's cot-death bereaving young parents may be no less baffling theologically than the deliberate genocide of millions. Indeed, the former, because it is entirely beyond human design and control, may present an even more direct confrontation with divine inscrutability.

Yet if he is right within theology, it only means that theology is not right for a humanity which cannot, in our time, subsume the ultimate or the single tragedy under the answer of divine inscrutability. Perhaps that is why the poets and writers have come to be our guides, enlarging, at the least, the areas where one might find answers. As Lord Jakobovits points out, even the theologians have listened to Elie Wiesel and others who speak about the 'Silence of God . . . as a mystery that will remain seven times sealed for all time to come'. But the theologians come to this statement in order to close the debate and push away the question. Elie Wiesel and the poet-prophets use the same idea in order to bring it out of the closed realm of dogma, into the daily discussion of the problems of existence which follow us on our way outside the academies.

Immanuel Jakobovits is not a university lecturer. He is more rabbi and pastor than he is a theologian. And so he turns away from this often technical discourse of the theologians and asks the question of 'religion' – which is not theology. There, the question becomes 'Where was Man at Auschwitz?' Here, he can confess that the poet-prophets had a sounder reaction in the strength of their expression than the religious leaders, who often under-reacted. Indeed he has indicated that the religious leaders were often silent. But then the Chief Rabbi turns to the 'Torah-true' communities of Eastern Europe; and he finds a remarkable testimony of faith in the lives that were to be terminated by the terror of the Holocaust.

Ninety per cent of the sages, academies, communities, and actual numbers of that heartland of Jewish life were swallowed up by the darkness of the Holocaust. Yet the few who survived, who carried on and rebuilt their religious structures were less concerned with the attempts to create memorials in prayers, institutions, or monuments than those who were far more distant from the tragedy. How can this be?

Some of the responses Jakobovits has cited in answer to this question are listed in the next chapter on rabbinic responses. Yet it adds to our understanding of Immanuel Jakobovits, and to our understanding of the stance of the believing Jew, to refer to the quotes he brings from the 'Brisker Rav' (Rabbi Welvl Soloveitchik), and the 'Hazon Ish' (Rabbi Abraham Yeshayahu Karelitz), who both reject new liturgies or commemoration services.

The 'Brisker Rav' follows the words in an eleventh-century elegy for the victims of the Second Crusade:

> ... *since we may not add an extra fixed season* for the destruction and conflagration ... therefore I will cause my cry of woe to rise *this day* [i.e. *Tisha B'Av*, the day of mourning the *Churban* of the Temple of Jerusalem] ...
>
> Take this to your hearts, and prepare a sad funeral oration; put on mourning and roll in the dust, for their massacre weighs no less than the burning of the House of God ... and since we may not add an extra fixed season for the destruction and conflagration ... therefore will I cause my cry of woe to rise this day and I will wail, howl, and weep in bitterness of soul.

After the war, the 'Hazon Ish' replies to an inquiry:

> The fixing of a permanent fast day is in the category of a rabbinic enactment, and what we have nowadays goes back to the time when prophecy still existed. How, then, dare we, a generation best silent, have the effrontery to contemplate establishing things for future generations? Such a proposal would testify against us as denying all our guilt and lowliness, at a time when we are soiled in our iniquities and transgressions, poor and empty of Torah and naked of good deeds ...

Perhaps, suggests Immanuel Jakobovits, he was afraid that such innovations might be appropriated by secularists. Secularists have taken over the commemoration of the Holocaust! The traditionalists, he feels, were right in standing firm against such prayers, to this day.

Needless to say, the 'Hazon Ish' pains me deeply in assigning guilt to the Jewish community – and, if the profoundly Orthodox do not have special commemorations for the Holocaust, one can applaud the 'secularists' in 'whose doubt is more faith than in all your creeds' (Emerson). It is true that there are historical precedents where, after calamities suffered, the rabbis and their communities either refused to install commemorative rites or abandoned the few that took place (commemorative prayers for the Cossack massacres soon dropped out of the prayer books). Those who strive to establish a special time of commemoration for the victims of the Holocaust argue that this time is different; that the Holocaust is in some ways unique. But this is precisely what traditional Judaism rejects.

Perhaps, in our age, as Immanuel Jakobovits suggests, we have a built-in aversion to new rituals (within traditionalism!). A compassionate thought of his is the suggestion that the most observant – and most deeply injured element of Jewish life – cannot bear to ponder upon the fact that the most observant Jews, the great centres of traditional learning, were wiped out. Why they? The answer sprang up among them: 'For those with faith there are no questions, and for those without faith there are no answers' (attributed first to the noted rabbinic scholar 'Chofetz Chaim' and later used by the Nitra Rav). When that community did ask the question 'Why?', blame was often apportioned to their opponents – the Zionists, secularists, and Reformers. Certainly Rabbi Yoel Teitelbaum of Satmar felt that the Jews were being punished for the sins of the Zionists while, as we have seen, Rav Hutner blamed the Arabs and the Mufti. Most of the attacks were directed against the 'assimilationists', which could include the mild rebels in the Orthodox community. Lord Jakobovits quotes the Maggid of Chelm, who attacked one of the leaders of German reform in the middle of the nineteenth century: 'Because of this sin of Geiger's Reform Code of Jewish Law, another law will emerge from Germany. It will say that every Jew without exception, must die. May God protect us!'[2] He quotes a number of such 'remarkable prophecies' but disassociates himself from them: 'I could not accept blaming any Jewish shortcomings as a specific cause of the Holocaust.' For him the doctrine of collective reward and punishment is invariably restricted to the Jewish national experience in the land of Israel only. And he also points out that these 'reasons' for the Holocaust do not represent the majority view.

In spite of our fundamental disagreement on the 'uniqueness' of the Holocaust, I am perfectly in accord with Jakobovits when he quotes authorities who direct our attention to the victims rather than the prosecutors, who remind us of their greatness and decency rather than dwelling upon the evil done to them. And it is of course true to point to their responses during the Holocaust and afterwards, to the great re-creation of Jewish life. Jakobovits quotes Rabbi Hillel Goldberg here:

The struggle simultaneously to remember, to transmit, and to interpret the Holocaust belies the notion that the Holocaust was unique . . . the persuasiveness of the argument for uniqueness is fading as time passes, as Jewish life perseveres, as the dialogue between the memory of death and the living of life endures in the usually inarticulate struggle of the survivors . . . Holocausts – and continuities – have come and gone in Jewish history. For this particular Holocaust of our time to have been unique, it had to have been not only more horrendous than any previous disaster, but also beyond interpretation, beyond response, beyond attempts to integrate it into the long chain of Jewish faith . . .[3]

The Jewish community has come out of the darkness and has rebuilt much. It has changed. The Chief Rabbi could express his hope in his community and its future when he said: 'The postwar period is the first in modern times when the leakage of defection has almost totally dried-up within the observant community, whether among survivors or thanks to their influence.' While it is clear that observant Judaism has grown far more than other segments of Jewish, this may be viewed as an overstatement. And if, as he really comes to suggest, the community has partially solved the problem of the Holocaust by isolating it, ignoring it, breaking with that aspect of the past and trying to live without that knowledge, one must worry about their future. A trauma can be isolated within the body and hermetically sealed off from mind and soul. Eventually, it breaks through – and no antibodies have been prepared to cope with the anguish that then fills the person. This, too, is something which we have seen.

*Yizkor*, remembering, is more than the charge 'to the survivors to rebuild what has been destroyed and to ensure the continuity of Jewish life through the blessing of children perpetuating and enriching their heritage'.[4] It includes the pain of being remembrancers, the knowledge of evil, and the determination not only to carry on, but also to live with the knowledge of human imperfection and with the awareness of the *tremendum*, the total evil which came upon us.

### Eliezer Berkovits

Eliezer Berkovits is the last of our witnesses for traditional Judaism as it attempts to create a pattern of life after the Holocaust. Once again, we come to see European thinking, even Germany, in this philosopher-theologian who studied in Berlin, at the famous Hildersheimer Seminary

– a few steps away from the Liberal Jewish Hochschule, a life-time removed from that tradition we come to see in Leo Baeck or Emil Fackenheim. Professor Berkovits became a central figure in the American traditional community, and was the teacher for more than one generation of rabbinical students at the Hebrew Theological College in Stokie, Illinois. Israel has also had its impact upon him, and he upon that land. One of the most often quoted works in the field of 'Holocaust theology' is his *Faith after the Holocaust* where he tries to see the Holocaust in terms of Jewish history as well as through the wisdom of the Halachah. When he wrote this text, he found himself confronted with the 'death of God' theology of Rubenstein. Without directly answering Rabbi Rubenstein (he was more concerned with Altizer and the Christian thinkers) he confronted radical theology by examining the problem of the *deus absconditus* of metaphysics in terms of *El Mistater*, the 'hiding God' of the prophets of Israel. To Altizer's claim that God is simply hidden from view '. . . that to the contemporary Christian . . . the death of God is accepted as a final and irrevocable event', Berkovits replies:

> Altizer believes that the Christian dogma of God's descent into the flesh represents the death of God as an event in history. At that moment, the transcendental God actually collapsed into immanent humanity. Thus he perished . . . the radical theologians all have in common the inability to acknowledge the concept of a 'hiding God', so important for example, in the theology of an Isaiah . . .[5]

and Berkovits celebrates the presence of the God who can and does hide in the world even when man is unaware of him. It is part of his approach to the anguish of the Holocaust, his attempt to delineate the role humans have to play in their freedom of making decisions – which is where God hides: in human responsibility and in human freedom. This is an aspect of Jewish thought which Christians have not really discovered or taken to heart, although Berkovits recognizes Dietrich Bonhoeffer as one who has travelled a long distance along that way.

Berkovits sees clearly that the notion of *El Mistater*, the 'hiding God', is far from being an answer to the generation after Auschwitz which questions God's silence in the face of the agony of the concentration camps and the crematoria. How could the redeemer of Israel be silent? In trying to give an answer, this text attempts to weave three factors of Jewish existence into one pattern: the *hurban*; the theological disagreement within Christianity as revealed by radical theology; and the rise of the state of Israel, the

59

antithesis to the *hurban*. And Berkovits stresses in particular Israel and Jerusalem:

> At this very moment in history, divine providence has placed into the hands of the Jew, in the form of the State of Israel, the secular city of man – for us to turn into a City of God on this earth. Quite clearly, we have been called. How shall we, the post-Auschwitz generation, respond to the call of the – after all – not-so-silent God of Israel?[6]

This was written in 1973. It may be an even greater challenge now.

Berkovits accepts Wiesel's query in *Night*: 'Where is God now?' since this is the right question to be asked now. 'Not to ask it would have been blasphemy'.[7] Faith, for Berkovits, is wrestling and arguing with God in the tradition of Abraham and Job . . . 'because of his faith Job cannot accept a defence of God that implies an insult to the dignity of God in whom he believes'.[8] Berkovits recognizes the anguish of faith in the concentration camps:

> If there were those whose faith was broken in the death camps, there were others who never wavered. If God was present for many, he was not lost to many more. Those who rejected did so in authentic rebellion; those who affirmed and testified to the very end did so in authentic faith. Neither the authenticity of rebellion nor the authenticity of faith is available to those who are only Job's brother. The outsider, the brother of the martyrs, enters upon a confusing heritage. He inherits both the rebellion and the witness of the martyrs . . . he is not attempting to steal a glance at 'the hand' of the Almighty – to understand is to justify, to accept. That he will not do . . . He desires to affirm, but not by behaving as if the Holocaust had never happened. He knows that this generation must live and believe in the shadow of the Holocaust. He must learn how this is to be done. If his faith is to remain meaningful, he must make room for the impenetrable darkness of the death camps within his faith.[9]

Here, we did find an openness to the total dimensions of the Holocaust, an understanding that the response of those who can no longer believe is as authentic as the faith of the true believer. Berkovits cannot go along with the total negativity of those who feel that God abandoned Israel, or who move into the courageous non-belief and acceptance of absurdity seen in existentialist thinking. He quotes Camus:

I know that heaven, which is indifferent to your horrible victories, will
be equally indifferent to your just defeat. Even now I expect nothing
from heaven.[10]

Berkovits sees the nobility of Camus who can move from a rejection of a
divine plan to a celebration of human integrity and independence, and who
can therefore assert that 'the world has at least the truth of man, and our
task is to provide its justification against fate itself. And it has no justification
but man . . .' Yet he limits this 'truth' to a 'good' person like Camus himself.
Berkovits only sees 'the truths of men' which can become a frightening
distortion when Himmler expresses his truth to the assembled SS leadership: 'to have gone through that, and to have remained an honest man just
the same . . . that is what made you tough and strong. This is a glorious
page in our history, never before, never again to be written . . .'[11] Berkovits
sees no hypocrisy in this: it is the truth of Himmler, alongside the truth of
Camus who opted for the oppressed. In a universe where all values are
based upon human choice anything may become a value. And yet, for Jews
to affirm religious denial accepts Nazi thinking, denies the Holocaust.

Berkovits looks at the past in order to put the Christian Church on trial:

The truth is that, apart from the Germans, the heaviest burden of guilt
rests on the Christian teaching about the Jews and on their persecution of
Christians through many centuries. Whether or not the Nazis considered
themselves Christians or not is beside the point. Christianity has poisoned
the very soul of the Western world with Jew-hatred . . .[12]

Here, Berkovits remains unforgiving. The Pope's visit to the synagogue,
and his often quoted remark that the Jews are 'the older brother' of the
Christians, only brings to Berkovits memories of Cain and Abel – except
this time the younger brother committed the crime of fratricide! Berkovits
does not include current changes within Christianity in his vision; yet Bonhoeffer and Niemoeller cannot serve as an excuse for Christians: a path of
two millennia needs to be expiated before it can be removed from the
agenda.

Jews who are involved in the struggle for civil rights for other minorities,
and keep insisting that others suffered, also miss the point, according to
Eliezer Berkovits, for these secularists cannot acknowledge that the Jews
are a unique people.

Berkovits joins his Orthodox partners in condemning the notion of the
Holocaust as unique. For him, it is basic that Jews understand these events

in the context of history, of a morally bankrupt West; the search is for the role the Jew has to play here.

For Berkovits ponders upon the relationship between the Jewish people and God. Has the Holocaust destroyed it? Seen as history, the Holocaust raises the question of the Jew's relationship to God along with the relationship to man. Within the world, Jews were powerless and harmless (Greenberg's point), dependent upon the flawed ethic of their society. This must, in the end, lead them to disassociation from that society: would they raise their children in a society which murders them? But has that society been changed by Jewish suffering? Must we not ask what the term 'chosen people' means in the world today, if we want to begin to understand the Holocaust?

> Why is anyone chosen? Why did God create man? Why did He create at all? No one can know it. But one thing we do know; no other nation on earth could have endured what we have endured and remained loyal to its calling as the challenge and warning to mankind. He has chosen one Jewish people for a purpose He is pursuing with the creation of man. The purpose of the Creator is, of course, a universal one. Thus, the function of the Jew is also a universal one . . . God chose us to be his partner in the inscrutable goal for man . . . [The return to Israel] . . . is a God-directed indication of the path of renewal. Some of the fundamental principles of Judaism have to be rethought to teach us the way of life for a Jewish people in a Jewish land. One thing is certain; nothing could be more foolish than to believe that finally the time has come for the Jews to become a nation like other nations . . .[13]

And the State of Israel still puzzles Berkovits. It has little power, limited national resources, and the size of the population and land are small. Has Israel entered the world of nations to play a weak and insignificant role? Even Israel's friends do not understand its weakened and endangered situation. The people who condemn Israel's 'acts of cruelty' would, in even less dangerous situations, commit once more acts of incomparable cruelty and humanity. The State of Israel – confronting its neighbours – is as homeless as any Jew ever was in exile. And this, as he sees it, is the anguish of the Jewish state today; its existence continues to be a challenge to the conscience of mankind; but it can easily be ignored.

Berkovits, then, has little confidence or hope in secularism or in 'humanitarianism' – but he lives in a world where he sees this as the majority option within a humanity which seems to have lost its way to God. Jews are too much like their neighbours; and Berkovits returns into his citadel of faith, waiting for the repentant Jew to return to him.

## Irving 'Yitz' Greenberg

Rabbi Greenberg is unique: a person, teacher, leader, and Socratic gadfly. Almost all of the Orthodox thinkers define themselves through him; challenge him, argue with him – and yet feel in some way he is on their side. On the other side, he is welcomed within Reform and Conservative circles as a traditionalist who shows compassion and understanding for the Progressive cause, and welcomes them to his own school with irenic confidence. Whoever – and whatever – he is, his approach to the Holocaust has been developed within most of Western Jewish thinking. He cannot and should not be defined institutionally. For that reason, I would only turn to one concept of his which has had a seminal influence on both tradition and Progressive Judaism; his notion of the Covenant.

The Covenant is the central notion of a Judaism which sees God's acts of redemption within history. Judaism wants to develop that history, even if it is shattered by it, in what Greenberg calls 'an enormous wager of faith', as Christianity often does. Nor does it follow Buddhism's approach of taking humanity itself out of life, into nirvana. As all religions do, Judaism has a final goal. But how is that goal to be reached?

> Nothing less than a partnership between God and humanity will achieve the dream of perfection. By a process of voluntary self-limitation, God summons humanity to participate in the process of creating a redeemed world. Each partner enters into his treaty to total redemption; each brings a pledge to this binding Covenant. God pledges that seeking perfection is not an exercise in futility. God promises to accompany humanity every step of the way. The human partner pledges to start the process of redemption, to go as far as possible in his or her lifetime, to create life and pass on the vision and the responsibility to the next generation – and not to relent or settle until the final goal is reached.[14]

This, with all its confidence in man's abilities and all its reverence for God's divine plan, immediately challenges many of the Orthodox preconceptions we have been examining. The process of 'voluntary self-limitation by God' is actually permissible in a traditionalism which reluctantly allows mysticism and Kabbala to use a language where *tzimtzum*, the contraction by God to make room for humanity, is at least a mythic hyperbole by which the mystery of Creation is allowed into human speech. Yet the way Greenberg develops it clearly fights for human autonomy which is more amenable to the thoughts of a Reform theologian like Eugene Borowitz and not really part of a traditionalist's conversation. And the Biblical scholar will note that of the various 'covenants' made available in the Scriptures, it is not the Covenant between 'superior and inferior' which is discussed here, but a covenant which seems to be made between equals – and that is a limitation of God which is not permissible to the tradition. Does God submit to a binding covenant? (Abraham had already bidden God to do so: 'Should not the Judge of all the earth act justly?' – this daring challenge to God is part of Greenberg's approach.) The challenge to humans is just as strong, particularly when Greenberg demands a renewal of the Covenant to be initiated by humans, since the Covenant was broken by the Holocaust!

In his construction, Greenberg sees God accepting human agency, which leads to a further covenant between God and Israel. Israel will walk in the way commanded by God, to accept a covenant task which will bless humanity. Any God is committed to protect the People Israel forever. Under this covenant, Israel forms a community to work out the task of salvation, and the covenant becomes a treaty for all generations. The generations are bound to the covenant, and work of each generation is linked to past and future. But, in each generation, there will be tragedies to test humanity. Suffering and defeat are part of human life, and must somehow be reconciled with the Covenant of Exodus and Sinai. Despair can be a natural reaction to catastrophe, and clash with the faith in the Covenant. After 70 CE some fell away, some became Christians – but most Jews refused to quit. They decided that the destruction of the Temple was a call to serve in a new way. A type of 'secularization' took place where God became more distant; but the Covenant was still renewed. In a new approach to the Purim story, the Jews looked for help and salvation within themselves. The Covenant came to mean new responsibilities.

Then came the Nazis. They tried to destroy all Judaism, and all Jews (whether those Jews 'believed' or not). And a total contradiction of the Covenant which had God as its protector in it took place. Auschwitz was not opposed. As Jews were killed, it was right to ask: can there be a Covenant without Jews? In Elie Wiesel's words:

The Jewish people entered into a Covenant with God. We were to protect his Torah, and He in turn assumes responsibility for Israel's presence in the world ... Well, it seems, for the first time in history, this very Covenant is broken.

Or, as Jakov Glatstein put it:

> We received Torah at Sinai
> And at Lublin we gave it back
> Dead men don't praise God
> The Torah was given to the living[15]

If the Covenant was a moral relationship, says Greenberg, it cannot ask the other to die. Could the Holocaust really be the price of the Covenant? Is the Covenant not at an end? And if Auschwitz did not mean the end of the Covenant, what does it reveal to us about the Covenant and God? Here, Wyschogrod's challenge comes to mind. For Greenberg, it is clear that God does not depend on prophets or interpreters of events. He speaks to us directly, he can speak through events. The Holocaust is 'an even more drastic call or total Jewish responsibility for the Covenant'.[16] 'If, after the Temple's destruction, Israel moved from junior participant to true partner in the Covenant, then after the Holocaust, the Jewish people is called on to become the senior partner in action.'[17] This is the message 'Yitz' Greenberg sees when the divine presence was in Auschwitz, suffering, burning, and failing to stop the Holocaust.

We were to stop the Holocaust. And, in Greenberg's view, part of our action to at least prevent future Holocausts was to create the State of Israel. And it was a Jewish community action, of believing and secular Jews. Here, to take it on again: we live in the age of the renewed Covenant. What had been a God-given task for the Jews now became a voluntary act of love as Israel decided to continue its mission, to still live within the Covenant.

The high hopes which Greenberg has for the State of Israel and its task in such a mission wait to be carried out. He demands a Torah for humanity, a healing which will go out from Jerusalem. Having taken on power, we now have to fulfil that task, with hope and realism until it comes to the final perfection. The Jewish people are thus an avatar of humanity, reflecting the anguish and glory of human life within themselves. And Israel can yet be a light unto the nations.

Where his critics worry about Rabbi Greenberg's flawed beliefs, I can only marvel at his unbreakable faith. His theology can be questioned, but his labour at bringing factions in Jewish life together so that they may share in the work if not in the word is the healing function of a great teacher who has begun to create awareness for what may in truth be a covenant of hope.

## The Halachah of the Holocaust

In the section which now follows, I have tried to bring together the insights of traditional scholars and rabbis (and sometimes their prejudices), in order to see how the challenge against the Holocaust could in fact create a company of observers who could show compassion and courage under unbelievable circumstances.

All travellers towards the dawn and the light must at times turn around and look into the darkness. And, as the psalm has it, even in the darkness there is light . . . God is there, and God is reflected in the lives that vanished into that darkness.

NOTES

1. I. Jakobovits, *Oxford Holocaust conference*, vol. 3 (1988), p. 205.
2. Ibid., p. 292.
3. Ibid., p. 294.
4. Ibid., p. 295.
5. Ibid., pp. 62–3.
6. Ibid., p. 66.
7. Ibid., p. 68.
8. Ibid., p. 69.
9. Ibid., p. 70.
10. A. Camus, *Letters to a German friend*.
11. I. Jakobovits, *Oxford Holocaust conference*, vol. 3 (1988), p. 205.
12. Ibid., p. 243.
13. Ibid., p. 246.
14. Ibid., p. 209.
15. Ibid., p. 217.
16. Ibid., p. 219.
17. Ibid., p. 219.

# [ 2 ]

# OUT OF THE ASHES

## THE HALACHAH OF THE HOLOCAUST

To continue rabbinic discourse we must be aware that the time barrier can be transcended. Moses can sit in the classroom of Akiva: the vision of the servant girl during the crossing of the Red Sea can communicate itself to anyone at the Seder today who recites 'this is what God did for me when I went to Egypt', and the rabbis who walk alongside the burnt Temple Mount can speak to the generation after the Holocaust.

> It is taught in Midrash Tanchuma;
> Three men saw three worlds,
> Noah saw the built world, the world destroyed by the Flood
>     and the world rebuilt after the Flood.
> Daniel saw the first Temple. He saw the first Temple
>     destroyed and he saw the second Temple rebuilt.
> Job saw his home established. He saw his home destroyed
>     and he saw his home rebuilt.

In our own time, the Book of Job is often used as a text in which we see ourselves described. It is true enough. Around the world there are many who saw a Jewish world which had moved towards greatness. Out of the *Yeshivot* of Eastern Europe, out of the deep piety of its sanctuaries, out of the scintillating writings of its Yiddish authors, something unique had emerged in which the tradition had shaped itself into new and glowing forms. And in Western Europe, a symbiosis between the Jew and his neighbour had moved into what should have been a golden age of creativity and achievement. But those who saw that world also saw it destroyed by a *mabul* of hatred, saw it drowned in blood. We saw the burning of the sanctuaries, the shattering of the pillars of the house. Of a certainty, we have seen two worlds. But have we seen the third world, the world rebuilt after the Flood, the new Temple constructed, the families returned to life? With Job, we can only place our hand upon our mouth.

Nevertheless, there are those who will claim that they have seen three worlds. It is a claim rising out of the basic optimism which informs our faith, a claim to be welcomed; it must be treated with great care. Not unnaturally, it rises out of the atmosphere of *Eretz Yisrael*, a beleaguered land which gains in strength with adversity.

Traditional Judaism expresses itself more in the response and in the practices of Jewish life, particularly when it confronts the most profound problem of our times; and we shall turn to these expressions. This does not mean that we can ignore the attitude of the modern traditionalist as it finds expression in the *shakla v'tarya*, the conflicts, resolutions, and discussions of daily life. Ancillary conflicts between the position of a progressive rabbi who affirms the Diaspora and the traditional Rabbi Amital's must be noted, though these should not distract us from the basic issues under consideration. Also, some of these differences are more a matter of emphasis. Rabbi Amital's formula of Israel and the Diaspora does not rule out its converse: if the State of Israel confronts its citizens with the historic Jewish essence, it cannot deny the reality of those living in Israel who run away from the essence, hiding in the deepest recesses of empty identities. If a Jew can live in the Diaspora without having to confront his past, the reality of those who come to terms with their Jewish identity while affirming Diaspora life cannot be denied. If we accept the indisputable assumption that a Holocaust can happen again, we need not accept as a *kal v'chomer* that Israel is a people which must dwell alone (*am l'vadad yish-kon*). On the contrary, we can argue that the need to reach out towards our neighbours and establish contact with the righteous of all nations has never been greater. It is vital for our continuance in the Diaspora, and essential as an outer line of defence for the State of Israel. We do move towards a fundamental disagreement here in the reading of history, since traditional rabbinic thinking would support the assertion that the re-emergence of the State of Israel should be seen as an act in the drama of *am l'vadad yish-kon*.

Within Israeli ambience, the assertion that 'the State of Israel is certainly part of the birthpangs of the Messiah' affirms the reality of a new life, of a new family and a rebuilt home. In this new world, the optimistic dimension which can also be part of the experience of suffering must be stated. Israel can affirm the suffering which helped to produce it. The survivors who are so essential to the spirit of Israel must receive due recognition. Despite all of the attitudes which make up *sh'lilat ha-galut* (the rejection of the Diaspora), despite the tensions between generations, there is an attempt here to see the good which comes out of suffering – 'God meant to bring good out of it by preserving the life of a mighty people'.[1] It is a cautious approach. Rabbi Amital is quite clear in his statement that Israel does not serve as a balance to the *Shoah*. Nevertheless, he wants to proclaim the good which emerged out of evil.

There are legitimate challenges to this type of thinking: and there are also illegitimate attacks upon it. I do not really want to enter the dark world of the *Neturei Karta* here.

We reject the wild fanatical hatred against fellow Jews. We do not reciprocate it. In those same pages, there is a deep and profound mourning for a world that has been destroyed. It is the awareness of Jewish suffering which causes Reb Shonfeld to strike out blindly against his fellow Jews. The theme of *mipne chattaenu* is sounded again, although the *Neturei Karta* really do not feel this world advanced enough to merit the *chevlei hamashiach*. We must turn back to Rabbi Amital here and, let me say it, we do so with some relief. But how can either *mipne chattaenu* or the *chevlei hamashiach* be applied to the Holocaust? In all periods of rabbinic thought, God's love and compassion have been central to the rabbi's discussion. God does not inflict needless pain. Then why is it necessary for the Messianic age to be born out of travail? Why must mankind suffer, either now or in the movement towards the time of perfection? Why? Because we are flawed tools. Suffering is part of human life. The easy definitions of early Reform Judaism rejected any notion of the evil resident in man. To this day, we make facile comparisons with our neighbours, explaining that they believe in original sin and we believe in original goodness. The rabbis had a different understanding. They appraised humanity in terms of what they could see, and they saw evil. Evil led to suffering, and the Jews were not exempt from this. Contemplating the destruction of Jerusalem, they did not enumerate the political and military factors which led to the burning of the city. They found the reasons in the moral decay of the populace. And even there in the face of the Roman oppression, there were interpretations of that *Shoah*, that *Churban*, which linked the sufferings of the Jews to the coming of the good times. 'Foxes playing among the ruins of the Temple? Let us rejoice ... if the dark prophecies have been fulfilled, the bright visions will also come true!' Rabbi Akiva, the greatest Jewish teacher at the time of the revolt against Rome, carried this concept of suffering into all areas of life. When the students of Rabbi Eliezer saw their teacher struck down by painful illness, they mourned. Akiva laughed. Why? 'Whenever I saw the flax, oil, and honey of my teacher flourishing ... I worried that it was a prepayment from the world to come. What would be left? Now that I see his suffering, I am reassured about his future world'. Eliezer could not contain himself[2]:

> 'Is there a single law I have transgressed?' he demanded of Akiva. Akiva answered 'You yourself, our teacher, often referred us to the verse "The world contains no one so righteous that he only does good and never does wrong."'

There is a passion in Judaism to gain some benefit from the encounter with the deepest suffering. Rabbi Amital is part of this tradition when he emphasizes the relationship between the new State of Israel and the Holocaust; we cannot do so. That tradition does not speak to our needs; it has been shattered by the Holocaust. There is no comfort in placing the *Shoah* into a divine plan when we could not possibly understand such a plan or its maker. If that is the answer, we could only cover our mouth in the manner of Job; but we would not stop mourning.

But there are other rabbinic traditions which can help us confront the Holocaust, traditions in which we see God mourning: as He sees the suffering of Israel, as He sees the Temple destroyed:

> In that hour, the Holy One, Praised be He, wept and said: 'Woe is me; what have I done? For the sake of Israel I let My presence dwell below. Now, since they became sinners, I have returned to my first place. I would not be an object of laughter to the heathen, mocked by My creatures!'
> In that same hour came Metraton, fell down upon his face, and said before God: 'Master of the World, let me weep. *You* must not weep'. Said He to him: 'If you do not let me weep, I shall enter a place which you are not free to enter and I will weep there. As it is written[3]:

> > "Can you not hear this?
> > My soul weeps in the hidden place."'

The Holy One, Praised be He, said to the serving angels: 'Come. We will go, I and you, we will look around in My house to see what the enemy has done to it'. The Holy One, Praised be He, then went to the house, with the serving angels and Jeremiah in front of Him. When He saw the house, the Holy Sanctuary, he said: 'Yes, this was My house, this was my resting place, now the enemies have come upon it and treated it according to their desires'.

The Holy One, Praised be He, wept in that hour, and He said: 'Woe is me for My house. My children, where are you? My Priests, where are you? You who loved me, where are you? O, what I could have done with you. I warned you but you did not turn back in penitence.'[4]

The theme of *mipne chattaenu* is also stronger here. But the overpowering impact of the rabbinic teaching is of a weeping God, a caring God, a 'God Who Suffers' with the victims. The desolation and destruction is not part of a divine war-plan, but rises out of human action. Once again, that line of rabbinic thought which makes our sins the cause of the Holocaust is manifest here; but there are certain subtle nuances present which somehow fade away in later times when Israel berates itself within its liturgy:

Because of our sins have we been reduced to captivity and to pillage . . .

chants the prayer. And Richard Rubenstein is right in pointing out that this continuing sense of unworthiness weakened the Jew in his confrontation with the persecutors. In the Midrashic text there lives the awareness of who is hated by God and who is loved. The guilt of the perpetrators is not ignored. The touch of vicarious atonement present in later texts is absent here. And what matters most is that the *Shechina* will go into exile with the children of Israel. There is the knowledge that God suffered as God suffered in the concentration camps. God mourns: shall we not mourn?

How does God mourn?

Rav Shmuel bar Nachman said: 'The Holy One, praised be He, called the serving angels and asked them: "On earth, when a king of flesh and blood comes to mourn, what does he do?" They answered Him: "he clothes himself in black garments and covers his head with sackcloth." God said: 'I also do this, as it is written[5]:

> "I clothe the heavens in darkness
> And make covers for them out of sackcloth."'

Another time He asked: 'One earth, when a king of flesh and blood comes to mourn, what does he do?' They said: 'He extinguishes all the lights.' God said: 'I also do this, as it is written[6]:

> "Sun and moon grow dim,
> And the stars shall withdraw their shining."'

And again He asked them: 'On earth, when a king of flesh and blood comes to mourn, what does he do?' They said: 'He walks barefoot'. God said: 'I also do this, as it is written[7]:

> "The Lord has His way in the whirlwind and the storm,
> And the clouds are the dust of His feet."'

And once more He asked them: 'On earth, when a king of flesh and blood comes to mourn, what does he do?' They said: 'He sits in deep silence.' God said to them: 'I also do this, as it is written[8]:

> "He sits alone and is silent
> For He has taken it upon himself."'[9]

Moving through the *Shoah* and its clouds of dust, drawn into silence, the God of the rabbis has been rediscovered by our generation. But our modernity has built new walls between ourselves and the rabbinic tradition – we have not heard God weep. And it is only because the rabbis of that time heard God weep, because the *Shechina* went into exile with them, that they could find their way to comfort.

Rabbi Joshua went to those who wept and could not be comforted. He said to them: 'Come, my children, I will now tell you what your actions must be. It is impossible for us not to mourn, for our dark fate has come upon us. But it is also possible for us to mourn too much; for no *takkana* can be established for the whole community if most cannot follow it because it could endanger the existence of that totality. But this we shall do, according to the words of the wise. When someone paints his house, he must leave one spot bald and unpainted. In memory of Jerusalem. If someone prepares a festive meal, let him make all proper preparation, but he must omit one of the customary things, in memory of Jerusalem. If a woman puts on her jewellery, let her never put on complete adornment; something should be omitted, in memory of Jerusalem. For thus is it written[10]:

> "If I forget thee, O Jerusalem
> Let my right hand forget its cunning

Let my tongue cleave to the roof of my mouth
If I remember thee not,
If I do not set Jerusalem
Above my highest joy."'

But he who mourns Jerusalem in the right manner will also be found worthy to see the joy of Jerusalem. For thus it is written[11]:

"Rejoice with Jerusalem and exult in her
All you who love her:
Share her joy with all your heart
All you who mourn over her." '[12]

There are other Midrashim to be cited here, Midrashim of lamentation of consolation, as Max Dienemann called them, texts which in the time of the Nazi Holocaust became part of the spiritual resistance of the Jew against his persecutors. But we have enough words from the time of the Roman Persecution to come to some understanding of that generation of rabbis and its confrontation with the Holocaust of the burning Temple. Set along-side the exultation of an Israeli rabbi who has completed the road into *olam banui*, the rebuilt third world of Noah and Job compared with the dark world of the teachers of the *Neturei Karta* filled with hatred and vengeful thoughts we come to see the unique character of Akiva and his generation – Akiva who laughed. One more text may serve to emphasize the difference. The rabbinic comment on the following verse in the Book of Lamentations[13]: *Lo aley-chem kol ov-rey derech* – 'Is it of no concern to you who pass by' (NEB).

Stubbornly, running against the basic spirit of the Book itself and against all later translations, the Midrash Rabba to Echa:

'May such not come upon you all you who go along the way.' The congregation of Israel speaks to the nations of the World: 'May there not happen to you what happened to me, may there not come upon you what came upon me.'[14]

How can there be such compassion in these texts, for Israel and for the nations of the world? How could the rabbi confront their desolation with such enlargement of spirit, with such nobility? These words are seldom said in our time. We live in an age which has lost its faith in man and in God. Even the traditionalist when he said, *Ha-tzur tamim po-olo* ('The rock,

His work, is perfect') senses an inconsistency between the world after the Holocaust and perfect creation. Our theology is a proud, logical edifice moving through the Greek philosophers and the scholastics and not averse to a touch of linguistic analysis. Omnipotence means omnipotence to us, and modern theology cannot separate itself from the problem of theodicy: 'If God is God He is not good, if God is good He is not God'.

The thought is not absent in the Jewish tradition. We delight in listing all the confrontations, from Abraham to the *Berditchever*, who have their *din toirah* with God, who call Him before the bar of justice. But the rabbis who comforted the generation after the second *Churban* used a different approach. They could not understand why Israel had to suffer so much. Why the Temple had to be destroyed. They did not seek the reason in the mind. They looked into their lives. Humanity had caused the Holocaust, not God, as it were. Israel had sinned: *mipne chattaenu*. Sin had removed the protective barrier – God no longer stood between them and the hatred of their persecutors. Those words, and those ideas, came to be debased in later interpretations, in later generations who confidently spoke of what was in God's mind and did not hesitate to identify the sinners of Israel in detail and felt ready to take over the divine function of judge and executioner. Frustrated anguish seeks targets in order to relieve itself. The earlier rabbis had a different task; they wanted to assuage grief, they saw that a generation had to be comforted.

What was it Rabbi Joshua said? 'Come, my children, it is impossible for us not to mourn, for our dark fate has come upon us. But we cannot mourn too much – for that would endanger the whole community'. And he gave them tasks to do as remembrancers: an aspect of desolation was to be part of all future creations. What thoughts motivated him and his colleagues? Looking at the Holocaust, he was not unaware of all the themes which have been pronounced in our modern discourse: the God who is hiding, who has turned away for a moment; the dark demonic side of power beyond human understanding: the incomprehensibilities of divinity without ending or beginning. But he also saw something else in the Holocaust: He saw God's suffering and God's grief. He saw God's loving kindness. Rabbi Joshua and his colleagues realized that they could build upon this. They could speak comfortably to Jerusalem, could bid her take heart. The advice given in our Midrash is based upon a profound understanding of human nature. It is informed by love and concern. And that love and concern would have been impossible for the rabbis if they had not come to understand that divine suffering and divine love was also present in the Holocaust. In our time, Wiesel saw God hanging upon the gallows

74

of Auschwitz. It was a way of saying that God suffers with us, that He identifies with the victims and not with the persecutors. We could not face such darkness if it were God's will. But God does not want it. He also suffers. He weeps for the destroyed Temple; He is desolated by the suffering of those who love him. He is with us. The *Shechina* is also in exile. Once this became clear to the rabbis they could begin to help their generation. They could again function as rabbis, and the open thinking of the Midrash could by-pass theological conundrums about omnipotence and could concern itself with the needs of the individuals caught up in the whirlwind of evil.

The rabbis of our time have continued this tradition.

Perhaps we spend too much time listening to the scholars who try to deal with the theological problems of a tragic and absurd world; although their work is necessary, and intellect and the quest for truth demands it, yet the tradition of Akiva and the generation after the second *Churban* shines forth most clearly in the actual decisions made by the rabbis in the ghettos and concentration camps. The dimension of truth shown us by the victims and survivors of the camps cannot be matched by their epigones, by those of us who follow in their steps and try to understand the nature of the Jewish tradition and of the Jew who entered hell and re-emerged from those depths.

A relationship does exist between the Halachic decisions made by the rabbis in the death camps and the Midrash of the days of the second *Churban*. The rabbis used psychological insights in many Halachic decisions which often moved beyond the letter of the traditional law; this was particularly true when the law had no answer to the problem rising out of the depths of hell. When the law which was to be applied was so cruel in the unique situation of the victims that pronouncing it would have destroyed them, silence or equivocation was used by the rabbis. The classic case is of the man whose only child was to be sent to the ovens. Was it permitted to the father to rescue the child through bribery, knowing that this would doom another child to death? Rabbi Hirsch has to give a negative answer to the petitioner. He cannot do so without destroying both the man and himself, so he gives his answer through silence, enabling the father to reach a tragic decision which cannot be made for him by the rabbi. This story is placed into a theological dimension when we realize that this is Rosh Hashana, and our final glimpse of the father sees him wandering about the camp in mystic anguish, crying out 'I am Abraham! I am Abraham!'. Rabbi Meisels had not used psychology, he had shown the ancient rabbinic concern and love.

Rabbi Oshri permitted suicide on one occasion. Rabbi Meisels was confronted with a case that entered upon this area:

A young man close to twenty years of age, Moshe Rosenberg of Salgotar-jan, Hungary, was to be sent to an extermination camp. Akiba Mann, a boy of about fifteen, wanted to take Moshe's place, so that he could die in the flames instead. Moshe was an outstanding student of the *Yeshiva* and his life, thought Akiba, was more valuable than his. The only request of the boy was that the rabbi would promise him that he would be able to go to heaven, unlike ordinary suicides.[15]

Here, Rabbi Meisels refused permission and would give no assurances about life in the world to come. For the child, ready to make this sacrifice, this was a world which has turned so perverse that the traditional theological structures had become far more real than the dark environment, a place where the traditional virtues and values still existed.

One final case:

On a death march, a man said to his younger brother that he should sleep a while and he would wake him when the march resumed. The older brother also fell asleep. He awoke to the command *Los!* and in haste and fright rushed off with the others ... while not fully awake. The march started. Then he remembered his brother whom he had forgotten to awake. He could not turn back without getting killed ... and never saw his brother again. Since then ... he has felt guilty ... and seeks atonement.

Rabbi Breisch concluded that the younger brother would have fallen asleep anyway and that the older brother was half asleep when the march resumed. But sleep is recognized in the Talmud as an *onus*, a *force majeure*, and this holds true, according to Breisch, for a short time after the person wakes up.

Thus we conclude that our man does not need to have pangs of conscience because this would lead to sadness which is an even greater sin, because it harms him and diverts him from the service of God which has to be done joyfully.

The surviving brother was enjoined to live a normal life, to raise orphans in his home, to support students. The rabbinic decision is more concerned with removing anxiety, with restoring an individual fully to the community. The rabbinic concerns are with the effects of the suffering, and rabbinic law was used to restore and not to punish.

The rabbis making these decisions were *b'nei rachamim*; they were men of compassion. They are the true inheritors of the rabbinic teachings pronounced in the shadows of the burning Temple Mount. Halachah becomes more than a measure of conformity; it grows to fit the circumstances, includes within its domain the awareness of God's love and compassion which is evident to the believing eye in the time of Holocaust. The rabbis of all ages know that grief must be shared. They also knew that hope must be shared. And they knew that when there was no hope, and when the outer darkness could not be dispelled, there still remained an inner dimension of courage and of faith which linked the Jew to a caring God who suffered alongside of him. Akiva laughed on the Temple Mount where foxes played. He also laughed when the executioner lit the fires which were to burn his life away. Rabbi Akiva died, affirming God, and not denying him. And that is the rabbinic teaching of the Holocaust.

NOTES

1. Genesis 50:20.
2. (Koh. 7:20) Sanhedrin 101a.
3. Jeremiah 13:17.
4. Petichta Midrash Rabba to Echa 24.
5. Jeremiah 50:3.
6. Joel 2:10.
7. Nachum 1:3.
8. Echa 3:28.
9. Midrash Rabba to Echa 3:10.
10. Psalm 137: 5–6.
11. Psalm 66:10.
12. Tosephta Sota 15:11–13 (Baba Batra 60b).
13. Book of Lamentations, 1:12.
14. Echa rabbati, 1:12.
15. H. Meisels, *N'kadshe ha-shem*, pt. 1, p. 9.

# [ 3 ]

# THE CARTOGRAPHERS OF DARKNESS

## EXPLORING AN UNKNOWN WORLD

IN the earlier maps of the African lands, unknown places were sometimes left blank, with only the inscription 'Here there be tygers' added. The fear of the unknown was thus expressed and, gradually, those maps came to be filled in. In our time, maps have been drawn up which might have carried similar inscriptions – but they would have concealed far greater fears and areas of totally unknown darkness. The historian Martin Gilbert, who has studied the Holocaust, also published a book of maps, trying to clarify the Holocaust by means of this graphic process. Thus, we come to see a landscape of Europe filled with squares, oblongs, small stars: the various types of concentration camps and death camps fashioned by the Nazis in their attempt to destroy the Jews, the gypsies, Communists, homosexuals, less than healthy children and adults, enemies of the régime, or those who simply came into conflict with members of the 'master race'. To put the inscription 'Here there be tygers' upon these places of darkness would have been a delusion – and a beautification. The historians, practitioners of a noble craft, have explored these areas from varying disciplines; but they were all cartographers of a world filled with too much darkness to permit them full access into that area of evil.

There is good reason to include them among our Riders Towards the Dawn, since they are often the most instructive guides of the past, and have clearly expressed approaches towards the future. But none of them were or are objective scholars, for we no longer accept the naïve presumption of nineteenth-century historians who felt they could write history *wie sie eigentlich gewesen ist* – how it really was! The Dutch historian Pieter Geyl

78

tried to write a totally objective history of Napoleon while he was imprisoned in one of those camps; it was to be his escape from an impossible reality. Later, looking at the text, he saw the subjectivity which had crept into it. Historians from the time of Plutarch have tried to give images of leaders and heroes which might cause later generations to emulate them. Or, as participants in a war – Thucydides is an example – they wanted to show that war 'as it really was'; and they wound up writing the speeches which should have been given, and the way in which they would have wanted events to have taken place.

Historians of the Holocaust find themselves in similar situations. First of all, one must determine the organizing principle which was central to the texts they wrote. There was Lucy Dawidowicz, for example, one of our great historians. As a young person, she went to Europe shortly before the war, and explored the Jewish community structures and their failures. Long after, when she came to write her brilliant and authoritative study, she called it 'The war against the Jews: 1933–1945'. The title conveys her basic concept: the war was, first of all, the basic concept and work of Adolf Hitler who planned the Holocaust as a 'War against the Jews' which had to take precedence over all else. There was ample material to substantiate Lucy Dawidowicz's theory, from the speeches of Hitler to the overall policies which could turn the railway system around at the time when the 'Second Front' started, in order to ship Jews frantically to the East in trains which were supposed to carry arms and reinforcements to the German armies trying to hold back the Allies in France. The notion of the influence of certain persons and individuals who shape this dark history for us is central to a presentation which gives us an outstanding overview of the events.

But can one really understand the events, the six million individual tragedies which come together in that kingdom of death? Can history be written in that way? We look at another historian, Richard Rubenstein, and see this understanding begins with a different concept, that of *triage*. Here, one begins with an idea from an earlier time, the notion that human beings could be seen as 'surplus', could be set against the value of land. The enclosure laws, the Irish famine, the blood count of the trench warfare of World War I where a score of the dead on both sides was kept and humans were reduced to cyphers – all become part of a technology of death where it was the system, rather than one person's evil imagination, which was at the centre of the Holocaust. (In another area, the historian Ellis Rivkin could write an incisive book on the death of Jesus labelled not 'Who killed Jesus?' but 'What killed Jesus?' Quite apart from the *angst* of Jews which filled Hitler, one could also proceed to concepts of 'utility' – what were the economic benefits of killing Jews? The *Kristallnacht* was the only way Goering could pay for the vast re-armament programme which had been carried out in Germany – the confiscation of Jewish resources, to which was added the insurance money which came from abroad to pay for the destroyed shops, enabled him to pay for the promissory notes which had been issued by the German government. Later, this mentality manifested itself in the running of the extermination camps. The Rubenstein–Roth book *Approaches to Auschwitz* gives a stark testimony of the work of the *Wirschafts-Verwaltungshauptamt* (WVHA):

> Calculating that a concentration camp inmate could be expected to work for nine months – a figure that turned out to be too high – SS economists reckoned that a total profit of 1631 Reichsmarks could be forecast for an inmate's labour. The calculation figured the cost precisely: food, clothing and RM2 for burning the corpse. Included on the profit side of the ledger were the benefits of an efficient use of the inmate's effects: gold from teeth, clothes, valuables, money. Though no cash figure was mentioned, this report noted that additional income could be realized from utilization of the corpse's bones and ashes.[1]

These historians were not drawing a picture of the absolute evil of Germans in all of the professions and institutions involved in the death camps. Rather, they were pointing to the system, to the potentialities which exist in every modernized society. They showed that genocide can be and will be carried out by a society which can ultimately only be stopped by intervention – armed intervention, not economic sanctions – from the outside.

Richard Rubenstein is too important as a theologian not to be studied at every turn of his development. His seminal work *After Auschwitz* (1966) has just appeared in a second edition[2] with a new subtitle: 'History, theology and contemporary Judaism'. The difference between the texts, as he notes, is 'the difference between the spirit of opposition and revolt . . . and the spirit of synthesis and reconciliation'[3] which draws upon the historical events from the Six Day War of 1967 and the events of contemporary history leading up to the present. The old text begins with the events of the Holocaust and the creation of the State of Israel. These are still intertwined for Professor Rubenstein, who sees the total destruction of the State of Israel as the current ultimate objective of Israel's Arab neighbours. For that reason, 'Holocaust theology' remains his current teaching, placed solidly into the teachings he has developed over the years: a view of the kind of world, and the systems operating within it, which made a state sponsored programme of mass extermination possible. Against this background, where history and theology intertwine, a shift in theology takes place for him where the immanence rather than the radical transcendence of God is more emphasized. Also, the notion of the Covenant emerges more clearly. Yet it seems to me that the very notion of the Covenant implies an entrance by God into the sphere of history where a partnership between humans and God can be established. The Ten Commandments commence with the teaching that God entered history to take Jews out of Egypt, and every Passover Seder recreates that event. In that context, it is harder to stress the 'absence of God' as clearly as the 1966 version of his *After Auschwitz* presented it to us. And, indeed, the new emphasis on the Immanent God moves away from the earlier radicalism. Those who deny God's role in history cannot ignore that redemptive moment of the Exodus from Egypt. In effect, they are thrown back into the position of asking: 'But what have you done for me lately?' which could make a mere bodyguard out of God. This, of course, is not Professor Rubenstein's position, who now says:

> In contrast to apocalyptic Jewish Messianism, which I view as a disguised form of Jewish earth paganism, I have stressed a form of nature religion in which *all men and women understand themselves as children of Earth*. The renewed contact of an important segment of the Jewish people with the land of Israel has contributed greatly to my appreciation of nature religion.[4]

The basic issue is not the change and development in Professor Rubenstein's writings: the thrust of his teachings remains the same. It is perhaps more that historiography and theology within the Jewish community has come closer to Richard Rubenstein, even when I cannot fully go along with his militant stance.

Just one glimpse into the heart of the darkness suffices to make us see that this landscape of hell might be sketched onto a map, but will not be totally open to any of us who have not actually encountered this situation in our own lives. The historians are still needed, and we can and should find a particular guide with whom we can walk through a gate that will either say 'Abandon hope all ye who enter here', *Arbeit macht frei*, or other litanies of evil. My own guide, for many reasons, would be H. G. Adler, whose work *Der verwaltete mensch: Studien zur deportation der Juden aus Deutschland* is a keystone of that dark historiography. The title indicates that humans were destroyed by bureaucracy, which fits the previous approach to the history of the Holocaust which we have discussed. Adler was not only an inmate of the camps, moving from Theresienstadt to Auschwitz with his wife. He was also one of those rare individuals whose work stretched over many areas, and his own account of Theresienstadt is painful in its truth and revealing in its accusations. *Der verwaltete mensch* remains his greatest contribution to our time. It looks at records, documents, the odds and ends of history which most of the practitioners avoid or throw away. Carefully, he picks up the little facts, the forgotten letters, until the mosaic was complete and we could see the face of evil. He traces the small bank account of a Jewish soldier who died in World War I, a hero at the front who had no family. The account remains dormant, growing slowly by accumulating interest, until, after 1933, it attracts the attention of the Nazis. First, the name 'Israel' is added to that of the dead soldier; and then, gradually, a correspondence accumulates as one department after another takes an interest in the small account. The file grows and grows until, at the end, we see bureaucracy in all its evil. All of the anonymous underlings, the little people who do their best to show themselves good Nazis, are revealed in these bits of paper; and we see how almost anyone can become part of the machinery of death. The small account did become state property; the expenses incurred far exceeded the sum collected!

Nevertheless, those cartographers of the external landscape can only direct us towards the evils that lurk outside, within our civilization. There is another type of cartographer who should be recognized: the scholar and physician who views the interior landscape of our mind in order to remind us that the animals we fear are part of our own self. Many of these did not survive. Just as the greatest of the Jewish historians, Simon Dubnow, was shot by the Nazis in Eastern Europe when he was ninety years old, with his last breath admonishing the Jews around him to 'Write it down, write it all down', so many healers of souls, psychiatrists and analysts, entered the camps and died alongside their patients. I talked to one survivor, an analyst who was taken at the same time as his patient, and then separated from him. After the war, they met again, and decided to resume the analysis. And they discovered that the analysis resumed at the same point where it had been interrupted by the arrest! The dark passage between then and now had been blotted out.

Among those persons, those who have wandered from the darkness towards the dawn, there are some remarkable individuals who deserve our closest attention in terms of what they had to give to us. Viktor Frankl, still alive at the time of writing; Bruno Bettelheim, who committed suicide in his old age; and Eugene Heimler, who died before his time. All of them have something special to transmit to us, whether or not we agree with their teachings. They all entered the hell of the concentration camps, and the experience of those days became part of their teachings. Yet these experiences differed widely. In 1938, when Bruno Bettelheim was thirty-five years old, he was taken by the Nazis and sent to Dachau and afterwards to Buchenwald. On his release, in 1939, he went to the United States and became one of the great psychiatrists and healers of our time. His experience of the concentration camp was vastly different from the innermost circle of hell, Auschwitz, where Viktor Frankl and Eugene Heimler survived until the end of the war and came back to their communities, totally changed, but with the need to move towards light after that darkness and to take the world along with them. Their teachings and their understanding of the Holocaust were far different from the position taken by Bettelheim, who in a sense left the field of healing at this point and made historical judgements which link him to the scholars mentioned above. In his books (for example, *The informed heart,* 1960) Bettelheim tries to analyse the reactions of Jews caught in the Nazi net. His stern and often cruel judgement is that any attempt not to engage in active resistance was a moral failure, and that the decision of Anne Frank's family, for example, in choosing a hiding place rather than fighting or fleeing sealed her fate and that of the family. Here, he might well be charting the interior geography of the human mind under relentless attack from the forces of evil; but he entered the field of historiography without obeying the basic rules of that craft. Lucy Dawidowicz, in her book *The Holocaust and the historians* (1918) on the other hand, dealt sharply with those who analyse this period of history without a solid knowledge of the situation or without an understanding that historians have to accept rules of evidence, make logical assessments of specific situations, and not assume their own areas of scholarship give them full authority.

How can Bruno Bettelheim be accused of a lack of empathy, since he himself had been in Dachau and in Buchenwald? His initial mistake, as others have argued, is that he was even less objective than most of the historians. He assumed that the observations regarding the passivity of camp inmates which he had noted while incarcerated held true for all inmates in all Nazi camps, and for the situations outside the camp. Bettelheim did not come to terms with the fact that Dachau and Buchenwald in 1938 could not be compared with the extermination camps of the 1940s. He did not understand the historical situation; and his deep understanding of the human mind under stress did not make any allowances for changing conditions or even of the sometimes unrealistic appraisal of those conditions. Of course, that is the accusation he makes against the Frank family. Yet it can be argued that it was Bettelheim who appraised the situation in Amsterdam falsely, and not Otto Frank.

In my initial book on the Holocaust, *Out of the whirlwind* (1968), I opened the first section of the book with an excerpt from Anne Frank's diary – and followed it with a selection from Bettelheim's *The informed heart*. There, he dealt with the behaviour of inmates in the extermination camps who made little effort to rebel, even if there were only a few guards in control of them. Yet, within the victims, hostility was repressed and the terrifying image of the SS was inflated. Terror indeed ruled the camps, and lead to a passivity which accompanied the prisoners on their certain way to death. In some ways, said Bettelheim, this was an ingrained passivity. In Buchenwald, he had talked to hundreds of German Jews and asked them why they had not simply left Germany and its appalling conditions. 'How could we?' they replied; 'we could not leave our businesses and all our material possessions.' (This answer, in late 1936, was when most of those who wanted to leave found that they were already prisoners in some way.) Bettelheim mentioned a number of individual situations where such passivity manifested itself; and he turned them into a general rule. The one judgement on which he was most often challenged was his condemnation of the Frank family, where he had this to say:

> There is little doubt that the Franks, who were able to provide themselves with so much, could have provided themselves with a gun or two had they wished. They could have shot down at least one or two of the 'green police' who came for them. There was no surplus of such police. The loss of an SS with every Jew arrested would have noticeably hindered the functioning of the police state. The fate of the Franks wouldn't have been any different, because they all died anyway except for Anne's father, though he hardly meant to pay for his survival with the extermination of his whole family. But they could have sold their lives dearly instead of walking to their death.[5]

Alexander Donat, a survivor, has given a clear and concise analysis of how and when resistance was possible, and why Bettelheim had not only wronged the Frank family, but the European Jewish Community whose resistance – *whenever possible* – had been stronger than that of any other people. This question is seldom raised when one looks at the countries occupied by the Nazis, where only a very small percentage of the total population engaged in active resistance.

And yet, to me, this was not a central issue. The image of taking one or two Nazis along into death has something appealing to it – for the onlooker. Our sense of guilt is assuaged, and one deals far more easily with the image of the Warsaw Ghetto than with the camps where, it was claimed, 'the Jews walked like lambs to the slaughter'. A photograph exists of an old man walking along to the gas ovens, with his young grandchild walking alongside. The old man has one arm over the boy's shoulder and the other hand is pointed to the sky. Yet 'that man had more important things to do than to attack the SS man in charge, or to rush against a machine-gun emplacement. He had to give comfort to his grandchild, had to assure him with his love and with his religious faith!' I believe that this was a valid answer not seen clearly by Bettelheim, who had little concept of a spiritual resistance against evil which was so clearly evident in the places of death. Eugene Heimler came far closer to this realization in Auschwitz; and Viktor Frankl, basically non-religious, also responded to the greatness of the human soul discovered at Auschwitz, and did not equate the victims with apathy and despair. Why, in our time, is spiritual resistance so often misunderstood and branded as weak passivity? Taken into the streets, it is honoured and compared with Gandhi – but it is just as heroic in the bleak barracks of the concentration camp.

Bettelheim's special field was the healing of children, as he demonstrated in his work as principal of the University of Chicago's Sonia Shankman Orthogenic school. And he understood dreams, whether dreamed in the Israeli kibbutzim[6] or the dreams and myths of our Western civilization. I am not certain what went wrong with his analysis of the Jew under Nazi pressure, but must resist the temptation to analyse him, too, in terms of what was a transforming experience in Buchenwald. I know that it must not be compared with Auschwitz, a different camp in a different time. And there were other experiences of that time and place encountered by great Jewish minds which reached different conclusions. One thinks of Emil Fackenheim, for example, who analysed what was a degrading experience for himself and came up with a positive evaluation of his fellow prisoners. Perhaps part of the difference rests in the fact that Fackenheim was a rabbi and Bettelheim an analyst: conflicting Jewish religions, as someone has argued.

Bettelheim's name can be put into that list of great minds who were exposed to the Holocaust, shattered in some hidden corner of their being, and ultimately found the dark of the camp breaking through their defences and swallowing up the vital spark of life. But Bettelheim was a terminal case; he suffered greatly from his pain, and found that there was no more 'quality time' at the end of the road. He wanted to leave the stage with dignity, and his model was Socrates and the cup of hemlock. His death, like that of Koestler, was an example of excessive courage, rather than of fear. In a key essay by Bruno Bettelheim: 'The Holocaust – one generation after', he finds that resistance did not develop; the victims only hardened. He dismisses a Hungarian survivor who said she did not know about the concentration camps before she was deported. Hitler and the Nazis had made their position against Jews clear: how could she not know? It simply gave support to Christian Germans who claimed not to have known; lies, or conscious denials which by their very nature become unconscious denials. This may be a sound observation by a skilled analyst, but it cannot be made the unswerving rule. The fact that Jews escaped, came to ghettos and saw their warnings spurned or denied, can rightly be viewed as a tragedy of Jewish life; but it should not become a moral condemnation of the Jewish communities in Europe. I can and do agree with Bruno Bettelheim's statement that:

By calling the victims of the Nazis 'martyrs', we falsify their fate. The true meaning of 'martyr' is: 'one who voluntarily undergoes the penalty of death for refusing to renounce his faith' (OED). The Nazis made sure that nobody would mistakenly think that their victims were murdered for their religious beliefs. Renouncing their faith would have saved none of them. Those who converted to Christianity were gassed, as were those who were atheists and those who were deeply religious Jews. They did not die for any conviction, and certainly not out of choice.

The use of the word 'martyrs' obscures the fact that they were all *victims*, who did not want to die. Heroism has to be seen in different ways which does not obscure the issue for the next generation, who can live much more comfortably with the notion of martyrs than with the truth of the Jew as a victim in the world. Yet I cannot go along with Dr Bettelheim when he objects to these victims being thought of as superior human beings in some way. It is a fact that there were heroes in those days, among those who lived and in those who died. Bettelheim does not give sufficient credit to those who offered spiritual resistance, whether they lived or whether they died. I do agree with him when he draws Elie Wiesel into the discussion and notes that, in the end, there can be no discussion – only silence. As Wiesel said: 'Those who have not lived through the experience will never know; those who have will never tell; not really, not completely.' And still, we must be remembrancers who do not judge harshly, but with compassion.

Viktor Frankl also observed his fellow inmates in the concentration camp. This time the camp was Auschwitz, during the war which was intended to destroy the Jews; and Frankl's conclusions were totally different from those of Bruno Bettelheim. Frankl was also the product of Vienna; and he returned to that city after the war and his release from Auschwitz. There, he founded what has been called the third great Viennese school of psycho-analysis. Logotherapy, an existentialist psychotherapy which drew upon his Auschwitz experiences, rejected the Freudian teachings which saw human behaviour in terms of determinism, the sex drive, and the suppressed experi-ences of the past. It also refused to conform to the individual-analysis of Alfred Adler with its emphasis on human self-assertion and the drive for power. Instead, this 'third school' of logotherapy understood humans as beings who 'can be masters in their own home' and who can be free even of themselves. They can be responsible for themselves, and thus they can confront the present-day danger of feeling that there is no more meaning in their lives. The need for purpose, for self-fulfilment, for a higher meaning of life is at the centre of human aspiration. Frankl's new system, emerging out of the concentration camps, tried to address itself to these needs.

In his classic best-seller *Psychotherapy fuer jedermann*, Viktor Frankl writes about the human fear of nothingness, nihil, expressed in contemporary nihilism. Against the image of a Pavlovian system of reflexes or a Freudian mechanism, Frankl wants to assert human freedom:

Man denies his freedom, when he always flees into fatalism and lets himself be driven and pushed by outer or inner forces. Finally, he denies his *responsibility* through a collectivism which makes it possible for him to submerge himself within an anonymous mass instead of serving a true community with a conscious sense of responsibility. Our chief task – for psychotherapy as well – is to give the human being courage to be himself. Only when he has the courage for himself will he overcome the fear he has of himself.[7]

Man's search for meaning had been at the centre of Frankl's quest when he came back to Vienna out of a kingdom of hell where there was no meaning or where, at least, the inmates of the camp were denied meaning. It was there that he realized that those who were denied meaning have not necessarily become cyphers – they, and contemporary man, can regain meaning in life. This is not a Jobean task of wrestling meaning from God, but the exploration of inner human resources: love and faith are part of the ultimate human resources, the most private part of the self that cannot be exposed. It is not Freud's 'pleasure principle', or Adler's 'will to power' – the human 'will to meaning' which made him name this therapy logotherapy (from the Greek *logos*). If it was the 'third method' in Vienna, it did not estrange him from his teachers Freud and Adler (even when their schools drew away from him).

Viktor Frankl had several opportunities to leave Vienna, even after Anschluss when the Nazis were in full control. He felt that he must honour his parents, and stayed with them. Then, the road lead to Theresienstadt and, three camps later, he was in Auschwitz. With a clinical eye, he observed himself and his fellow inmates suffering under the inhuman assault waged against them which stripped them of their possessions and their identity. He saw that, often, it was the unscrupulous who survived, and felt that he and others who had survived needed chance, luck, and all manner of unpredictable events to escape death. Frequently, he said: 'We who have come back know: the best of us did not return.' And yet, alongside this humility, he also saw that this unbearable suffering could bring out the best in human beings, and that there was an inner freedom which endured and helped humans to confront suffering and death. These were the insights he brought to his healing practice, deeply aware that this understanding had to be invoked out of the innermost recesses of his patients, and that he could not impose his own values upon any of them.

The uniqueness of every human being is a principle of Judaism. Yet religion holds no monopoly upon that insight, and to understand Frankl one must not put him into the framework of a 'Jewish thinker' working out of the tradition, but rather one must honour him as a survivor who learned this truth in the camps. Each person there was possessed of an inner truth and core of meaning which could be armour and shield. Often, it was something which accompanied him to death, since it was the few who survived. The various patterns of spiritual resistance which we have examined in the Theresienstadt camp through which Frankl passed ran parallel to one another. The deeply religious self-assertion which could be traditional or progressive could be expressed by Leo Baeck and his 'secular' lectures or by private and group prayer. There were others who clung to a way of thinking which gave meaning to their lives: as communists, as Zionists – one had to reach out for meaning in any corner of the Holocaust kingdom. Somehow, there has to be an inner commitment to a goal which gives meaning, to other human beings who give love. In an interview printed in the *Observer* magazine[8] Viktor Frankl stressed his own need to reach out to others out of the obligation to help:

There is ultimately only one power, and that is the power to rescue!

I grasped the meaning of the greatest secret that human poetry and human thought and belief have to impart: the salvation of man is through love and in love.

I understood how a man who has nothing left in the world may still know bliss . . . In utter desolation, when man cannot express himself in positive action, when his only achievement may consist in enduring his sufferings in the right way, man can achieve fulfillment. For the first time in my life I was able to understand the meaning of the words, 'The angels are lost in perpetual contemplation of an infinite glory.'

This is not a retreat into some inner dimension of contemplation, but an opening of the self which takes the innermost resources residing within a human being and applies them to the darkness through which one has to pass. It is a text to set against the dark judgement of Bruno Bettelheim, who wanted a final, violent, self-assertion of the captured individual who should not be permitted to 'go gentle into the night' but should offer a fierce resistance which might have accumulated within the hell and become a stumbling block for those committing the evil. Standing on the outside, one cannot make prescriptions for what should have been done. And both Bettelheim and Viktor Frankl were healers who left the darkness and moved into the dawn of a new and creative life where they could help the next generations who could not fully understand what happened in the days of their parents. Our own days carry their own anguish and, in his text on psychotherapy, Frankl refers to our 'age of anxiety'. He also deals with the prevalence of suicide, but points to an interesting statistic which seems to indicate that the suicide rate drops in areas where the living standard also drops. And he writes:

How can one explain this? In my opinion, perhaps best through a simile: I was once told *that a building which has become dilapidated can be supported and strengthened* – paradoxically – *by having extra weight placed upon it.* It is similar with the human being: as outer difficulties grow, so do his inner powers of resistance.[9]

This is an insight rather than an absolute rule. The prevalence of the *muselman* in the camp, the person who had resigned under the heavy burden and was just marking time until death, shows us that suffering does not automatically ennoble and give strength to a person. More often than not, suffering destroys us. Yet the healing teaching of Viktor Frankl is that this need not happen, particularly in our own world where suffering is more limited and often of our own making. In the camps, Viktor Frankl saw base powers predominate – but he caught a glimpse of the uniqueness of the human being, of the power to love and to find meaning in life. He is one of the most important persons we have encountered in our search, someone who finds light after darkness and who brings healing and love into the world.

The third healer out of the camps was Eugene Heimler, a poet, a novelist, psychiatric social worker and, in every sense of our quest, a Dawn-Rider. Of the three, he is the only one with whom I have come into close personal contact. Almost a quarter of a century ago, Eugene ('John') Heimler started a small therapy group for rabbis in London, and brought some of the profound insights he had acquired in the camps to the special needs of the rabbis. Heimler had come to England from Hungary in 1947, two years after he had emerged from the camps. I had first met him through his writings, since his deeply moving account of this Holocaust, *Night of the mist*, had been one of the first works I had selected for my Holocaust anthology. One of its passages, a dream he dreamt as a young man in Hungary, can be linked to the notion of Bruno Bettelheim that physical resistance was the best possible response to the Nazis:

I was on the way to the pit in which heaved the dark sea of doomed bodies. There was a shovel in my hand, the kind that grave-diggers use in the cemetery. Slowly the thought came to me: 'You must die, you will die – but why die alone? The shovel in your hand is a weapon. You will have the strength to strike. If you must die, make certain that this murderer dies too.' I turned my back, lifted up my shovel and with upraised arm ran towards him. Suddenly everything appeared formless . . . when my frenzied rush had brought me up to him I saw that it was indeed only an unarmed figure of clay which stared witlessly into the world . . . and my arm was lowered without effect. I woke up.

The following morning, the 19th March, when my sister, deathly pale, announced to us the news that at 5.30 that morning the Germans had crossed the border, and occupied our country, I was not even surprised.[10]

Nor were they surprised when, not that long after, they were gathered up and sent along the road which lead into the death camps. His sister with her 2-year-old boy Gavriel died there, as did his father, uncles, aunts, cousins, and his own young wife Eva. After the dream came the reality, and it was worse than any nightmare built upon the news the wind had carried to him out of the shattered Jewish world into which Hungary was now precipitated. In *Night of the mist* the narrator reveals himself in such a way that the remembered evil is contained and somehow kept separate from us by a great spirit which takes the pain into itself and does not transmit all of it. Decades later, Eugene Heimler spoke on the theme 'Memories without hate':

> I am a man who was caught up by great historic events which were beyond my comprehension, and because I did not choose any of what has happened to me, for a long time after my liberation I had difficulty in accepting that a living and loving God would permit such global tragedy. Yet hardly eight years after the event I had the urge to build on the ruins of destruction . . . the prayer which I had been told as a child came to me: 'Let me be silent if people curse me, my soul still and humble and at peace with all'. But how could my soul be quiet when I was cut off from my roots, my family, my friends: how could I be at peace with all when my days seemed numbered and when death lurked in every corner and in every eye? Yet eight years later this prayer had become very significant and relevant to me.[11]

Heimler came to London, went through his analysis (in 1949). He learned to trust himself and his intuitions, just as these intuitions had saved his life in the camps when he instinctively gave different answers from his fellow prisoners and was not sent to the gas chamber; just as, one night, he refused to go back into his barracks which was emptied in the morning – and he had somehow survived. Now, in England, a new life started for him with his new wife and sons.

Eugene Heimler began working as a psychiatric social worker in 1956 and, in the course of this work, began developing what was to be called the Heimler Method. It began with the question he had asked himself when he left camp and started a new life: 'On what does it depend whether life defeats us or whether we succeed?' His personal answer was that he could find satisfaction through the personal positive experiences of his past, and of his childhood. One had to keep remembering this. At the same time, recalling the meaninglessness of camp-life which destroyed the individual, he came to stress the *meaning* of one's work as a vital ingredient to success. He had seen many prisoners die after being forced to carry sand and rubble from one part of the camp to the other – and then returning it. But now, in

London, working with the unemployed, he saw that meaninglessness was also destroying them. His job consisted of introducing meaning into their lives, through a psycho-social feedback system which utilized the self-knowledge of his clients who were unaware of these hidden resources within them.

Heimler's own words:

> Instead of trying to talk people out of something they consider bad or evil, or negative, we should help them to think of how he or she might use this for her or his own good. We don't analyse its roots, why and how it all came about, but rather try to establish that it is there, and what we might do in order to connect this to the reality of that person's life with genuine victory.[12]

The method is always action-orientated, rising out of Heimler's conviction that action is the end of persecution. Confronted with the machinery of the camps, knowing that it would destroy him as a person even before the end of the gas chamber, Heimler tried to rebel, attempted to escape, and turned to his hidden self, where he found the necessary vitality to survive from day to day.

Part of the Heimler method appears similar to Frankl's logotherapy, but it is on a much simpler level, without a large intellectual superstructure. It works. As a lay parson, standing outside this particular discipline, I can only venture my own opinion which deals with the therapist far more than with the therapy. I find that the great healers of our time work perfectly within their own system – or even outside of it. And no system will work without a capable therapist.

Each of these, then, has had remarkable success as a healer, although Viktor Frankl is in a class all his own, towering over this generation of analysts. They all entered the universe of the concentration camps and suffered in an unimaginable manner. That kind of pain cannot be quantified, particularly from the outside. While Bruno Bettelheim judged later camp experiences with an insufficient yardstick, that does not diminish the suffering he endured, the attack upon his psyche, his response to it. His judgements in the field of history and his assessment of other sufferers and of the Jewish community of that time does not diminish the appreciation one must have for a man who came out of hell and was able to give another lifetime of service to humanity. This, in fact, is what these three healers present to us with absolute clarity: the Holocaust and its suffering could not destroy the love for humanity which existed in the deepest recesses of these individuals. Even where it was recognized that the suffering could

destroy altruism, that it often led to bitter battles for survival – one survivor
records an incident of a father who murdered his son for a piece of bread
and was then killed by the others in the barracks who had seen this –
there are remarkable testimonies of humanity reasserting itself in that hell.
Eugene Heimler records that when the victims discovered one another as
human beings, suffering became more bearable:

> It was in Buchenwald that I learned, from Jews, Christians, Moslems
> and pagans, from Englishmen, Serbs, Romanians, Czechs, Frenchmen,
> Dutch, Russians, Greeks, Albanians, Poles and Italians that I was only
> one more suffering insignificant man; that the tongue my mother taught
> me . . . was an artificial barrier between myself and others. For essen-
> tially, as mankind, we are one. A slap on the face hurts an Englishman
> as much as a German, a Hungarian or a Negro. The pain is the same.
> That I was not in any way superior, that I am not different from others,
> that I am but a link in a great chain, was among the greatest discoveries
> of my life.[13]

Eventually, Eugene Heimler found himself, in the midst of the camp, in
charge of a group of children. He taught them. He comforted them, wept
with them, and prayed with them. As he shared his faith in God with them,
they grew stronger. In those moments, Heimler said:

> . . . I felt I was praising that Infinite Power which had granted me the
> opportunity of playing a positive role in this inferno. I felt that I had
> strength only because He was present in my blood and in my senses,
> and that so long as I realized this force within me, the Germans would
> be unable to touch me.

There are different discoveries to be made in the dark midnight of the
soul. Individuals can discover their own hidden resource; some can discover
God, while others find the neighbour, although God is there too. Religious
or non-religious, these responses link humanity together so that they
become more than the one person sinking under the weight of suffering.
One cannot speak of a true community of sufferers helping each other
when one looks at the camps. The pressures were too enormous and the
evil of the persecutors could penetrate the persons caught in their web.
What is more remarkable to us who look back from a great distance is that
there is so much testimony of goodness in the midst of that evil. If the
Holocaust were an unrelieved image of total darkness, we could not bear

to look back to it, to recall it. And there are many who, for that reason, want to walk away from it, do not want to traumatize the next generation. This can simplify life, can permit us to cauterize the wound of a people and of a world. Yet it ignores the wounds left in our civilization, in the world itself, and in healers who came out of the camps cannot simply be accepted as a gift of our own time. The darkness lives in them as it lives in us. We are all maimed by what has happened, and the current acts of terror that live in Europe and in the rest of the world are not unrelated to the evil of the time of darkness.

The historians have charted the outlines of that kingdom of hell for us with varying success. 'Here there be tygers' might still be the correct inscription for each book which charts out its own programmes and tries to give a definite answer where no answers can be given. The last time I visited Buchenwald I saw that the old, dreadful inscription was still upon the gate: *Jedem das seine* – to each his own. The total cynicism of the Nazis can be seen here; but one may also feel that the three healers who walked out of those gates had their own answer which went beyond the theories of the historians. They found that each human being is a container of love, a free soul searching for meaning in this world. At this point, one does move from the darkness towards the dawn.

Healing comes much slower than the dawn. But it does come.

NOTES

1. R. Rubenstein and J. Roth, *Approaches to Auschwitz* (London, SCM Press, 1987), p. 230.
2. R. Rubenstein, *After Auschwitz* (London, Johns Hopkins, 1992).
3. Ibid., p. 11.
4. Ibid., p. 14.
5. B. Bettelheim, *The informed heart* (Glencoe, The Free Press, 1960).
6. B. Bettelheim, *The children of the dream* (1969).
7. V. Frankl, *Psychotherapy fuer jedermann* (Freiburg, Herder, 1971), p. 115.
8. *The Observer*, 21 June 1992.
9. V. Frankl, *Psychotherapy fuer jedermann* (Freiburg, Herder, 1972), pp. 31–32.
10. E. Heimler, *Night of the mist* (London, Bodley Head, 1959).
11. E. Heimler, 'Memories with hate: the Kaufman memorial lecture', *European Judaism*, vol. 21, No. 2, p. 7.
12. B. Heimler, 'E Heimler: in memoriam', *European Judaism*, vol. 24, No. 2, p. 57.
13. Heimler, *Night of the mist*.

# [ 4 ]

# THE OTHER AUSCHWITZ

CHRISTIANS AND THE *SHOAH*

THERE are so many ways to find our Dawn-Riders, the guides to the future who have left the darkness of the past behind them. Some, we find posthumously: they died in the darkness, but their teachings have endured for us. Some, we find inside our own tradition. It brings them closer to us, but at the same time presents its own problems if we have broken with that tradition or have emended it in our own way. My own approach is not to look so much for a system but for some insight, some special teaching which I can incorporate into my life and, perhaps, into a system all my own.

What happens when we meet teachers from another tradition? Knowing that we are not bound to take on the full load under which they travel – the 'house of the turtle' – we can fully accept what they have to give us. More often than not, this consists not only of a single insight, but also of a way of life which we admire, and which inspires us. The fact that a Christian willingly enters the concentration camp in order to proclaim his or her solidarity with the Jewish community is so remarkable that I will always stop, revere, and light a candle of memorial for that person. Some of my friends cavil at this response on my part. 'How', for example, 'how can you celebrate Maximilian Kolbe when he was the editor of an anti-Semitic paper before the war?' Or 'But Bonhoeffer came late to the knowledge concerning Jews; he was at first only concerned for baptised Jews!' Or: 'Niemoeller? Didn't he offer to command a U-boat for Hitler to prove his patriotism?' *Und so weiter* . . . and so on.

To answer these questions, we look at the facts, and then try to ascertain not only what is true or false in those charges, but the conditions under which this type of flawed action could still fashion acts of heroism and of deep spiritual commitment to God and to humanity. Sometimes it is hard to look at Christianity and the burden it carries in terms of the *Shoah*. Yet this deserves special examination in our search for guidance. First of all, we have to look at the darkness. We have to understand Auschwitz not only in our terms, but also in terms of the Christians whose lives were also touched by that darkness . . .

Auschwitz is more than an incurable wound in the Jewish soul. It is a trauma, hidden or open, which exists in our civilization. In an era which has begun to show awareness of the dispossessed, the enslaved, and the minorities which have been persecuted and permitted to suffer, other aspects of the kingdom of hell have begun to receive attention. The persecution of homosexuals has not ceased; AIDS as the new plague has made them targets in new areas. Yet there is now at least some knowledge now of their presence in the concentration camps. The fearful Nazi doctrine which attacked them, the mentally sick, the handicapped – the whole concept of racial superiority and of the *mastervolk* – is re-encountered in contemporary attitudes. The knowledge of what happened to them during the Holocaust may act as a corrective to the present; it cannot undo what happened in the past, or give recompense.

Then there are the gypsies – the *Sinti-Roma*. In terms of percentages, the gypsies suffered most in the Holocaust. And, after the war, they discovered that even in the new democratic West Germany some of the racial laws of the Nazis remained in force or were reintroduced. 'What? Let the gypsies, the "travellers", occupy camping spaces which would bring in hard currency from tourists?' And so they were chased away; something which happened with monotonous regularity not only in Germany, but throughout Europe (including England), where 'travellers' were viewed with fear and contempt by a comfortable society which often paid only lip service to their right in a world which had ostensibly accepted the 'Declaration of Universal Human Rights' written for the UN by Rene Chassin.

For more than a decade, I have talked with one of their leaders, Romani Rosa. Romani and I have met, and exchanged our writings and sorrows. It was important for him to be in contact with the Jewish community which had at least begun to receive some restitution for the days of the *Shoah*. No restitution had been given to the *Sinti-Roma*, and they needed help to process claims. The late Heinz Galinski, the chairman of the Jewish community (first in Berlin, then in all Germany) had joined them in their fight.

More than anything, they needed to know that the world cared; that people knew what had happened to them. They do not forget; they had their own writings, recollections, memories of Auschwitz and Buchenwald. Perhaps more than others, their fate is a touchstone and test for our time: as long as they are still persecuted, Auschwitz lives in our midst.

The current upheavals have touched them in particular ways. Romani Rosa is now being torn apart by the new persecutions in Central Europe. A huge group of *Sinti-Roma* had come to Germany from Hungary and Romania. What could one do for the new refugees? The whole agenda of the *Sinti-Roma* was changed; and they split apart. As a historian, I recalled the problems besetting the Jews of France at the time of the French Revolution. The Sephardi Jews, long established and comfortable within French life, now wanted their rights and French citizenship. But there was the problem of the Alsatian Jews, impoverished and more German than French – Ashkenazi Jews. Sadly, some of the leaders of Sephardi Jewry tried to ignore their needs, wanted the assimilated French Jewry to receive their rights, even if it meant postponing the Alsatians' claims to a later time. Something akin to this situation confronted the small, well organized community of *Sinti-Roma* in Germany who did not want to see themselves swallowed up in this new wave of the needy. In the end, French Jewry united and established itself; one must hope that the same pattern will work for the *Sinti-Roma*. What can and must be stressed, of course, is that their problems are not of their making. A just society must meet their needs, both in terms of a past which most people do not want to remember, and in terms of the present which most people do not want to see.

Auschwitz lives in the present. It is particularly alive in the Church; more specifically, in the churches. It is difficult for an outsider to be fair to the many varieties of Christianity, but I speak as a friend rather than as an opponent. Part of the problem with contemporary Christianity is its alliance with the political structures of the world in which it lives. Often, nationalism and Christianity grew very close together, particularly in countries where both were suppressed by political systems. The re-emergence of the Russian Orthodox Church, for example, brought with its new power the ancient superstitions which had been engrained in Russian peasant life but also in the teachings of the church: anti-Semitism. The new openness of the Western Church teachers had not penetrated. The Jews 'had killed Christ'. The Holocaust had been their punishment (when the Holocaust was recalled at all); Jews were still enemies. Part of the Auschwitz 'problem' for the Poles, as we will explore, was their need to make that place of death both a national and a Christian monument; the Jewish experience had to be ignored. And a Christianity, which is built upon Calvary and the suffering on the Cross, cannot easily assimilate the awareness of Auschwitz as the absolute evil for which there is no explanation. The Cross, for Christians, must be both the ultimate suffering and the expiation and the redemption of human suffering – at least, for Christians who have not relearned their faith after Auschwitz. Later, we can explore the new Christian post-Holocaust theology. Here, we are still in the process of learning from human experience, from those who entered Auschwitz and did not emerge again; and from those who were as brands plucked from the fire with a survivor's message to the rest of the world.

It is invidious to choose from survivors, since each one has a personal and unique message either locked up within the soul or ready for communication. Sometimes, a wrong choice is made. Edith Stein was a Catholic nun who was taken from her convent and murdered in the camps. Christians surrounded her life and death with particular concern, viewing her as an authentic Christian martyr particularly acceptable to the world and to the Jewish community because Edith Stein had been born and raised within the Jewish faith before converting to Catholicism. Jews were appalled. Edith Stein had been taken from her convent because of her *Jewish* background; the other nuns were left alone. No one would deny her tragedy and the rare shining of her Christian faith. Yet she died a Jewish death among her people, and it was at the least highly insensitive to make her a voice of Christian suffering. She still remains a symbol of *shared* suffering for our time, and a reminder that a whole history of Jewish-born Christians who went into the darkness because of their family history remains to be written.

Who are the Christian messengers of that time? There are of course the great names to which one must now turn: Dietrich Bonhoeffer, Martin Niemoeller, Maximilian Kolbe and many more. There are arguments and questions concerning each of them, important not because they diminish these men in the end, but because of the very flaws of the imperfect person enhance their greatness. A man can edit an anti-Semitic paper when young and place himself next to the Jews in the death camps when that time comes. One can be selective in the support one gives to the suffering; one can be blind in some time and some place. The key to those great lives was that they stood firm in a time of evil; and that they were good.

What about the unknown, unsung, or almost unbelievable lives which come to us when we examine this darkest period? As a Jewish chaplain of Columbia University, I welcomed Rolf Hochhuth to the campus, so that he could discuss his play *The representative* with the students. The play was based upon an unbelievable premise: someone working within the SS would find out the truth about the camps, and would approach the Church and the world in an attempt to have them intercede. The play was a bitter attack against the Pope, but also provided the image of a good priest, Father Riccardo, who would express his solidarity with the suffering Jews by entering freely into the camps. Reality is stranger than fiction: these things happened. The true story of Kurt Gerstein may not be a theological statement of Christianity in the time of crisis. But Gerstein was a member of the 'Confessing Church' as a young man who, after a study of medicine, joined the SS in 1941. He achieved a responsible position within that criminal organization, and came to discover the technical details and the extent of their plans for mass murder. He then did try to inform the world: church officials, politicians, anyone who might have helped prevent some of the crime – it is said that he contacted over a hundred people. Then he disappeared again from the historical stage, although there is a story that he committed suicide in a French prison in 1945.

There were individuals, questionable in their motives at times, flawed characters, who tried to fight evil where men of good repute and fine character failed. Oscar Schindler, setting up factories for his own profit and providing an 'ark' in which he saved hundreds of concentration camp inmates, must be honoured for his achievements. We cannot be ungenerous by picking out flaws in those who saved lives. In our view of Christianity, we can and must see an overall pattern of concern and justice, of high ideals and the intense love for God which it tried to establish within the world. Any religious structure will contain the flaws of the world into which it is placed. Evil and unworthy men and women will be part of its machinery – which itself can be used for harm instead of good. With the best will, recognizing the invincible stupidity of morally blind functionaries, I try to excuse the Church of some of its excesses. Yet, when I reflect upon the 'underground railroad' which smuggled Nazi criminals into South America after the war, I cannot maintain such a position. It was an evil act, a perversion of justice, possible only because those involved had once again surrendered moral judgement to the organization and had become robots inside an amoral transportation machinery.

One turns to the great lives with relief: individuals justify an institution more than the institution justifies its members. Dietrich Bonhoeffer would have been a great teacher and human being in any age. The Bible says of Noah: 'He was a righteous man in his generation. He walked with God.' The rabbis argue a great deal about the phrase: 'in his generation'. Some say that his goodness is only relative – where everyone is wicked, even a weak person can be considered good. Others feel, and their view prevails in the rabbinic text, that goodness which prevails in an evil society must be even greater than the easy, comfortable acts of goodness possible in a gentle environment. Certainly, Bonhoeffer was a good man in an evil time. His teachings and beliefs belonged to a Church which had not yet rid itself of a violent animosity against Judaism and the Jews, but it was dominated by the 'teaching of contempt'. Here, we look more at the person and his actions in a world where the flood of hate had swept across his land. Dietrich Bonhoeffer openly expressed his resistance against the 'Arian Paragraph' which removed the Jews from the protection of the law, in April 1933. Over the years, he showed increasing concern for the fate of the Jews; first, more clearly, for the 'Christian' Jews who were part of the Church; and, later on, for all Jews. Late in 1939, he came to recognize where obedience to the state had to end – not an easy insight for the obedient Christian – and he began to involve himself in the conspiracy against Hitler which ultimately led to his death.

*Kristallnacht*, 9 November 1938, is a proper place to take note of Christians and ask about their silence or their activities. Coming out of my hiding place on that night, wandering through the streets as a child seeing the synagogue burning and the unconcerned church nearby, I had come to believe that we were all alone, that no help could be found in those places termed 'houses of God' by my neighbour. Was Dietrich Bonhoeffer among the silent, unconcerned onlookers? Certainly, in those days he was not like Helmut Gollwitzer, whose sermon in Niemoeller's Dahlem Church let the reality of that time shimmer through opaque language. Nor was he Karl Immer in Wuppertal, with his straightforward question to the congregation: 'The question is simple: how deeply rooted is the evil?', which his congregation interpreted correctly. The early history of Bonhoeffer and the events which follow that day in November let us see this questioning Christian scholar in a positive light.

In 1933, Bonhoeffer had already demanded that the Church act against the persecution of the Jews. In that same year, he refused to sign the 'Bethel Confession' since the section on Israel had been cut by his more cautious colleagues. During his years in London, Bonhoeffer had been active in the help given to German-Jewish emigrants; and there is his 1935 statement: 'Only someone who speaks out for the Jews has the right to sing Gregorian chants!' Eberhard Bethge was with Bonhoeffer on 10 November, travelling from two small communities Bonhoeffer served where no actions had been taken, and where the reports were sparse. The two of them travelled to Berlin, where as an already suspected person Bonhoeffer was not permitted to preach. Bonhoeffer had Jewish relatives in Goettingen, and he asked Bethge to find out whether their home had been attacked (it was spared).

Bonhoeffer returned to Koeslin, where he was conducting his study group, illegally, two days later. There, his students had now learned how the local synagogue had been burned, and a long discussion took place among them. One of the students reported the discussion in a later book:

> A great discussion commenced among ourselves as to how to assess this action. Some spoke about the curse which had rested upon the Jews since the crucifixion of Jesus Christ. (Bonhoeffer had returned to us by then.) Bonhoeffer now turned against this, rejecting the interpretation that the destruction of the synagogues by the Nazis was the fulfilment of the curse against the Jews, in the sharpest way possible. 'If today the synagogues burn then, tomorrow, the churches will be set on fire!'

Bonhoeffer knew that the Church (and some of the students he was instructing) was unclear within itself how to deal with the persecution of a people constituting a challenge to current Christian theology. Even the 'Confessing Church' of that time had no trouble in accepting the dogma of the Jews as a 'cursed people', as deicides. Luther's anti-Jewish teachings had been republished in 1937, and there were few, like Bonhoeffer, who slowly and hesitatingly began to move towards what was not yet called an 'Israel theology' within the Church. Bonhoeffer turned to the Bible in prayer during dark times; and he marked Psalm 74 for himself that week, a psalm which speaks of the Babylonian attack upon Israel 'they burn all the houses of God in our land!' In a pastoral letter, immediately forbidden by Goebbels but copied and sent around by his students, Bonhoeffer then added a sentence: 'In these last days I have thought much about Psalm 74, Zacharias 2, 12, Romans 9, 3f and 11, 11–15. This leads us profoundly into prayer'. It does not say that much to us, perhaps, in our time; in that time, it was more than might have been expected. And, by 1940, Bonhoeffer was part of the conspiracy. I personally find it significant that members of the Church had to enter the political area rather than explore possibilities for actions in a church grown weak.

Can a rabbi invoke the New Testament against the Church? When I look at the events of 1939, I tend to see the story of Peter who denied his saviour thrice. After Austria had been annexed, the 'official' national church had demanded an oath of allegiance to Hitler as a 'birthday present' – and even the vast majority of pastors in the 'Confessing Church' joined in this betrayal of their faith (Hitler was not impressed). Then, many of them distanced themselves from a 'peace liturgy' created by some church synods who were promptly accused of treason by the SS. And then, the church groups clearly rejected Karl Barth's counsel that a war against Hitler was a just war. The cock crowed more than three times in those days.

In a text written on Christmas, 1942, entitled *Nach zehn jahren* and hidden within the rafters of his parents' home, Dietrich Bonhoeffer described his views on the inner life of the conspiracy against Hitler. He had little time left before entering his cell.

The text deals with the individual who is also German and who is, as Bethge notes, perhaps himself, *Civil Courage*.

Who would deny that the German always fulfilled the utmost: in obedience, in his task, in his profession? He offered his total life here, and all of his courage. Nevertheless, the German safeguarded his freedom – and where in the world has there been more passionate discussion concerning freedom than in Germany, from Martin Luther to the philosophy of idealism? – safeguarded in that he strove to liberate himself from the expression of his own will in the service of the totality. His calling and freedom were to him two sides of the same coin. But, in that he misguided the world. He had not counted on the fact that his readiness to subjugate himself, to give all his life to the task, could be misused for evil. When this happened, when the exercise of his calling became questionable in itself, all of his moral preconceptions tumbled. It came to be seen that the German still lacked a decisive, basic understanding; that of the necessity of free responsible action even against a calling and a commanded task. In its place there established itself on the one hand an irresponsible lack of scruples, and on the other hand, a self-lacerating sense of duty which never led to the correct action. But Civil Courage can only grow out of free responsibility of the free man. Only today are Germans beginning to discover what free responsibility means.[1]

Here, then, is a text taken out of a situation of anguish. It is essential that the content of such a text should not be divorced from the existential situation out of which it was created. The history of a people is addressed, but beyond that Bonhoeffer appraises the nature of the human being. A Christian preacher-prophet castigates his people for losing their freedom by failing to exercise it, by permitting injustice to be done to their powerless brethren.

Do words help us to understand the historical situation, both then and now? Dietrich Bonhoeffer saw the fusion of nationalism and the Church in Germany, and fought against it to the point of the ultimate sacrifice.

For him the predicament is prefigured by the debate between Moses and Aaron. He shows the conflict between them in his sermon on 'The Church of Moses and the Church of Aaron', preaching on 28 May 1933, in the *Kaiser-Wilhelm-Gedächtnis-Kirche* a few days after the 'German-Christians' had named Ludwig Muller as their national, nationalist bishop:

> Moses and Aaron, the two brothers, from the same seed, the same blood, out of the same history, walking side by side for part of the way – then torn apart. Moses, the first prophet, Aaron, the first priest. Moses, called by God, chosen without respect of person, the man with the heavy tongue, the servant of God, who lives totally in listening to the world of his Lord. Aaron, the man with the purple vestment and the holy crown, the sanctified and sacred priest, who has to preserve the divine service for the priest . . .[2]

In the confrontation between the brothers, Bonhoeffer sees the internal conflict of the religious institution. Moses is on the mountain, waiting for God's word – which cannot be hurried. Aaron wants to serve the needs of the moment, the impatient congregation which would reject the universal for the particular. They want to pray. They want to sacrifice – is it a bad thing to serve their limited needs? Let them have the Church of Aaron: the Church without God! Does not a 'National Church' bring sacraments to the devout? And they are eager. Bonhoeffer preaches:

> Humanity is ready for any sacrifice, and sacrifice in which it can celebrate itself, can worship the work of its hands. In front of the god fashioned by the work of our hands, after our own desire, humanity and the worldly church sinks to its knees, joyous, smiling. [Everything] is offered up to it . . . everything thrown into the fiery oven of the idol . . . everything that has value, that is holy . . . all their ideals . . . and then comes the intoxication.[3]

Moses can do little against this escape into the world of emotion. The Church of Moses, the vision of God, is far away – until it returns from the Holy Mountain, until the tablets are smashed, the golden calf lies shattered upon the ground, until the world Church has been judged and God rules again. The Church which presumes to make God out of its priest is omnipresent in the world seen by the preacher. It has to be torn apart, so that the congregation might reassemble as the Church of Moses. And he preaches:

Out of the impatient church there comes to be the church of the silent waiting, out of the church of stormy striving for the fulfilled desire, for seeing, there comes the church of sober faith, out of the church of self-dedication there arises the church which prays prayers to the one God. Will that church receive the same dedication, the same sacrifices (spent for the church of Aaron)?[4]

The caesura does not remain. Again, Moses climbs the mountain. This time to pray for his people. He offers himself as a sacrifice: 'Do not reject me with my people. We are one, O Lord. I love my brethren.' But God's answer remains dark, awful, and threatening. 'Moses could not achieve the atonement. Who achieves atonement? None but the man who is both priest and prophet . . . the man with the crown of thorns . . .'

Looking at the Dawn-Rider, Dietrich Bonhoeffer, we see a man who understood the suffering God, as he had come to understand the suffering of Israel. This is Eberhard Bethge's account:

Immediately before the failed Putsch, Bonhoeffer, in his letter of 18 July 1944 wrote statements which bring the Messianic suffering event of Christ and of Israel, as well as the happenings of the present, into full inclusivity. Metanoia, in this place, is a 'letting oneself to be pulled along into the way of Jesus Christ, into the Messianic event, so that Isaiah 53 will now be fulfilled.' Isaiah 53 as vicarious suffering of Israel for the nations is not fulfilled within those days but in a now, in the present, as 'life participating in the Ohnmacht Gottes, God's weakness in this world' (WEN 396). It is thus the Jews who keep the Christ question open.

Two days earlier, Bonhoeffer had fashioned the formula which has now become famous, 'Before and with God we live without God' (WEN 394). Interpreting it 'Before and with the Biblical God we live without the Greek God'; 'Before and with the crucified God we live without the enthroned God'; 'Before and with the suffering God we live without the omnipotent God'. The poem written in the same days, *Christians and Heathen*, belongs to this, particularly the second verse (WEN 382):

To God in his weakness humanity goes. Find him maligned, poor, without shelter and bread. Sin, weakness, and death held him in their throes. Christians stand by God, in his pain, in his dread.

There are signposts here, pointing in the direction of a theology after Auschwitz.[5]

'If there was a God, how could I bear it not to be a God.' Nietzsche.

Nietzsche's saying was written into one of Martin Niemoeller's diaries; and it is at least a hint that we are dealing with a complex being, a war hero and U-boat captain in World War I, and who was a different kind of hero in World War II – as Hitler's 'personal prisoner' in a concentration camp. He was also a great preacher and pastor, the central symbol of the 'Confessing Church' which represented the conscience of Christianity during Hitler's time; he remains an enigma to me.

After the war, he was one of the first to admit that the 'Confessing Church', with all the credit due to it for its stance against Hitler, had done far too little to combat the evil of Nazism as it appeared within society itself; they had fought for themselves, their own freedom, and had fought nobly. It is true that a memorial address to the Fuehrer, with which he was involved, had clearly pointed to the attack upon the Ten Commandments taking place within the whole land; and that had been in the summer of 1936. This memorial was also read from some pulpits. The German Church today, and many of those who knew him and understood what he was trying to do, have no hesitation in seeing him as a moral leader who inspired his own generation and those who succeeded in the years that followed. I do not challenge this – particularly since all our quest has convinced me that we are not looking for saints, but for leaders and teachers who could rise above their own weaknesses, and the flaws built into the religious structures they served, in order to make a statement which stood out in their time and which will stand above time. Niemoeller's last sermon before his arrest makes a similar point:

> In these critical days in which we live, we have wished for ourselves that there might be today a single, respected, leading man like Gamaliel who, as a decent man, might summon us to be truthful, who, as a pious man, might call us to give honour to the will of God.[6]

The qualities of the former U-boat captain and leader in the Church shone through that dark time; his courageous and angry fight against Hitler, his attempts to protect the Church from the Nazis, his role as the genial friend and pastor who had reached out to his flock and had comforted them in the time of terror were all recognized. Niemoeller had been slow to recognize the total evil which Hitler represented, in part because he was a

German patriot and Hitler, after all, was the head of the state. Patriotism, despite the positive qualities inherent in it, can blind or at least distort the vision.

A traditional, fervent religion could, perforce, accept many of the judgements of an earlier time, the time when the Church was engaged in a fight against the Jewish people and against Judaism. Some of Niemoeller's sermons echo those traditional sentiments, but only rarely. The fact that his last sermon, cited above, shows the rabbi, Gamaliel, as a pattern of righteousness, is an indication that Niemoeller could and did separate himself from that Christian 'teaching of contempt'. And his stance after the war, when the confession he wanted the Church to make begins with himself and his own sins; clearly, the image of the High Priest in the Bible who first confesses for himself and his family, before turning to the necessary confession for the community, is not far from the Christian statement. Even then, one must state that the Stuttgart Confession in 1945, with all its humility, in no way comes to terms with the Holocaust in which the Church *had* to see itself involved in some way.

In an essay on Niemoeller, Thomas Mann has pointed to the impact and personal charisma of a man who at an earlier stage was even acquitted by a German 'people's court' of the charge of having misused his pulpit for political purposes – particularly since he was guilty of that 'crime'. He had challenged the puppet church which had tried to establish a 'German Church' as a support group for Hitler. In the old conflict between 'Caesar and God' he had declared:

> Without grumbling, we will give to the world that which belongs to it. But when the world demands that which belongs to God, we have to turn to courageous resistance. We cannot give that which is God's, cannot, for the sake of living well in a foreign place, surrender our native place, our home . . .[7]

According to Mann, any German pastor had to become a resistance fighter. At this point, Martin Niemoeller *did* become a political agitator; and the court which refused to convict him was touched by the message which could even penetrate the minds of those who had basically surrendered themselves to the state. In this instance, it did not matter: once outside the courthouse, Niemoeller was picked up by Hitler's secret agents and transported to the concentration camp. As the 'special prisoner of Adolf Hitler' he occupied an unusual position in that kingdom of death: condemned to death, and yet somehow not to be killed. A hostage against the Church, a reminder to Christians that they must not rebel; and yet that very reminder strengthened them in their resistance to the evil regime. In this penultimate sermon from his pulpit Niemoeller preached:

> We have to do our (Christian) duty. Whoever wants to preserve his life must lose it . . . which, in practice, means: I have to speak in this manner again; perhaps, next Sunday, I can no longer do so. I *have* said this to you once more, today, in all clarity, for who knows what will happen next Sunday?[8]

Two Sundays later, the pulpit was empty.

Looking at the life of Martin Niemoeller, one is first struck by a quality of his person which one might call 'loyalty', although this does not express the full power of his the German word *treue*. He was faithful: to his conservative Prussian family, to his country, his ideals. He had joined the German navy in 1910. At the end of World War I, he had become known as a daring U-boat captain. Perhaps the disillusionment and defeat brought him into the ministry, although there had been clear signs of his interest in religion. At any event, by 1931 he was the pastor in Dahlem, a fashionable part of Berlin, with a large following of congregants who admired the sermons and the concern he showed his flock. His criticism of the Nazis became more pronounced after 1933, and, in 1934, he was summoned to appear before Hitler. Goering personally read out the transcripts of his 'bugged' telephone calls; and he was prohibited from preaching.

This did not stop his religious work, although, in later years, he again accused himself for not having done enough for others outside the Church. A classic comment has been attributed to him which, in one version, reads:

> First, they came for the Jews. I did not speak out because I was not a Jew.
> Then, they came for the Communists. I did not speak out because I was not a Communist.
> Then, they came for the trade unionists. I did not speak out because I was not a trade unionist.
> Then, they came for me. And there was no one left to speak out for me.

I must note that this is too good a text to be left alone. In recent years, I have seen it quoted in a version which also contains reference to the homosexuals who were mercilessly persecuted by the Nazis. And I have seen an earlier version in which the Jews were not mentioned. Personally, I would go for the text as it is given above, since it certainly represents Martin Niemoeller's thoughts and teachings after he had been saved from the concentration camp at the end of the war. In the Stuttgart Confession, Niemoeller and ten of his colleagues who had been active in the resistance against Hitler and had suffered, were able to say:

We confess that we should have witnessed more bravely, prayed more faithfully, believed more joyfully and loved more fervently.

– an attitude which fits the earlier statement. Again, the narrowness of Stuttgart can be seen to rise out of an incomprehension of the enormous darkness from which they had emerged. The Stuttgart Confession was the last statement of the old church. The new awareness, which had to include the Jewish dimension and which had to change their theology, still waited for them in the years to come.

Niemoeller has been called a 'prophet for our times'. He ruled over the Province of Hessen Nassau from his episcopal residence in Wiesbaden, and was an efficient and yet warm-hearted administrator, perhaps with little time for 'democratic processes'. His pastors were still crew members on the ship which he commanded. There was also the second life on the international scene. Martin Niemoeller was the first President of the German Church's office for foreign relations. Once a strong Conservative, he had moved into the field of ecumenical dialogue. And then, with the evangelical tradition still very close to his heart, Martin Niemoeller became an international evangelist.

Niemoeller moved around the world: America in particular, but he was also the first prominent West German to visit the Soviet Union. In 1961, Niemoeller was elected president of the World Council of Churches. He felt comfortable in that role, and remained close to the figures within the ecumenical world well after his retirement. And then there came the third stage, a complete break with much of his past history: Martin Niemoeller became an ardent pacifist, and a strong voice for disarmament. Since this was precisely the time when West Germany became an active part of NATO, a collision course was set for this pastor who 'simply would not stay out of politics'. Well ahead of his time, Niemoeller pleaded for a rapprochement with the Eastern bloc, and opposed German rearmament (together with his friend Gustav Heinemann, who later became the West German president).

The Church pulled away from him, disagreeing with his pacifism. And, by 1959, his public pronouncements and speeches had become so opposed to current politics that the Defence Minister Franz Joseph Strauss tried to have him prosecuted for 'defamation of the armed forces' – a far cry from the U-boat captain. Perhaps he was more mellow in his last years. Certainly he recalled the occasion when he offered Hitler his services as a U-boat captain again, and reflected how fortunate he had been that Hitler had not accepted this offer.

I have said that he was still an enigma to me. Behind this, I see my own disability to enter completely into the thoughts of a Christian, even when I respect that person deeply. There is also, I confess, a sadness that Niemoeller did not reach out to his Jewish brethren immediately and fully. Yet for the majority of his life, if one thinks about this, he fought against the flaw in his church. He remained a dedicated Christian who believed in challenging a world which had strayed from the Biblical vision. Any company of Dawn-Riders would be enriched by the presence of Pastor Martin Niemoeller.

*The Christian and Jewish Community Today:*
*find a joint way towards the dawn*

Jewish and Christian teachings meet along the frontiers of the dark experience we call the *tremendum* and the *Shoah*. We have listened to the Dawn-Riders of Christianity, especially those who also entered the concentration camps, with reverence and with the knowledge of our shared suffering. Since they have brought us closer to one another, we can then also begin to examine the present, particularly when we still find areas of confrontation between Christians and Jews related to; the Holocaust. The most recent controversy in the 1990s, which has brought anguish to both sides, is the story of the Carmelite convent at Auschwitz. The spring of 1993 saw new discussions take place in London and in Cracow, and new words of reconciliation have been uttered, particularly by Sir Sigmund Sternberg in London whose close contacts with the Catholic Church have kept open the vital channels of communication. Yet much remains to be done; and the earliest correspondence between Sir Sigmund and Cardinal Glemp, which produced the Cardinal's conciliatory letter, is only the first stage of a journey towards reconciliation which still has to take place. And yet, when we summarize the teachings of our Christian and Jewish guides in this dark period, we see that there are possibilities of understanding one another.

One thing remains: Auschwitz can *never* be comprehended. It is a place of broken silence, a dark hole of evil in the world. Those who were there and died took the mystery of its evil with them in order to present it to God. Those who survived can at best give a stammered testimony which the world can respect even when it cannot understand it. It is the testimony of Jews and Christians, of Baeck, Bonhoeffer, and Niemoeller – but also of Communists and Social Democrats, of homosexuals, of the *Sinti-Roma*, of groups as well as of individuals. It belongs to everyone; and it belongs to no-one. We cannot understand it because our minds cannot grasp the totally demonic; but we must not forget it, for that would bring Satan into the world. But when we stare at Auschwitz, we freeze into statues. Auschwitz, Treblinka, Mauthausen, Buchenwald – Stheno, Euryale, Medusa – the eyes of the Gorgons look at us through the smoke of the chimneys that still travels back and forth through the atmosphere. I do not wonder that the good Carmelite nuns who planned a convent on the site of Auschwitz, staring as they did at the hell of the camp day and night, became programmed into a pattern which could not look outside itself, which ignored Jewish thought and feeling. As of old, they had taken the shield of their religion as a mirror through which to see the unseeable. And so they survived. But they were trapped in that mirror image that had coped with evil by contracting it to the point where they thought they could control it. They wanted to pray it away. That is a glorious task. And out of a tradition that believes in the 'Thirty-Six Righteous' for whose sake the world is preserved, I can only treat such prayer with awe and respect. Their prayers came before God to be accepted. I cannot speak for God. But the prayers did not come to us; not to the families of the victims; not to the victims. It was not the right place. It was not the right time. They were not the right prayers. The evil has remained in the world and in that place. Auschwitz is not the place where prayers remove darkness. It is the place where one can remember the evil and walk away maimed. Out of that encounter can come good, but not in Auschwitz. The story of the *Akedah*, of God testing Abraham by demanding his son Isaac as sacrifice, has received different interpretations within Judaism and Christianity. But Mount Moriah became a holy place – with sanctuaries built there by Jews, Christians, and Muslims – because the tragedy did not take place: father and son walked down the mountain hand in hand. Auschwitz is not Mount Moriah, nor Calvary. It is an evil place and will remain an evil place, empty and desolate, salted with the tears of mourners, where no sanctuary can stand. A place of worship there becomes a place of self-deception. And so it is not a matter of politics, of hasty actions in creating a place of worship at Auschwitz without consulting others, which is the issue here.

The cup of human suffering overflowed. If Jews and Christians are to talk together about the nature of suffering as seen in Auschwitz, both must first learn to speak a new language.

We can no longer view suffering as a divine punishment. We can no longer see Jewish suffering as part of the plan for the redemption of humanity. And we cannot, must not view Auschwitz as a restatement of Calvary.

The nuns – and Christians as such – have failed to understand the nature of the objections against the convent at Auschwitz as expressed by Jews. Deeply hurt, good Christians have pointed out to the Jews that their actions were motivated by concern and compassion for the Jewish victims: that their prayers were intended as a balm to assuage the wounds of suffering humanity. They saw the wounds of Christ at Auschwitz. They wanted to pray for him and to him; and they wanted to pray for the Jews. How could the Jews reject their prayers? Would that not be, in some ways, a Jewish triumphalism?

One cannot deny all aspects of their case. Every religion has a touch of triumphalism within itself, wants to assert itself against the neighbour. But in the matter of mourning for our dead, Jews do not ask others to say *Kaddish*. We pray as a family, we are remembrances with a particular need to say *Kaddish* or the millions who have no descendants left in this world who could fulfil that religious obligation. And we do not wish those who have died to become subjects or symbols for another faith that in some ways challenges their status as *Kedoshim* – holy ones who died in their purity.

At a symposium many years ago on the Holocaust, Dorothee Soelle addressed the central problem. In a way, she anticipated the controversy of the Auschwitz convent when she said:

> As I see it, the great danger of Christianity is in its open or latent anti-Judaism, which distances itself triumphantly from the pain of God and comes down on the side of the victor. This . . . appears everywhere where Christianity makes definitions of itself which are not legitimate, ie. which are not in accord with God's social, political, and historical will . . . a Christianity which excludes the Jewish interest destroys itself: it excludes justice from redemption, politics from theology, this world from the presumed other world, recollection or deliverance from individual suffering, and death and any meaning from non-thermalized collective suffering.[9]

Both the positive and negative aspects of Christian thought, as they can be applied to this particular controversy, come into play here. Positive Christian thinking brings the teaching of the suffering God into the human situation, where divine pain can be alleviated by human action that directs itself to the removal of evil in the world.

The final question at this point is 'Are there lessons Jews and Christians can learn as a result of the recent nuns at Auschwitz controversy?'

I do not really think that I want to answer this. Religionists always tend to be didactic, to leave the scene with a moral trailing behind them. For myself, I have certainly learned something – about myself. I was amazed at the anger I felt against what was certainly the innocent piety of the nuns. But then I consoled myself with the final words in Spinoza's *Ethics* which assure us that one must struggle greatly to attain what is worthwhile.

NOTES

1. D. Bonhoeffer, *Widerstand und ergbung* (Munich, New Edition, 1970), p. 15.
2. D. Bonhoeffer, *Predigten (1925–1935)*, ed. Otto Dudzus (Munich, Kaiser, 1984), pp. 364–365.
3. Ibid., p. 368.
4. Ibid., p. 370.
5. E. Bethge, 'Dietrich Bonhoeffer und die Juden', *Konzequenzen*, ed. E. Feil and I. Toed (Munich, 1980), pp. 206–207.
6. M. Niemoeller, *Dahlemer Predigten 1936/1937* (Munich, Kaiser, 1982), p. 193.
7. Thomas Mann, *Dahlemer predigten 1936/1937* (Munich, Kaiser, 1982), p. 185.
8. Niemoller, *Dahlemer Predigten 1936/1937* , p. 190.
9. D. Soelle, 'God's pain and our pain', *Remembering for the future* (Pergamon Press, 1989), vol. 3, p. 241.

# PART 3

# PROGRESSIVE AND RADICAL
# JEWISH THINKING

THE radical and liberal philosophers and theologies trying to find a way out of the shadow of Auschwitz and into the twenty-first century do not all come out of the camp of Progressive Judaism. Nevertheless we come back to the rabbis of the Progressive movement for an understanding of the way in which the Jewish community has moved from Orthodoxy when confronted with the realities of our time. The Orthodox thinkers we have studied have done nobly in terms of the tradition which they defended and which defended them in a time of spiritual crisis. They absorbed the teachings of the past and attempted to make new interpretations for the present age. They did not succeed. The question which remains is whether or not the Reform thinkers can do better in adapting their inheritance to the anguish of our time.

All of them are inheritors of a past which belonged to all of Jewish life. The thinkers we shall presently consider: Eugene Borowitz, Stephen Schwarzschild, Arnold Wolf, Richard Rubenstein, Marc Ellis, Dow Marmur, Emil Fackenheim (some of them recur for they belong in other chapters) all built upon the Jewish thinkers of the first half of this century. Hermann Cohen, Martin Buber, Franz Rosenzweig, and Leo Baeck were part of the great tradition of German Jewry which was destroyed. Their teachings endured. Other teachers cannot be ignored, and scholars like Ignaz Maybaum formed a bridge to the German tradition which linked the present generation to that past. That past has not disappeared. One of the natural flaws of contemporary writers is their conviction that these past teachers, tied to older cultures and patterns of thought, have lost their relevance. Oddly enough, this reasoning is not applied to Biblical texts which also rise out of the culture and mores of another time; but then, these texts are considered sacred. Yet contemporary scholars, particularly those raised in or aligned to the Progressive community, should not hesitate to challenge these texts as well; the conclusion should not be that the older texts lose relevance when contemporary thinkers disagree with them, for that is a dangerous way to treat the past. It comes back to haunt us, and insights from another time and place are not necessarily erroneous. The teachers of the past with profound insights remain the teachers of the present.

One of the most intriguing thinkers of the immediate past was one of that company of German Jewish thinkers who came to England rather than to the United States. A disciple of Franz Rosenzweig whose original thinking moved him some distance from his contemporaries, and whose life was a testimony to the vitality of the German Jewish *émigré* who could and did establish new roots and had a profound effect upon the host community into which he entered. This was Ignaz Maybaum, still challenged and attacked decades after his death, but listed in most summaries of what is termed Holocaust theology.

## Ignaz Maybaum

In Auschwitz, I say in my sermons – and only in sermons is it appropriate to make such a statement – Jews suffered vicarious death for the sins of mankind. It says in the liturgy of the Synagogue, in reference to the first and second *Churban*, albeit centuries after the event: 'because of our sins'. After Auschwitz Jews need not say so. Can any martyr be a more innocent sin-offering than those murdered in Auschwitz! The millions who died in Auschwitz died 'because of the sin of others'. Jews and non-Jews died in Auschwitz, but the Jew-hatred which Hitler had inherited from the medieval Church made Auschwitz the twentieth century Calvary of the Jewish people.[1]

What rabbis say in sermons is even more important than what they say in print, although Ignaz Maybaum was one of the rare rabbis who did not hesitate to publish his sermons. He could say these and other frightening things about the Holocaust in his sermons because of an 'I-thou' relationship which existed between himself and his community, for they felt the compassion which went alongside the intellectual challenge he hurled at his listeners. Who else would dare say:

Would it shock you if I were to imitate the prophetic style and formulate the phrase: Hitler, My Servant? In the Book of Job Satan is there, among the servants and messengers of God. Hitler was an instrument in itself, unworthy and contemptible. But God used this instrument to cleanse, to purify, to punish a sinful world; the six million Jews, they died an innocent death; they died because of the sins of others. Western man must, in repentance, say of the Jew what Isaiah says of the Servant of God: 'Surely, our diseases he did bear, and our pains he carried . . . he was wounded because of our transgressions, he was crushed because of our iniquities'.[2]

One sees why these texts rise out of sermons. They are challenges hurled at the worshipper. They awake and present him and her with something which is basically unacceptable but which, in that context, simply cannot be ignored. The teaching of Maybaum is summed up in the words he uses. He will not use the words *Shoah* or *Holocaust*, part of a later language which tries to deal with the incomprehensibility of the past. He used the word *Churban*, because that term *is* understandable. It lives in history, it has occurred before, it will occur again if God so wishes. There is a traditional thinking here, but it is transformed into utter radicality by the mere fact that Maybaum not only accepts it as God's plan, but sees this as something good.

But how can that be? Is not each *Churban* a tragedy? Jerusalem (in 586 BC)? The second *Churban*, when the Romans again destroyed Jerusalem and the second Temple (in 70 CE)? And this third *Churban*, when six million Jews, among the other victims, fell to the evil actions of the Nazis? And yet, for Maybaum, each *Churban* was the destruction of what was old and had to go, was the advent of something new which had to come into the world. This third *Churban*, Auschwitz and the death of six million Jews, was seen by him as part of the death throes of medieval evil; and the State of Israel emerged out of this.

Maybaum could not be viewed as a Zionist, although, in his youth, he had been part of the *Blau-Weiss* youth movement in Germany. It was not that he hated the State; he could and did rejoice in the state of Israel and in Jerusalem the holy city. But the closing words in Maybaum's *The face of God after Auschwitz* are:

The strongest fact which can make Israel a centre is the miraculous way in which this biblical country has constantly remained the Holy Land. 'If I forget thee, O Jerusalem!' We who must sometimes repeat to our kith and kin in Israel Einstein's words to Ben Gurion, 'Curb Jewish nationalism', say the Psalmist's prayer for the Holy Land:

> Pray for the peace of Jerusalem;
> may they prosper that love thee.
> Peace be within thy walls,
> and prosperity within thy palaces.
> For my brethren and companions' sakes,
> I will now say: Peace be within thee.
> For the sake of the house of the Lord our God
> I will seek thy good.[3]

But Jerusalem was not *the* centre of Jewish life, as far as Maybaum was concerned. He was a Diaspora Jew who felt that when the Jew had entered modernity he had not become assimilated, had not become less; he had reached another stage of development. For Maybaum, the Jew lives within and for the Diaspora environment – even in his suffering the Holocaust.

The traditional system of ritual and liturgy *also* has a function for the neighbour, although Maybaum came to be less involved in this. In contrast to Rosenzweig, Maybaum moved from traditionalism to Reform, whereas Franz Rosenzweig came to affirm more and more of the tradition. Another difference between them, not unimportant, was that Rosenzweig basically concerned himself with the dual Covenant he saw for Judaism and Christianity, and was blind to Islam. Maybaum made a deep study of Islam, even if, in the end, he comes to challenge the structure of society which emerges out of Muslim teachings. He compares the Halacha with the Sunna and, ultimately, criticizes Jewish Orthodoxy as 'Islamised Judaism'.

The image of the *Akedah*, the testing of Abraham who brings Isaac to the mountain as a sacrifice, becomes an image of the *Churban* for Maybaum; but he also uses it as a touchstone for the three faiths confronting this challenge.

History devours its hecatombs of sacrifices. Youth, above all, is sacrificed. Each generation goes like Isaac to the altar, where a voice says: 'Give me your son!' This story, the *Akedah*, the 'binding of Isaac', is told in two narratives, one in Genesis, the other in the Koran. In Genesis we meet a father who represents both law and love. In the Koran, there is a father who stands for law, but for law without love. In the first case, the home of man penetrates history, in the second history goes on in inevitable tragedy without the intervention of love. In Genesis Abraham hears a voice not recorded in the Koran: 'Do not raise your hand against the boy; do not touch him'.[4]

Mohammed tells the story about Isaac in Sura 37 without mentioning any intervention from outside history. Only a history far removed from the home which harbours love determines the fate of the Koranic Isaac. The story as Genesis tells it is known wherever the redemptive power of God is praised. The story in the Koranic form is shortened and records the bitter command: 'Give me your son!' Abraham obeys. This is all and this is enough. The rescue of Isaac is added like a postscript which does not really belong to the story.

Yet it is Christianity which is most bitterly criticized by Maybaum's use of the *Akedah* image. The Christians *demand* the sacrifice because they need it, because they need Jesus sacrificed for the sins of humanity. The text is appropriated by Christians as a prefiguration: it is the story of Jesus on the Cross. Here is where, for Maybaum, Auschwitz becomes Calvary, and where Christian guilt comes to be clearly established. The Crucifixion must take place, is desperately desired by Christians – but the Jews can be made responsible for this and be branded deicides! In that way, Christian guilt is removed. Maybaum saw this particularly as the mythology of the medieval Church which so infected Europe that Auschwitz was almost inevitable. With the removal of that Church when dawn arose upon the bleak scene, he finds Christians and Christianity a partner with whom one can live in amity. But the myth of the deicide still lives. It was typical of the medieval mind of the Church which participated in the Holocaust; and Maybaum firmly states:

> I accuse not the Christian, but the Christian who thinks on medieval lines. He is guilty of complicity in Hitler's final solution.[5]

Thus, Maybaum felt that if the turmoil of the third *Churban* had made the medieval Church irrelevant, it had had a positive effect.

A modern scholar, Steven Katz, has expressed himself outraged at this notion of a positive role in God's plan for Auschwitz:

> . . . if the Holocaust is the price of freedom, or in this case progress and expiation, then better to do without such evolution and reconciliation – the price is just too high. It is morally and theologically unacceptable.

To insist on it is to turn God *Kivyachol* ('as if one could say this') into a moral monster.[6]

An impossible irony also discloses itself as a corollary of Maybaum's suggestion that God used Hitler for His purposes. If the *Shoah* is God's will, if Hitler is 'My Servant', then to resist Hitler is to resist God; to fight the Nazis is to fight the Lord. As such the Warsaw Ghetto resisters, the inmates who rebelled at Treblinka, the righteous of the nations, who risked death, and more often than not died, to save Jewish lives, all these were rebels against the Almighty.[7]

Dow Marmur, in his 'Holocaust as progress'[8] places Katz into that line of thinkers who proclaim Israel as the moment when the Jews moved out of powerlessness (cf. Irving Greenberg) and who can therefore reject the Maybaum stance permanently:

> We have suffered enough, died enough, been put upon enough; we wish to reject forever our state of powerlessness.[9]

Rabbi Marmur is right in that assessment; it brings us back to the question of Jewish life in the world after Auschwitz – and whether or not we want to exercise secular power in a world which has rejected so much of the spiritual vision. Is Israel's exercise of that power a continuation of the task of the Jew? Dr Maybaum's acerbic judgement of the state comes from an earlier time but the earlier vision is not necessarily wrong. Franz Rosenzweig's concept of the Jew standing 'outside of history' came before the time of the Holocaust and of the State of Israel. Maybaum, who saw both, can still define himself within his teacher's vision.

In my own assessment, I find the conjunction between Calvary and Auschwitz too dangerous a tool for Maybaum's self-definition for either Jew or Christian; I see use of the *Akedah* as a brilliant attempt to ascertain the inner identity of Jew, Christian, and Muslim – but it is too wide, too sweeping, and ignores the variances of each faith. And, with great reluctance, I cannot see the term *Churban* giving us the true definition of the Holocaust. It is not that other terms are better; they may, in fact, be worse. But the very weakness of the other terms reminds us that the event is indescribable and that it cannot be understood. Maybaum places it into the plan of God which is also beyond understanding; but he gives us a religious definition in which it seems to make sense according to the ancient tradition. I reject it – not because it is tradition but because the incomprehensible darkness of Auschwitz breaks all current definitions. The strength of

Progressive Judaism is that it can still believe, but it can also reject. So I in turn reject the notion that the death of more than a million children was punishment or test, or even a necessary step towards a better world.

Ignaz Maybaum surrounded himself with disciples who saw him as the link with that past which had its golden period in German Jewish life. Teaching the *Churban* as an aspect of the divine plan which had positive features, he could at least assert a new Jewish world which was one that was better than what had preceded it, and that is a comfort.

I teach his classes now, at the Leo Baeck College, part of the later generation which escaped from Germany. And I am painfully aware that I do not have this depth of learning or his serene confidence in progress. I teach doubts more than certainties. And I still find that the strength of my instruction comes from the conversations we have had, from the books – sermons or not – which he had scattered as seeds into an alien soil. Ignaz Maybaum was very much part of a totally different world which existed before Auschwitz; and he is part of that vastly different world which exists now.

In our modern world, Islam has become far more important in terms of its confrontation with Judaism. Maybaum's knowledge of Islam, and his reservations, have something to say to us here. On the one hand, dialogue with the Muslim community becomes more of a possibility where Jews have taken the trouble to acquaint themselves with basic Islamic teachings, following Maybaum's example. But there was also Maybaum's awareness of the Islamic faith constricted within the structure of the legal system which exists within the Muslim states, and which politicizes Islam's encounter with Judaism: the status of Jerusalem is only one example of many. Political fanaticism emphasizes the rejection of the neighbour's religion, and suppresses the openness with Islam which had been able to acknowledge at least parts of Judaism and Christianity. Maybaum saw flaws within fanatic Jewish Orthodoxy and with current Israeli thinking regarding the Palestinians. Excessive legalism and intolerance are not necessarily acquired from the outside, but can be aspects of any beleaguered faith. Maybaum's critique of the Jewish community in Europe as in Israel acquires a new relevance here; and he continues to be our teacher.


*Dow Marmur*


Marmur's ideas are as adventurous as his life which has moved through the experience of persecution in Russia; Siberia in the days of the USSR; a refuge in Sweden after the war, and service with the Israeli Consulate;

London and the Leo Baeck College in the days of Maybaum; and a brilliant rabbinical career which has now moved from London to Canada, where he leads one of the largest American congregations (Reform) in Toronto.

Here, we are concerned with his writings which, in Great Britain, already established him as a Reform thinker who collected and directed the searching minds of a revitalized Judaism which tried to focus upon life after the Holocaust. Dow's own considerable contribution was a book, *Beyond survival* (London, 1982), which tried to build upon Fackenheim's insight that, at the very least, Auschwitz gave us God's revealed commandment 'to survive'. Rabbi Marmur, as the title shows, felt that this was not enough: there had to be a purpose for survival. Fackenheim's brilliant philosophic texts, and the love for Israel which became central in his work, had its influence upon Rabbi Marmur, just as the mediated thoughts of Rosenzweig which had come to Dow Marmur through Ignaz Maybaum.

In line with Fackenheim, Marmur has affirmed the centrality of the State of Israel for the Jew of today. Fackenheim sees this as the one guarantee for Jewish survival after Auschwitz. Rabbi Marmur replies:

> The theme of my book stresses the centrality of Israel – not because it guarantees Jewish survival, but because it defines Jewish purpose, which by inference also guarantees survival yet goes beyond it.

Marmur also uses Rosenzweig's image of two triangles, the 'Star of David'. On one triangle, there are the sides marked 'Faith, People, and Land' (alien to Rosenzweig or Maybaum, but central to Fackenheim). Dow Marmur sees the need for the three foundations. Faith alone would only lead to Moses. We cannot reject the parents – Abraham and Sarah – through whom we become a people, one that cannot live without the faith. Yet it *has* to live upon the soil of the land given through the Covenant which unites these triune aspects of Jewish existence. If our land, as the teachers through the generations have instructed us, has been the text of the tradition, Marmur insists that the Jewish people have stubbornly kept their faith in the land that would one day be theirs once more; and that faith was rewarded. The new reality now denies the old classical Reform approach with its anti-nationalism. It challenges secularist insistence upon peoplehood in the Diaspora; but it also rejects Israeli nationalism which would immerse itself in the land and fail to see the people of the Diaspora or the faith of the generations. In the postmodern world, the realities have shifted and changed; and so has Judaism. In what one might judge a passionate overstatement, Dow Marmur says:

The simultaneous erosion from within – in the form of the loss of Faith – and attack from without – in the form of persecution – were too much to withstand. When Hitler was finally defeated, Judaism was so weakened that he may have been close to his posthumous victory. One dare not speculate as to what would have happened to Judaism had there not been a Zionist movement to point camp survivors in the direction of the Land of Israel.

It is of course true that the creation of the Jewish State and the emergence of Israel as a haven and as a place of physical and spiritual renewal had the enormous impact – not only upon camp survivors, but upon all Jews looking across the barren landscape left in the grey dawn after the darkness. Yet the suggestion that without the light shining from the East Judaism might have perished ignores the realities of history which Maybaum sketched for us in describing the first, second and third *Churban*: Judaism not only renewed itself; it became deeper, more profound with the passage of time. After the first *Churban* came the time of Talmudic greatness; after the second, a brilliant Ashkenazi Jewish life (and Sephardic Jewry, despite oppression, remained more than viable!). Yet it *is* proper for Marmur to indicate that this third *Churban* was different in quality and quantity – Jewish life was shattered. This does not mean that revival of Judaism will not take place in the Diaspora. Indeed, one can say with some sadness that it has suffered more in Israel than outside of it, partly because religion and the state have made a concordat which is injurious to both parties.

Rabbi Marmur's lecture underscores the 'paradigm shift' which takes place in science but also in religion:

The scientist does not make new discoveries by moving step by step, but by approaching the subject of his research within a given framework, a paradigm. Progress is made when one paradigm is abandoned in favour of another paradigm that makes it possible to view the problem in a new light, within a different framework ... Finally, the old paradigm is no longer tenable, a revolution takes place, and the new paradigm becomes the norm ... this explains, I believe, the shift from a Judaism centred on survival – the ghetto – to a Judaism centred on purpose – the Land.

It is here, I believe, that Rabbi Marmur makes his most significant contribution to contemporary Jewish thought. We move from this paradigm to another as we try to understand the meaning of contemporary Jewish life. Eugene Borowitz and other Jewish scholars who dismiss earlier Jewish thinkers are right in reminding us that some approaches in theology are time-bound and immured in the patterns of the world in which they were created, even if I would insist upon basic, enduring truths which move through generations and their teachers and maintain themselves as affirmations of Jewish life. We live within the state, within the legal structure which maintain societies even when they place strait-jackets upon the individual who has to conform to imperfect patterns. One of the most profound teachings of Judaism was the Babylonian sage's injunction: *dina d'malchuta dina*: the law of the land in which you live must be obeyed! Yet this does not apply to thought patterns; and there are also times when the law must be disobeyed, even when one stands within it: marching from Selma to Montgomery to fight for black civil rights, we willingly took it upon ourselves to go to prison, if need be, in order to effect changes eventually. And the 'righteous gentiles' who disobeyed the Nazis at the risk of their own lives to save Jewish lives certainly set themselves against 'the law'.

In a land where a religion has something of a concordat with the state, the enforcement of a dogma can lead to an immobile faith which becomes its own prison; and it becomes important for the believer to recognize that the contemporary pattern, particularly if reinforced by the state, is still a 'human pattern' which can inhibit the quest for the ultimate. The religious search for the ultimate must continue, even as we recognize that it is only touched upon in an imperfect manner within each age. With this recognition comes the affirmation of revelation within faith, our own relationship to an enduring Covenant made at the beginning and reaching us through time and space.

These assertions lead me to express some worries about Dow Marmur's placing the new centre of Jewish faith and religion into the State of Israel. The importance of that state to the Jewish people cannot be over-emphasized; but to make it *the* purpose of our existence once again concretizes the revelation within a human structure which cannot be given absolute authority, particularly in our time when a semi-concordat between traditional Judaism and the State exposes Orthodoxy to political criticism which can and perhaps must corrode that faith.

When we affirm the world in which we live, we are basically expressing our belief in a human environment where love and compassion, justice and truth can be found. The broken faith structures of religion are no longer able to express this confidence fully. They can retreat into an enclave surrounded by the high walls of religious practice and law – a traditional option which Rabbi Marmur rightly attacked for its myopia as well as for its ineffectiveness. The true believer can shrug this off; living in a closed structure of faith, he can ignore the imperfections of the surrounding society, or find fulfilment in a future world in which the Messianic dream will be realized. There, the wicked are blown away as chaff, or will at least receive the punishment due to them. But the Progressive thinker, the radical, the unbeliever, and the secular person established in this world, in this place, cannot accept this comfort of religion.

The Enlightenment attempted to establish moral principles as a separate realm of reason, independent of revealed religion. David Hume pointed out that empirical evidence does not become a moral code. Nevertheless, we can still turn to Kant in our belief that the rational person can decide between the good and the bad. If we deny that the distinction between right and wrong, good and evil, is *valid*, we simply deny the very possibility of a morality in the normal sense of the word; and if we deny that, there is no longer any way that respect for the moral law can be distinguished from fear of legal punishment. But we affirm the moral law in this world; and we live within a society of laws to which we can and do appeal quite independent of our religious convictions. If we did not believe that there is justice in the world, we could not believe in life itself.

## Simon Wiesenthal

Simon Wiesenthal, one of our Riders Towards the Dawn, would not be recognized as a philosopher, a radical thinker, or an Orthodox or Progressive spokesman; he is a man of action who also instructs through his writings; a passionate man in search of justice who is often misunderstood. Our own concern is how and where to live in a world after the Holocaust which has forgotten the victims and has not punished the guilty. Traditionally, religion comforts the suffering, and expects the State to punish the guilty in this world, even if God's punishment will await the sinner in the world to come. There are also those who believe that divine punishment will overtake the evil person in this world, whether through bodily afflictions, bad luck, or through legal procedures. When the wicked seem to prosper, one might mutter that 'God's mills grind slowly, but they grind exceedingly deep'; and one settles down to wait.

Wiesenthal wanted the murderers of the Holocaust to be found and punished. In this, we can see a faith in a society and a world that had persecuted him mercilessly. Like Job, he still believed in justice. He addressed himself to a society and legal system which had enormous flaws, but which was not rejected by him. Simon Wiesenthal had started life in

Lemberg, Galicia, and had been a successful architect before he was swept up by the war and entered the Holocaust kingdom. He moved through many of the concentration camps, and the story of his survival is a miracle in itself. In May 1945, he was freed by the American army when it occupied Mauthausen – one of the worst camps. Most of his family had died, some in front of his eyes; and he wanted to see the murderers punished. His Jewish Documentation Centre in Vienna, the Wiesenthal Foundation in California, and the many reports of his work in discovering the Nazis who had gone into hiding after the war ended, have made his life's work familiar to the world. To some, he represents the avenging angel in all of his fury; to others, he seems a monomaniac who cannot let go of a project where the enemies are already dead or in their eighties, and where the world has long forgotten what they have done; more, where the witnesses which a legal system needs in order to proceed are no longer available.

One can simply, dispassionately, look through the records and mark the achievement of his Vienna Centre: the criminals who were traced, the witnesses who were found, and the meagre end result. Or one can look at the work of the Wiesenthal Foundation which has gone far beyond the initial goals set for it and is now more involved in fighting anti-Semitism wherever it reveals itself. Yet none of this gives us those aspects of Wiesenthal I would consider important: this quest for justice and the asking of fundamental questions which, since Socrates, has also been the philosopher's task.

Some of Wiesenthal's friends want him to be the avenger, the voice of justice. As a prisoner of his Documentation Centre, and perhaps even of the Wiesenthal Foundation, he ceases to be an individual. But we can only marvel at the courage of a person who has been the subject of death threats, and of murder attempts. What the Nazis, old and new, think of him is easily imagined. Fear and hatred are there in full measure. When he dies, the criminals still in hiding will celebrate; but not for long. It seems to me that they will miss him. Criminals need their guilt, and they need those who know about it. There is a certain perverse pride in being the last of the Hitler gang. And in the quest for justice which I see at the heart of Wiesenthal's thinking there is also the compassion for the criminal who needs to expiate, even half a century later.

The Jewish tradition demands justice in the world: without it, there can be no compassion. And there will always be a special need for someone amidst the people, a voice crying: 'In the wilderness, make a way for the Lord!' The imperfect justice of the world is there but the moral vision stands behind it for a better world.

*Eugene Borowitz*

In the late 1940s, a group of young rabbis emerged from the Hebrew Union College in Cincinnati who had not only been taught by the American scholars with their insistence upon rationalism and social justice, but had also encountered the refugee scholars from Germany with their deepened awareness of evil and the sense that they were the final teachers of the European tradition. This combination of teachers produced a new type of rabbi who could address the next generation of American Jews.

One of the new rabbi-teachers who emerged in a role of intellectual leadership was Eugene Borowitz, who might be seen as a model rabbi for the twenty-first century. Over the years, he has gained a cult following for the controversial journal *Sh'ma* which is one of the few interesting periodicals cutting across the intra-faith boundaries of Judaism. Eugene Borowitz has written a dozen books which have expressed progressive Jewish thinking for laypeople and scholars. By now Eugene Borowitz has influenced more than one generation of American rabbis, convincing by intellect rather than by charisma – which lasts longer. Basically, Eugene Borowitz fulfils the role of the rabbi-teacher. As a professor at the Hebrew Union College and as a scholar, he also reaches out to the European community.

The strongly personal dimension of Borowitz's teachings became quite clear during his visit to London in 1967, at the time of the Six Day War. Speaking to an assembly of the British Reform Movement, he declared to them that the Israeli victory, at a time when it was not unlikely that Israel would perish, had convinced him that God was there, that God had intervened in human affairs. Had the outcome of the war been different, his faith would have been severely tested.

Borowitz makes a full analysis of the Holocaust seen through the eyes of Wiesel, Rubenstein, and Fackenheim, and accepts some of their insights. He cannot go along with theories which made the Holocaust the one reality which must be used to measure the rest of human experience. We have emerged from the shadows of that time, have at least learned that utter evil must be opposed absolutely. But then, as he says in his guide for today's theology:

> That mandate makes sense only if we can still honestly affirm the reality of unqualified good.[10]

In the end, while paying tribute to Feuerbach's view that human aspirations are at the heart of religious growth, Borowitz here comes to the full assertion of divine revelation. But where can this be found? The new spirituality of Jewish life is an inward search; but it cannot reduce God to a component of human beings. The positive response of survival after Auschwitz asserts our identity and sets good against the bad. This assertion of Jewish identity and existence is seen most clearly in Borowitz's relationship to the State of Israel. He had been deeply hurt by the world's apathy towards the dangers confronting Israel, and had looked in vain for Christian support. He doubted humankind; and then, in the victory, he experienced God:

> Then news came of the staggering Israeli victory. World Jewry experienced an elation that transcended relief from dread or rejoicing in Israel's prowess; the Bible calls it deliverance. Jews everywhere found themselves incomprehendingly overwhelmed by the sight of soldiers conversing on the Temple Mount's Western Wall; atheists, agnostics, and believers alike found themselves moved to prayer. I believed then and believe now that we had personally experienced God's absence during the Holocaust – but an experience I remain certain was not an illusion, one real enough that it moved a critical mass of our people to rededicate themselves to Jewish existence.[11]

This commitment to Israel has not blinded Borowitz to the weaknesses of the Jewish state; *Sh'ma*, his journal, has a distinctly 'peacenik' approach. And what was to a large extent a 'secular' encounter with God at a time of danger did not create an enduring reservoir of a Jewish identity which would assure a commitment to Jewish values. Ethnicity is not enough. Borowitz challenges Greenberg here and states:

> Where he (Irving Greenberg) and others believe we can separate the ethnic from the spiritual drives in the postmodern ethos, I believe this exclusively humanistic view of ethnicity returns us to the faulty premise of Jewish modernity, the humanisation of Jewish obligation.[12]

If Judaism just becomes a personal choice, he sees that choice exercised less and less, particularly in Israel. If Judaism is a command, this must be surrounded by a structure of Jewish duty to be effective. This becomes a central theme to which Borowitz returns in his efforts to link Jews and Judaism – folk and faith. Borowitz here unites the contemporary experience of Jews in the Diaspora and in Israel which yearns for a faith which can give meaning to the events which have battered and bruised the Jew in the world of today. And he tries to find a contemporary language which can address a generation which has moved away from despair but cannot find enough evidence in the world of today to entitle it to optimism. Eugene Borowitz lives in the postmodern world and is intensely aware of the political and moral problems of a State of Israel trying to deal with its complex relationship to the Palestinians and its Arab neighbours, to a Diaspora Jewish community confronting a new anti-Semitism and new doubts within itself as spiritual sensitivity which can create a synthesis with the past tradition and with the postmodern insights which shape the Jew and the Christian today.

Borowitz speaks as a religious thinker synthesizing past tradition with contemporary experience. He knows that human beings carry the spark of the divine within them, and much of Jewish life, particularly since the days of Jehudah Halevi, sees this quality particularly in the Jew with the Jewish genius for religion. He affirms the relationship between humankind and God as stated in the Covenant between them; but he recognizes that this historic relationship has changed. As a people, we hesitate to make this an exclusive claim of Jewish life; as individuals, we live in a democratic society where the dignity of the person demands the freedom to affirm or to reject. And so Borowitz wants to affirm both corporate Covenant and self-determination, recognizing that this dichotomy carries a conflict within itself which has to be resolved. The old struggle between the particular and the general comes to the fore. Polarities develop where the dynamic tension between the poles turns the religious quest into a dynamic search for new discoveries.

Here, Borowitz comes to propound a system of belief for the 'postmodern' Jew; but that system demands the participation of the reader from step to step. It approaches the new generation with the vision of individual freedom which this teacher values so highly, and the system does not demand to be the only 'way'. At its best it sees itself as one approach into that area where the individual has to confirm the Covenant for himself and herself. Some traditionalists will turn away from this approach, rejecting this 'autonomy' for authoritative guidance. But the key to Borowitz is his insistence that the individual exercises freedom built upon knowledge.

In so many ways, Borowitz is the authentic expression of American Jewish life. The Holocaust is a long distance away from him; but it is not absent. As a navy chaplain, Borowitz's commitment against the darkness which filled the world was active and non-pacifist. Some of his teachers at the Hebrew Union College were sparks saved from the fire. And it was the

Holocaust itself which challenged his theology and made him realize that the doctrine of the Covenant had to be restated for our time and place. Thus he became one of the Riders Towards the Dawn, a traveller who broke away from those who had not experienced the darkness and managed to enter the experience of European Jewry with empathy and compassion.

American Jewry is sometimes difficult to understand: there can be over-reaction. 'We will never forgive! We will never buy German goods! All Germans are anti-Semites!' And there are also thinkers like Borowitz who established a bridge between the insights and experiences of American life and the reality of the evil which had poisoned the world beyond the ocean. Borowitz never strays far from his American roots. At the same time, he tries to relate them to their Jewish roots, to the Bible as the foundation of American life.

God is encountered. But what does this *mean* for us? Borowitz gives an extensive answer :

> Our tradition supplies us with a most evocative metaphor for this awe-some tie between the transcendent and the human: *brit*, Covenant. The Torah daringly asserts that, despite the disparity between them, the one God of all the universe enters into intimate partnerships with humankind. It understood God's covenants with the Children of Noah – humankind – and with the Children of Israel as contracts between partners mutually bound by stipulations of their agreement. Non-Orthodox postmoderns find the term congenial to their mix of transcendence and self by reinter-preting Covenant as relationship rather than contract. This shift enhances the human role beyond what our tradition could grant yet acknowledges God's independence ... It also makes the Jewish people central, not peripheral, to our Judaism, for our historic Covenant was not made with individuals but with our folk corporately. And thus to share in the Coven-ant immediately involves us in the God-grounded, community-directed, personally appropriated sense of responsibility that creates the life of Torah.[13]

The transcendent and the immanent God, Torah as revelation, and the people of Israel who as a community but also as individuals have the freedom to enter into the Covenant. The Covenant, Borowitz indicates, is made with the People Israel (and a Noachitic Covenant assures the rest of human-kind of the same relationship). Yet in both cases one can separate oneself from the people; the autonomous decision of the individual remains.

Eugene Borowitz sees the word for our time to be Covenant, not 'chosen-ness'. Based on characteristic American pragmatism, he believes that this demands movement from the people, as from the single Jew, into that relationship with God. He had studied the European teachers with great care, absorbing the Hegelian insistence that the Jewish people has to identify itself with the Spirit (ie., monotheism) in order to live forever. And it is part of the Covenant to proclaim God in the world, as a choosing rather than as a chosen people.

I am uneasy about some of Eugene Borowitz's thought; but how can I reject a scholar who has listened to the contemporary world, has responded personally, and who concludes his book with a confession of faith that touches us with its truth and its inner commitment:

> Because I know myself to be related to God as part of the people of Israel's historic Covenant with God, I can be true to myself only as I, in my specific individuality, am true to God, to other Jews, to the Jewish tradition, and to the Jewish Messianic dream. And while that truth is found more in the doing than in the thinking, it is by reflection on what constitutes true Jewish doing that Jews in every age have kept themselves alive to their responsibility as partners in the Covenant . . .[14]

## Stephen Schwarzschild

One 'partner in the Covenant' whose life was closely linked with that of Eugene Borowitz was Stephen Schwarzschild. Stephen Schwarzschild and Eugene Borowitz worked together at the Hebrew Union College.

As a boy growing up in Berlin, Schwarzschild attended the Theodor Herzl Schule where his teachers directed him (and all the students) towards Zionism and *aliyah* (emigration to Palestine). At the time, he was undoubtedly affected and stirred by Zionism. Schwarzschild came to the United States in 1939. The family settled in New York, and he studied at the City College of New York, and at the Jewish Theological Seminary before coming to Cincinnati for further studies and for ordination as a Reform rabbi, although he soon joined the Conservative rabbinate without abandoning his Reform links. He returned to Berlin as the original 'iron curtain rabbi', ministering to all the Jews in that city and setting a high standard of community service which was continued by his fellow student from Cincinnati, Peter Levinson. Later, he had a Conservative pulpit in Lynn, Massachusetts.

Writing on modern Jewish philosophy, Schwarzschild in some ways sum-
marized his own rationalist approach in a trenchant survey:

> Among the devout there is the temptation to assert an at least equal, if
> not superior, realm of the numinous beyond the realm of ethics. Thinkers
> like Jehudah Halevi in the past and Rabbi Soloveitchik in our time, with
> his conception of a 'higher will', as well as Leo Baeck, with his duality
> of 'mystery and commandment', illustrate such a natural religious pull.
> When this pull is powerfully exerted, thinking tends to abandon what
> can still be called philosophy and becomes theology or even mysticism.
> The degrees of identification of 'the holy' with 'the good' . . . may be
> seen . . . as the measure of the power of the ultimate and dominant
> Jewish claim in its many different expressions.[15]

The problem of human suffering and the attempts to give adequate answers
to this human condition occupied him often. His friend Eugene Borowitz
had given a simple answer to the questioning lay person:

> Rabbi Yannai said, 'We cannot explain why some evil-doers enjoy
> satisfying lives while some good people endure severe suffering.' If you
> want a theory which ends all our questions about why God permits
> everything other than goodness, then that is more than Judaism, tra-
> ditional or modern, can supply.[16]

Schwarzschild's answer countered with what he saw as a profound doctrine:
that God withdraws from humanity the way a father sends his son away to
school so that he may grow up and learn to stand on his own two feet,
ie., that secularism is the process of humanity's growing up (Bonhoeffer's
doctrine of the 'hiding God' which leaves the world a place of total suffering). But, says Stephen Schwarzschild:

> . . . the doctrine of the *El Mistater* is considerably more searching and
> more humanistic than that of the 'Death of God'. In the first place, in
> Jewish tradition it is a hiding, not a hidden God – an *El Nistar umistater*,
> not a *deus absconditus* – it is a doctrine of an act not a state of God, a
> present process, not a completed one. In the second place, it is a doctrine
> of an absence, not of an emptiness . . . In the third place, whereas
> immanentism declares that there is nothing but what is and therefore
> celebrates it, those who experience the hiding of God know that there
> is an alternative and feel called upon humanly to overcome their present

condition. The hiding manifests transcendence, and out of it the imperative to ethics and revolution sounds forth – the commandment of lightning out of the darkness of the cloud.[17]

Schwarzschild cannot accept the current infatuation with the Kabbalistic doctrine of *tzimtzum*, God's permanent withdrawal from the world to make room for humanity and leave us in permanent exile, which sees God deserting the victims of the Holocaust. Schwarzschild goes through the list of Biblical figures who saw utter destruction and refused to give God full praise. Jeremiah and Daniel were overwhelmed by the evil, but the rabbis countered with the suggestion that the greater the evil, the more we can believe in God whose patient and loving kindness in the face of these evils is the only foundation upon which such a world can continue to exist. Israel must simply continue to cry out to their Father who will hear their cry.

It is not surprising that such a vision of future hope made Stephen Schwarzschild one of the few teachers within the non-Orthodox community to assert his belief in a personal Messiah. There is one message here which applies to all of the Dawn-Riders: it is the movement *towards* dawn that matters, the 'pursuit of the ideal', even if we do not enter the sunlight. Even when the world is doomed, when it remains unchanged despite our own efforts, there is movement within ourselves. Moral reality, Stephen Schwarzschild would say, is the morality of persons. Ethics are located in us and not in ages or ideas. The Messianic age is a Utopia; the Messiah is a concrete, though future, reality.[18]

In the end Stephen Schwarzschild wanted to be what Samson Raphael Hirsch called the *Yisrael Mensch*, a person filled with the truth of Judaism and expressing it in the world. Since for Stephen Schwarzschild these teachings were universal truths to be possessed by all, it can be seen as a preference for humanity.

Stephen Schwarzschild was a profound thinker who rescued truths from the past and made them relevant to the present. He was a Dawn-Rider who strove towards so distant a horizon that it was the journey and not the goal which ultimately mattered. But it was that goal which gave him the vigour and vision which animated him: his belief in the personal Messiah. It made him more of a traditionalist who could recite the Creed of Maimonides: 'I believe with perfect faith in the coming of the Messiah; and even though he tarries, yet will I wait for him!' This is the ultimate pursuit for the ideal, the knowledge that sunrise may be delayed, but will ultimately shine upon all humanity.

*Eugen Taeubler*

One of the most unusual scholars in the United States in our time was Eugen Taeubler, who taught at the Hebrew Union College. If we look for Dawn-Riders who bring the most stringent academic standards to the journey towards light, Taeubler would certainly be chosen. He was a most unusual man of letters: a towering figure in the field of Roman and Greek history who was also a Hebrew scholar. He concerned himself equally with the development of Jewish academic life. As late as 1938, Eugen Taeubler carried on a correspondence with Judah Magnes at the Hebrew University in which some of Taeubler's own blueprints for that university were taken up again. At first on the staff of the Hochschule in Berlin, long before Hitler came to power Taeubler sacrificed a brilliant academic career in order to dedicate himself to the *Wissenschaft des Judentums*.

Taeubler had much in common with Arnaldo Dante Momigliano – both were leading figures in the field of ancient history and in Jewish texts, both Riders Towards the Dawn, *but concerned with the past rather than the future*. This is important, for we need those who can and will explore the past to throw light on the company of travellers. Taeubler had a great vision of the past which offers comfort but also dismay. Taeubler moved eventually from Berlin to Heidelberg, the first Jew to be a full professor in what was at the time the greatest German institution of learning. He renounced all academic honours once Hitler's rise to power had taken place, and returned to the Jewish community. In an address, entitled 'Judaism as tragic existence', he confronted his students with the future as well as with the past:

> When I spoke to you, twenty-six years ago, few of you . . . had seen the light of day. Then, we all lived under the impression that the well-known sun of culture and of humanity – two words for the same thing – . . . was forced to keep climbing higher on the horizon and to remove the last traces of shadow from the earth. Since then, I have learned . . . to view life from a different aspect, that of *tragic* existence.[19]

'How did I separate myself from you, and how did I find my way back to you?' he asks the faculty and students. Freely and openly he confesses that he felt himself too much restricted in being bound to Jewish history. An inner drive towards the more general questions of history, towards interpretations of universal historical nature, took him into that outer world in which he proved himself one of the great historians, the successor, as he had been the amanuensis of the great Theodor Mommsen. At the same time, he discovered that he never left Judaism: it remained the starting point of his explorations. And his own fate was Jewish fate, with a 5000-year process having shaped him and strengthened him to ask those questions which were at the centre of the historian's quest. Searching for the meaning of the history into which he had become immersed, he moved towards universalism and existentialism.

Like Momigliano, Taeubler found particular relevance in the Hellenistic age. Its impact upon Jewish life in exile leads to re-examination and then into new territories. In that time of darkness, hope was found. Taeubler almost applies this insight in a Messianic manner for he demanded a new awareness and the unsealing of a new language in which humanity will receive the revelation of the most high God. But then, he says, he begins to stumble.

Whence do I journey? I have already crossed the border which the science I am to represent here has set for me. It is to be my task to teach that which is recognizable as history and to show how one can use scientific means to achieve knowledge – and I am to let you hear no more than that, dear students. But before I commence that task, it might be in place to indicate to you that which within me points beyond the boundaries. I trust that I will not only meet you in the lecture hall; and I hope that more than science will unite us. And, when I tell you what once was, you will forget as little as I will forget what it means *to live under the sign of a not yet completed fate.*[20]

This was the man who came to Cincinnati in the days when darkness ruled Europe and tried to teach a different type of student what he had wanted to proclaim to the German students on the brink of destruction. He lived out a tragic existence in which his scholarship was not appreciated. But he remained a teacher of rabbis and, on various occasions, he illumined the world for his students.

Eugen Taeubler came to America. What was he to America? Had conditions been different, he might have been a Boethius in the Middle Ages, helping a new world uncover the treasures of antiquity, the proud past of Roman Law, the rich sources of the Jewish spirit. More than serving as an object of reverence, he would have emphasized the validity of the past, its use as a foundation for the future.

Can this generation reap the harvest of Taeubler's teachings? Grave problems face us here. For the basic teaching of Eugen Taeubler, exemplified by his own life, is the demand of the scholar to attain universality.

And the world of scholarship today is one of specialization. Eugen Taeubler saw the past – Greece, Rome and Palestine – with the clear eye of genius viewing a unified field; and he loved what he saw with a strong and abiding love. We can admire this; can, perhaps, learn to utilize and to appreciate the last remnant of European scholarship which found its way to us; but it is difficult to emulate it – the present, with its noisy clamour, drowns out the past. And yet had it clearly heard this Dawn-Rider, American Jewry would have grown closer to its origins.

He saw history in terms of the totality of life. This was a philosophy expressed also in his Cincinnati classes on the Psalms, on Biblical Criticism, and most particularly in his lectures on Job, the 'universal man' to Taeubler. Throughout his lectures and private discussions, Taeubler called himself an existentialist. But if his philosophy was existentialism, it was one that denied Sartre's hopelessness, or Simone Weil's flight into Catholic mystery. It resembled more that of Tillich and his 'Protestant principles' – the recognition of the presence, behind all human affirmations and ideals, of the 'unconditioned'. But it moved beyond conventional existentialism by substituting hope for despair. Where existentialism, a child of its time, has exalted the most conspicuous feature of present day experience, suffering, into a primary aspect of the universe as a whole, Taeubler had the detachment of the classicist who sees the harmony of the universe behind the coda of suffering. He had experienced all the sufferings of the present; but he saw beyond them. Looking at the past, he had visions of the future. True, the existential situation of life was crisis and tension. But it was a creative tension, the quest after the *ens realissima*, after the enigma of 'The Being'. This quest, in Taeubler's mind, was approachable from two directions: through metaphysics and through religion.

Taeubler felt that, within Judaism, there was that which made it possible to connect it with metaphysics. 'The existential problem of Judaism is to be connected with metaphysics. This is the decisive point!' he would tell his Cincinnati students time and time again. The dark suffering of the present is part of the encounter of life, but it is not the totality. A living, vibrant Judaism, playing its needed part in a new Western renaissance, must become part of modern Jewish consciousness. Lecturing on 'Basic notions of Occidental metaphysics', Taeubler would show how modern philosophy was estranged from the reality of personal needs, and how a partial breakdown of culture could be the forerunner of a new renaissance. Judaism, a living force, was indispensable to this new world; but its carriers would have to rediscover the real sources out of which Judaism gained its living structure. The Jew must come to know himself; and, beyond mere historical knowledge, there would have to be the historical consciousness of a fate that would move him towards the future.

> To say No to misfortune, constantly
> To overcome that which presses us with pain . . .

> To say Yes to the tragedy of our existence
> Our fate, root of our being, the fullness of strength . . .

> Conquered Yes and No will both serve us, the victors.
> Both hold us, conquerors, in eternal arrest.

'Umbra Vitae'

There is a special teaching found here, rarely enunciated by others, and yet of particular importance to the present generation: the darkness which fills many lives, the daily attacks we face in a world which has lost its values – these are enemies to which we have to say 'no!', which we have to reject. We cannot deceive ourselves that they are not there: apathy to evil does not negate it. Taeubler teaches us to say 'yes!' to that tragedy, to accept our role as sufferers, which does not necessarily make us victims. Taeubler was familiar with the heroes of Greek and Roman literature who are subservient to the fates, but who nevertheless fight against them. It is our conduct in the road between darkness and dawn which matters, even if the final night falls before one has entered sunlight.

## Leo Baeck

Leo Baeck has been the central figure in my understanding of Judaism from my earliest days. As a small child, I would be brought to the Fasanenstrasse Synagogue in Berlin on special occasions, to listen to words I did not understand. High up on the pulpit, Rabbi Leo Baeck would give a sermon which, according to some of the board members of the synagogue, was a 'private conversation with God'. This was true, as far as I was concerned. It did not mean that I was not deeply impressed. Much later, after the war, Leo Baeck came to the Hebrew Union College as a teacher. And I came to see that he was truly someone who had come out of the uttermost darkness, had survived the concentration camp, and had preserved a faith and a serenity which placed its seal upon my life. Without having formulated the concept of Dawn-Rider, I knew that I was encountering a messenger, a classic teacher of Judaism who could lead us from darkness to light.

Baeck had been the teacher and leader of German Jewry since the days before World War I, and had seen German Jewry fall into the darkest pit of hell. More than being a teacher and academic like his comrade and friend Eugen Taeubler, he had also been active in every aspect of Jewish community life, president of most voluntary institutions, a rabbi who had served different Jewish congregations – in Oppeln, Dusseldorf and Berlin – with great distinction and dedication, but had also written classic texts of Jewish theology and history.

In order to understand this particular Dawn-Rider, one has to enter the darkness from which he emerged; one has to gain at least some insight into the ghetto-concentration camp Theresienstadt to see the way from darkness to light which he was able to teach even in that inferno.

In theory Theresienstadt was a 'model' concentration camp for the 'Prominent'. At times, Red Cross delegates would be seen, taken on tours where they could not see. And it was not an extermination camp. But then, it did not have to be one. Death came on its own. The daily fight against death, in the midst of suffering, was internalized by Baeck: vision and patience, the outreach of imagination necessary to endure suffering, comes to be stated with great clarity.

How does one escape suffering? Baeck lists various situations. There was the daily caravan of death. He describes the deep dark corridor of the fortress, where the long row of coffins appeared each day. Heaped on top of one another, the dead listened to the psalms – up to the final 'I will let them see my help' – and then the coffins gained their freedom. The officiant was permitted fifty steps out of the darkness; then he returned. The coffins continued to their place of burning, free at last.

There was the other way of 'escape' from the camp: the transports to the East. Month after month – often day after day. The question of what was known and what was guessed arises again here. In one text, three months after leaving Theresienstadt, Baeck again stresses the terrible suspicion set against the principle of hope, of a fantasy needed to survive each day and the next day:

No one knew for certain [where the transports would go]. One only knew: they went to the East. A cloud of sorrow, of fear, and of horror kept enveloping the camp. That, of course, was the password of the master-jailers: keep the Jews uncertain. Give them no rest.[21]

Baeck describes how those assigned to the transports were given new numbers, were isolated. 'As the lot came upon them,' he says. But he had removed himself from the areas of power where the lots were determined. Others describe in great detail how Baeck came to be the pastor, rabbi and teacher of the community in the midst of their extreme suffering. Baeck does not mention himself. In the text which follows, Baeck clearly describes his own work, but without mentioning himself. The conceptual structure of vision and patience as a bulwark against surrendering to the darkness turns into a description of the way in which the darkness was held back: the ideational structure and the experiences of existence come to join together:

> The battle between the 'mass' and the 'community' continued unabatingly. Humans who had not known one another tried to help one another physically and spiritually. They gave one another from their possessions, from their spirit. Humans found one another, here and there. In the early morning hours and late at night they came together for divine worship, wherever a room was available. Out of windows, out of the hallways of the houses, the voices of those at prayer, the sounds of the Torah-reading entered the streets. Or, they came together in the darkness of a long evening in the loft of a barracks, immediately under the roof. Pressed tightly together, they stood there to listen to a lecture on Plato, Aristotle, Maimonides, Descartes and Spinoza. They listened to talks on Locke, Hume, arts and poetry; on Palestine then and now, on commandments, prophecy, and Messianic ideas. These were hours, hours belonging to all, where a community rose up out of the mass, where narrowness became wide. They were hours of freedom.[22]

It was Baeck's prescription against the ultimate surrender to the suffering they were enduring. Here, he saw fantasy and patience reasserting themselves, as individuals and a community realized their inner capacities. The fact that it was Baeck who gave these lectures was not considered important by him, not worth mentioning. But it mattered to the group, who saw their faith vindicated by their rabbi and teacher. They might still recite their prayers 'for our sins are we punished', might still be aware of a tradition equating suffering with punishment for all who have done evil.

If we think of the Dawn-Rider as someone who leads us from the darkness into light, we must here consider the role of the teacher who is able to do this in the midst of an absolute darkness where there is little hope for anyone to see the morning light. Baeck stirred imagination and hope within those who knew that they *were* lost, but who could see, through him, that inner light within themselves which could sustain them. And those who survived with him – the very few – had changed along with him. Like Baeck, they were now less philosophical; but they had a different, a tested faith which enabled them to enter a different world.

The positive thinking of the 'early' Baeck had already distanced itself from the tradition in terms of the reasons for human suffering and in the way of coping with the tribulations of the Jewish people. And yet, bound to the motions of Covenant and the task of the martyr in the world, accepting the God who 'tests' his people and permits them to see virtue in their pain, Baeck had not broken with the past. It was more that his emphases had shifted: one did not ask for the reasons, but simply tried to cope with the human situation in which suffering was a given. After the Holocaust, this was no longer a tenable position for most thinking Jews. The death of a million children in the camps could not be a punishment for sins. It could not be a testing or a purification. It was simply monstrous.

There came a time, there *had* to come a time, when Leo Baeck returned to Germany and confronted the German community. The year was 1952. It was an important year for German–Jewish confrontation. Martin Buber had come to Frankfurt to accept the Peace Prize from the Frankfurt Book Fair. And he spoke words of reconciliation. In 1978, forty years after the *Kristallnacht*, the German Chancellor, Helmuth Schmidt, spoke at a commemorative occasion on the theme of 'Truth and tolerance'. The heart of the speech was an expression of hope for a new dialogue with the Jewish community, one which would build upon the candour expressed by Martin Buber:

> Fifteen years ago, the German–Jewish philosopher Martin Buber asked in the St Paul's church: 'Who and what am I that I could dare to express forgiveness here?'[23]

In 1939, Martin Buber had spoken of the end of the German–Jewish symbiosis, taking a position particularly espoused by Gershom Scholem in later days, although Scholem went further in his assertion that such a symbiosis had actually never existed. And it was not the intention of Buber's Frankfurt speech to renew the previous relationship. Buber saw Germany's guilt; he spoke of Auschwitz and Treblinka. But – and here he differed from many Jewish voices of that time – he did not demand that German opponents to Hitler should have chosen martyrdom. He saw them in their flaws, deaf, blind, unresponsible. And yet, unlikely as it seemed to those examining the situation from the outside, Buber did not rule out the possibility that there were those who simply did not know what was happening. Buber did recognize that there were a few non-Jewish friends who resisted, who saved lives, the *chassidei umot ha-olam* ('righteous gentiles'). For their sake – as Abraham pleaded at Sodom – he saw the possibility for a new beginning.

In October 1952, almost at the same time, Leo Baeck published an article in the *Merkur*, entitled 'Israel and the German people'. The opening lines of this important presentation bring together the themes of reproval and reconciliation:

> Only a profound, one almost wants to say, a loving, yearning, for inner openness and outer clarity can permit anyone to speak about peace between Israel and the German people. Only this truthfulness in which thought and speech join together as a specific particularity, which leaves no room for ulterior thoughts or excuses, gives a justification here to confirm or to deny, to hope or to doubt . . .

> But now for the other precondition. It is, as it were, the precondition of a Kairos-assumption with its question which must be asked: given that this foundation of a matter-of-fact objectivity together with a personal dimension is clearly established, should this dialogic confrontation really commence *now*? There is an old Jewish saying: 'If one tries to rush the hour, it flees away'.

> Has the time come? Some say . . . that the Jews should make their peace with this span of time, with the goodness and monumental sadness contained in it. Certainly with the good. But with the sadness? Sadness will come to join sadness. But was there not something else, something completely and utterly different in that time? Should peace be made with all of that otherness, with all the ways in which the image of God was destroyed at that time?

Quite simply, Baeck speaks here about honesty in human relationships, whether in a one-to-one confrontation or in the re-encountering of Israel with Germany. The time *was* early: 1952, and Israel and Germany were moving towards a grey area of an uncomfortable relationship which has not yet been fully resolved. Baeck's call for total honesty where the intellectual and moral dimensions could join together and where sentimentality could be avoided was not heard. Over the years, large reparations were given and accepted for (partly) wrong reasons; an element of guilt was present on both sides, and awkwardness and the uncomfortable skirting around issues continues. Yet it may well be argued that Baeck's call for honesty, if not heard within the political sphere, has been partly realized in the area of scholarship in its secularity. Yad Vashem (Israel's Institute of Holocaust Studies) presents the dimensions of horror in so far as one can look in the face of Medusa through a mirror. At the same time, the Avenue of Righteous Gentiles sponsored by that institute gives recognition to those whom Baeck already recognized as standing in the shadows of the Holocaust: the rescuers who cared and refused to go along with the multitude to do evil.

Baeck did not really write about his Holocaust experiences. He did not create a new theology of suffering or make radical changes in his teachings. The changes and new emphases had already been established in the text he finished basically in Theresienstadt: *This People Israel: the meaning of Jewish existence.* Shift from essence to existence (his first major work was *The essence of Judaism*). Yet the two works are one, a logical development of a clear, rational, ethical and pious approach to all of the Jewish tradition. All of Baeck's writings form a consistent, interlocking structure and are at the heart of Judaism.

Why did he still look at Germany and reach out hesitatingly towards a dialogue? One must remember Baeck's demand for truthfulness – the only pattern in which an eventual expression of repentance by Germans could eventually take place. And, as Baeck taught, there is no repentance without actions of atonement. He saw at that time that such actions had not come to the fore, and warned against rushing 'time'. A 'forgiving and forgetting' would not only be a dishonest obscuring of the past, but would also deny Germany the necessary acts of atonement.

At a later time, Ernst Akiva Simon, Baeck's friend and colleague, expressed this point of view in a statement on Germany in which he still searched for acts of atonement:

> The new Germany can only 'work through' or 'overcome' its most recent past (whatever the term is) if it is ready for a genuine task of turning back (*teshuvah*, return). The meaning of 'turning back' is that one attempts to undo the consequences of evil deeds, to the fullest extent possible. No one who died is awakened by a return, but the return can help avoid new murders and new war. A peace policy which brings Israel and its neighbours closer towards an understanding would be such an act of return. Then, Israel might be able to continue the task of rebuilding in peace and with humanity. If you (Germans) really want to return, do all in your power to let all the nations on earth find the way towards God's peace, not least Jews and Arabs in the Holy Land.
>
> We Jews were God's witnesses under the greatest oppression and

deepest suffering; we hope to remain God's witnesses, in our own state, under conditions of freedom.[24]

Whether or not the time has come; indeed, whether or not Ernst Simon's hopes for Israel as well as for Germany have moved closer to fruition, continues to be a question of concern to us. But the balanced hope and doubt of Leo Baeck in this area is still applicable today.

Baeck was a great human being with a hard core of inner integrity. He inspired his colleagues as much as his students. All of them knew: 'the day is short, and the work beckons . . .'

The current interest in Leo Baeck is an indication that his teachings have survived and can address contemporary searches after truth. He demonstrated through his life that evil need not stifle goodness, and that spiritual resistance is possible where there are no other weapons at hand. At Theresienstadt, he was a light against darkness by ministering to the intellect as much as the spirit. In the nights of Theresienstadt, he could teach Greek philosophy as one way of spiritual resistance.

If we are on a journey from darkness to dawn, we have to recognize that we journey along that way in the company of travellers – and that we have to sustain one another. One of the complaints made against Baeck in Theresienstadt was that he gave pastoral counsel and sustenance to Christians imprisoned there as much as to Jews. In the end, that may be the teaching most needed for our time: the truer we are to our own faith, the more we reach out to others – that is the way into the light.

NOTES

1. I. Maybaum, *The face of God after Auschwitz* (Amsterdam, Polak & Van Gennep, 1965).
2. Ibid., p. 67.
3. Psalm 122, 6–9.
4. Genesis 22, 12.
5. Maybaum, *The face of God after Auschwitz*, p. 13.
6. S. Katz, *Post-Holocaust dialogues* (New York University Press, 1983), p. 253.
7. Ibid., pp. 253–254.
8. D. Marmur, 'Holocaust as progress', *Oxford Symposium* (1988), vol. 2, p. 955.
9. S. Katz, *Post-Holocaust dialogues*, p. 260.
10. E. Borowitz, *Renewing the Covenant; a theology for the postmodern Jew* (Philadelphia, JPS 1991), p. 42.

11. Ibid., p. 44.
12. Ibid., p. 46.
13. Ibid., p. 107.
14. Ibid., p. 229.
15. S. Schwarzschild, 'Modern Jewish Philosophy', *Contemporary Jewish religious thought*, ed. Cohen and Mendes-Flohr, p. 633.
16. E. Borowitz, *Liberal Judaism* (New York, 1984), p. 190.
17. S. Schwarzschild, 'The lure of immanence', *Collected essays*, p. 79.
18. S. Schwarzschild, *The pursuit of the ideal*, p. 11.
19. E. Taeubler, *Aufsaetze zur problematik juedischer geschtsschreibung 1908–1950* (Tuebingen, 1977), p. 47.
20. Ibid., p. 51.
21. L. Baeck, 'Life in a concentration camp', *The Jewish forum* (London, 1946), pp. 29–30.
22. Ibid., pp. 31–32.
23. Buber, 'Acceptance speech at Frankfurt book fair', 1952.
24. E. Simon, *Das zeugnis des Judentums* (Berlin, 1980).

PART 4

# [ 1 ]

# AMERICA

## GOLDEN PAST, UNCERTAIN FUTURE

> Give me your tired, your poor,
> Your huddled masses yearning to breathe free
> The wretched refuse of your teeming shore;
> Send these, the homeless, tempest-tossed to me.
> I lift my lamp beside the golden door.
>
> Emma Lazarus[1]

THE 'golden lamp' is cited more often than the 'wretched refuse' these days; both lines are engraved upon the base of the Statue of Liberty in New York harbour. The compassion for refugees has been strong in the 'land of immigrants'; but there is a dark side to the 1930s when the Jews were trying to flee Europe. Before World War II, there was a certain naïvety in the American attitude to Europe. In principle, the land of the free was open to all who were oppressed; in reality, anti-Semitism and the fear of disrupting the economy were strong enough to close the golden door to many who wanted to escape from Hitler.

Franklin Delano Roosevelt appealed to much of America as the kind and liberal president who could be relied upon to give help; those immigrants who were able to enter the United States still hold him in reverence (I include myself in that number). But he was responsive to pressure. Roosevelt genuinely cared for the Jews and hated the Nazis; when he did help, he wanted it kept out of the public eye, lest his enemies' slogan 'Jew Deal' be utilized as an attack upon the 'New Deal'. Domestic issues were more important, and there was a great apathy concerning the fate of the Jews in Europe which was not confined to the non-Jewish community. Jews themselves were worried about an influx of new immigrants and were slow to show themselves as more than only American. As they saw their people attacked, they remembered that they were Jews; and they were proud of it.

Later on, 'Holocaust Studies' came to be established alongside the 'Black Studies' programmes that were to proliferate at the universities. But, even after World War II had ended, the American-Jewish action was to draw back again into the comfortable security of being 'American' – secure, rich (or confident that material security was available to them) and part of an accommodating society where even the changing patterns of life were supportive to the Jewish identity. The movement out of the inner city into the suburbs strengthened the new synagogues and temples where religious faith was well in retreat but where the sense of community was stronger than before, underlined by the many social functions which would flourish in a house of worship which was now a house of assembly – and of play.

Then came the full news of the Holocaust, and the creation of the State of Israel. One need just record the interpretations and instructions of the rabbis, theologians, and poet-prophets. That dimension was there, yet the centre of that experience is not so much within the literature which recorded the reactions, but in the reactions themselves. Immense scholarship has gone into examining the American and the Holocaust, but the dangers which arise out of a totally scholarly approach are probably the same as in most enterprises of this nature. The past is defined and agreed upon by the university, and is then filed under the approved rubrics of a system which discourages dissent. We are told what happened to us, and memory is displaced by the standard interpretation. The Heisenberg principle of uncertainty assures us that the individual unit may zig to the right or to the left. At the end of the day, it does not matter: the totality has gone along a certain road. And yet; the journey of each individual within that continuum was and remains unique, as the countless volumes of recorded 'oral histories' indicate, even if all that testimony is then smoothed down and placed into a pattern where the unique becomes one more cog of the machine. The *zeitzeuge* – the contemporary witness – can insist upon the claim that he or she is the only reliable authority for a world event. And that claim can be easily dismissed: did a foot-soldier at Waterloo really understand the battle, the issues involved, or the tactics? But the servant-girl caught in the midst of the Israelites moving through the path in the Red Sea – her direct experience of these events and of the revelation, can be set against the prophets and their experience of revelation. Of course, the girl did not go on to become a prophet; nor did the foot soldier become a historian. Yet to have shared a moment of history, can be one of the turning points of life. In Havana harbour, I was with my parents in a rowboat. We drew close to the side of the *St Louis*, that ill-fated refugee ship not permitted to land anywhere in North America, which had brought its load

of despairing lives back to Europe where many of them died. And I heard
the despair in the voices of our friends calling to us, and in my parents'
voices through the loudhailer which they used to talk to them. I saw life
and death separated by so small a margin; and I remembered my experience
as an 11-year-old arrested and held in a police station in Berlin. Reflecting
on this later, at least I knew that I was different. I had not been born into
the prejudices of my classmates in Vicksburg, Mississippi, blind to the
minorities, to the blacks who shared their community. As refugees, we lived
on the edge of the black community. The great difference, the basic one,
was the knowledge I possessed of who the Nazis were and what they did.
Once America had entered the war, Europe impinged upon the awareness
of the general community – but it still did not deal with the Holocaust.
The United States was living in the past, inside its 'Manifest Destiny'; the
good sheriff with the white hat would enter Dodge City to clean out a nest
of bandits. Pearl Harbor was a shock; but the Japanese were still the 'Yellow
Peril' who could only hurt America by a sneak attack. And the Germans
were the same Germans who had been taught a lesson in World War I
which would have to be repeated. Of course they were evil; they were the
'bad guys'. In the cinema, Erich von Stroheim resuscitated the Prussian
bully, the brutal and powerful general who would be defeated by clean
living American film idols. The radical evil that had emerged on the world
scene with the Nazis was not yet understood.

In New York, and in the large urban centres where refugees had arrived
in sizeable numbers, the knowledge of radical evil existed in the Jewish
community. Not totally; not completely. They had almost immediately taken
on the stances of the host community into which they wanted to be absorbed.
Even when they received some knowledge of the carnage wrought in Eastern
Europe, of the death of Jewish life, they did not go into the streets to
demonstrate. One did not yet do this in America. The Jews believed in
*statlanut*, ie., 'representation' by the powerful Jews within American society
who would act discreetly, behind the scenes. They were reassured when
Rabbi Stephen Wise could tell them that he had talked with Roosevelt.
Both of these men were folk heroes for the Jews: Stephen Wise, a tiger in
the field of social justice who had fought for the underprivileged and had
established his credentials; and the President who had taught them that
the only thing to fear was fear itself. They could not accept that their rabbi
could be deceived, or that Roosevelt would act out of political motives
rather than absolute ethics – that he could and did deceive Rabbi Wise.
Even now, as a 'child' of the democratic south, I find that I cannot remove
President Roosevelt out of my pantheon of heroes. I prefer to believe that

he did not fully realize the nature of the death camps, that he acted with good intentions, that sickness was already sapping his ability to make the right decisions. I find it harder to understand that he could sit down later, with Stalin at Yalta, and not see the tiger behind the face of 'Uncle Joe'.

The scholars who ask why six million Jews died and who see the complicity of the Western powers, the silence of the English and American politicians, as part of the answer, cannot be denied. But their answers do not deal with the reality of a decent and kind United States – South, North, East, Middle West and Far West, who applied nineteenth-century thinking and ethics to the twentieth century of brutality. There was little wrong with the ethos of 'our town' or even Ben Hecht's snarling, amoral Chicago of *The front page* – it was just totally outdated. It was all part of a United States defined and therefore partially shaped by Hollywood, sleepwalking along the rooftops of the world where God – the Wizard of Oz – was ultimately not needed. Little Judy Garland could click her heels together, and the wicked witch would be defeated. Until America came to understand the totally radical evil of the Holocaust, it could not do more than accept some – too few – of the refugees. It could not undo what had been done. Even afterwards, in conquered Germany, its naïve approach in 're-educating the Germans' with its *fragebogen* (questionnaires) and blindness in putting Nazis back into power, was a reflection of out-dated, Middle American thinking. America itself could not be re-educated to know evil. The study and identification of the *tremendum*, the total evil of the Holocaust, was within a sophisticated dialogue of scholars which did not penetrate the average American home.

I was nineteen years old when I came to the Hebrew Union College in Cincinnati, a graduate of the University of Chicago. This was 1945; and a number of the students who now came to be educated as rabbis had come out of Europe, out of the very same centre of the Holocaust. Gunther and Walter Plaut had come from Berlin (although Gunther had already finished his studies in Berlin, at the Hochschule). Stephen Schwarzschild was another 'Berliner'. There were other refugees: Eugene Weingarten (later 'Vineyard', with a successful business career to come in South America) and Hugo Gryn. Hugo Gryn had accompanied his father into Auschwitz, had learned from him in that life and in that death. Quietly, by his presence more than by presenting the facts of that reality of death, he educated his fellow students. I was 'adopted' and cared for by that triumvirate of senior students who later became the teachers of the next generation: Eugene Borowitz, Arnold Wolf, and Stephen Schwarzschild. One could say that the Holocaust slowly began to be part of the thinking of the students – but not through direct instruction. They observed their teachers, many of them refugee scholars from Germany. Hildegard and Julius Levy taught Assyriology and Bible (in Germany, as a secret language, they had interspaced their letters to one another with cuneiform texts which were actually messages). Samuel Atlas was the great philosopher who actually understood Solomon Maimon and Schelling, but taught Talmud. Franz Landsberger was the museum curator, the expert on European Art. Alexander Guttman from Berlin was also a Talmud teacher; his profound discussion of Jewish responses in the death camps only appeared a few years ago. Eric Werner taught music; Selma Stern-Taeubler, historian and novelist, was a librarian at the Hebrew Union College. Her husband, Eugen Taeubler, was arguably the greatest of the scholars assembled in Cincinnati by the president, Julian Morgenstern, who enabled refugee scholars to find a haven. Taeubler had taught ancient, medieval and modern history at Heidelberg, the only Jew to be a full professor and member of that Academy, as associate and then successor to the great Mommsen. The profound thinker Abraham Heschel had passed through the College on his way to the more conservative Jewish Theological Seminary; and there were other refugee scholars. But with the arrival of Leo Baeck, the first one (Werner Weinberg came later) to have entered the concentration camp and to bring the full knowledge of the Holocaust to that community, the awareness changed.

When we try to understand American life (and American Jewish life) before and after the Holocaust, we quickly learn that generalizations are more than fallible. The vastness of the land, the different indigenous cultures and the imported traditions created patterns which cannot be directed from the centre. No one normative pattern can be discerned, even though the WASP equation (the White Anglo-Saxon Protestants) was frequently deemed the model for the 'average American' – a person who did not exist. The Amish in Pennsylvania, Catholics in Maryland, French grandees in Louisiana, or Spanish cavaliers in the City of the Angels asserted an individuality and freedom for themselves which might be deemed the one aspect of American culture in which all minorities could participate. In Europe, the Jews had been a minority who could only survive by incorporating themselves into a watertight structure with a central authority. In America, they had to learn to live as free individuals in a free society.

Discussing the problems of American and German Jewish historiography Selma Stern-Taeubler wrote:

Whereas the German Jew was successful in adapting his commercial experience – inherited or acquired for himself – to the changed conditions of the Colonies, he failed in his efforts to transplant the old, communal forms to the new soil. It was not only that the centuries-old tradition was missing . . . but that the legal forms departed completely from those to which he was accustomed. The Jewish congregation, just like the Christian sect, was not a legal corporation, recognized by the state. No Jew was obliged to join a congregation. No elder had power to force members to pay dues, to control their settlement or departure, to regulate their relations with the authorities, or to watch over their moral behavior. The individual Jew was left on his own. He alone had to shape his new life in a new land, to look for a place in which to settle, to choose a profession by which to make a living, and to find a room in which to pray to his God.[2]

Over a century later, in the twentieth century, Jews were still independent. Isaac Mayer Wise had established the institutions which formalized an American Reform Jewish community: the Union of American Hebrew Congregations, the Central Conference of American Rabbis, and the Hebrew Union College. Consciously or not they had tried to conform to what they thought their fellow Americans wanted from them: an intense patriotism which had made their leaders reject the early Zionism; a respect for learning and for logic which linked them to nineteenth-century positivism and Kantian ethics; and a conviction that they were Americans and not Europeans (although they were less certain of this than their neighbours and were dimly conscious of the roots which had nurtured them). They were still a laity, who always respected their rabbis and often ignored them. The teachers at the Hebrew Union College in the middle of the 1930s had often been trained in Germany; but their allegiance had been given to radical developments of the 'Science of Judaism' rather than to traditional Jewish learning; and they tried to turn rabbinical candidates into modern scholars. A *mathmid*, a traditionalist Jew yearning for Talmudic learning who strayed into the school would soon leave or be converted. And yet, strangest of all, most of the rabbis ordained in the 30s and early 40s would go to congregations who turned them into devout and capable rabbis. Perhaps it was the openness to the needs of the congregants: pastoral counselling had become stronger as a discipline to be studied. In a time of war and postwar recognition of the Holocaust, in a changing society where conformity was no longer the ultimate good, American Jews now wanted the warmth of traditional customs; they recognized the need of European Jewry who wanted to rebuild the ancient land; and they had learned to distrust the goddess Reason. American Judaism became more existential, less concerned with essence, more involved with existence.

Few of the refugee scholars at the Hebrew Union College really felt at home in an atmosphere of Jewish learning which was curiously out of step with their own experience in the European institutions. It was a place of refuge and they were grateful for this. The College library was a place where books could be written. It was America. When the young chaplains came back from the war and appealed for student volunteers who would join them in smuggling refugees into Palestine, they found eager listeners. Americans still did not understand what the Holocaust had been, but they understood human needs and the sufferings of the People Israel hounded across the lands and seas of Europe. Leo Baeck himself, as witness and prophet, tried to instruct the College and its students in the fate of the Jewish people who were a revelation to the world. He did not really succeed in Cincinnati. The students were too impatient. They could not understand his accent, they would not struggle with his ideas. They loved and revered him as a person; but only a few of them would today consider themselves to have been his disciples. The finest minds among the students – one comes back to Borowitz, Schwarzschild, and Wolf – found themselves closer to the teachings of Martin Buber and of Franz Rosenzweig. And none of them, at that time, saw the Holocaust as a *tremendum* which rested outside understanding but demanded to be encountered as a reality of evil which had nullified many of their categories of thought.

I taught at an Indian College in Oklahoma, and even opened a rodeo with my prayers. This was in 1952 – and there was still a total silence about the Holocaust in that part of the world. No one was interested. Prayer books did not mention the Holocaust, although the lamentations for the destroyed Temple (in 586 BC and 70 CE) at times allowed a mention for the six million who died in the camps and ghettos.

Internally, a slow process of education was taking place wherever there was a large community containing survivors. Leo Baeck had expressed his hope for the vibrant, young (by European standards) American Jewry which was assumed to have taken over the leadership for the world Jewish community. He still had hopes for America, even if it only came to terms slowly with the true reality of the Hitler years.

Popular literature, rather than academic discourses, reflected the awarenesses of the public (television had not yet become the universal leveller of thought). It might have been assumed that Hollywood, where many Jews had established themselves in a new and open discipline, would deal with the anguish of Jewish experience. This did not happen. Occasionally, a 'brave' film like *Gentleman's agreement* in 1947 would deal most cautiously with anti-Semitism; but movie-makers were not concerned with educating the public. They wanted to give the public what it wanted and as one Hollywood adage spelled it out, 'nobody ever went broke by underestimating the public taste'. But books about the Holocaust did begin to appear.

In 1964, the Union of American Hebrew Congregations asked me to prepare a textbook on the Holocaust which could be taught to 16-year-old students; a history book. Initially, I refused the task. How could one have a history text dealing with Hitler, Auschwitz, the Nuremberg Laws, etc., which school children would accept? Then I proposed to create such a book based upon the literature of the Holocaust to which young people could respond. The result was *Out of the whirlwind: the literature of the Holocaust* (1968). The book's intention was clear: the Holocaust was to be described by those who had encountered it; and it insisted that the truth of the experience could be conveyed through fictional writings. The objections came from the parents, who did not want that 'terrible topic' to be taught in American schools. Even in the 60s, the Jewish community resisted the knowledge of Auschwitz. And they still reflected the outside environment. I received a telegram from my publisher, informing me that the book-of-the-month club wanted *Out of the whirlwind*. A short time later, an apologetic letter arrived. Someone, at the top of the book club organization, had vetoed this: 'The public does not want to read about concentration camps!' At the time, this was probably the correct judgement.

The relevance of this book to our exploration of the American awareness of Auschwitz rests in the fact that the work did become a standard text, and not only in the Reform movement. Conservative congregations included it in their curriculum and, for some reason, the book moved steadily upward, so that it is now a standard work for many Holocaust courses at universities. What is most intriguing is that it spoke to the next generation, rather than to the parents. The growing awareness of the teachings of Elie Wiesel contributed to this, and one of the opening selections in the text was from the *Diary of Anne Frank* where the continuous interest in the diary was supplemented by the Broadway play and the movie. But what should be underscored is the fact that it was not the 'theological' section, asking about man and God after Auschwitz, which was seen as the centre of the work. Rather, it was the awareness that it was the children of *Terezin*, the diary of a teenager, and the questions asked by the women and men encountered in the common areas of life who enunciated the pain and puzzlement of 'everyman' caught in the whirlpool of evil who spoke to the young Americans. Long after the theological 'answers' had been put aside, the persecuted children remained to awaken consciences; they established the links between America and the victims of the Holocaust. We have to turn to the serious thinkers upon the American scene, the professors and rabbis who came to articulate the faith and the doubts which then linked American Judaism with the reality of the Holocaust; but ultimately the emphasis is on the hearts and minds of the American.

Professor Mordecai Kaplan, the brilliant, innovative spirit at the heart of the Jewish Theological Seminary, whose Jewish Center reinforced the status of the laity, is credited with saying: 'There is one organic Jewish community in America. And then the seminaries send out their students who will tell them: ' "You are Orthodox", "You are Conservative"; "You are Reform" ' – and there was much truth in that statement. In practice traditional, in theology radical, this movement was in some ways particularly American in its pragmatism and its sociological orientation, its denial of supernaturalism and of the 'chosen people' concept. And yet, it has had little to say about the Holocaust. In its scientific orientation and dependence upon Emile Durkheim, it created a pattern of reason where the *tremendum* of Auschwitz seeps through its categories of understanding.

It is, perhaps, unfair to expect a particular position on the Holocaust from those seminaries which ordain the American rabbinate: the Jewish Theological Seminary (Conservative), Hebrew Union College (Reform), or the Orthodox houses of learning: Yeshiva University and its ancillary academies, the Skokie Hebrew Theological College, and the many *Yeshivot* in which Jewish learning has become more and more traditional. The Jewish Theological Seminary, started in some ways as an antidote for the Hebrew Union College, was tied to the new emigrants arriving in New York and on the East Coast. Its traditional approach, which could still accommodate itself to American culture, thus becoming a bulwark of American Judaism.

European refugees had also come to the Jewish Theological Seminary and occasionally, students also left the Hebrew Union College for the Jewish Theological Seminary as did Richard Rubenstein. Trained at the Hebrew Union College, at Harvard, and at the Jewish Theological Seminary, Rubenstein became the thinker who presented the Holocaust to American Jews and non-Jews with a pitiless clarity which did not shy away from the ultimate conclusion: if Jews, no matter what teachers and practices they followed, believed at all in a contract, a Covenant, between God and the Jewish people, they had to re-examine this belief. The Orthodox, still trained in a theology of suffering for the sake of God, were not as affected by this thesis. As we have seen, there were traditional answers which did not minimize the Holocaust but did stress an ancient, not to be challenged, belief in the divine plan. Richard Rubenstein spoke to all other Jews, but

particularly to those who felt uncomfortable with the standard synagogues
and the standard answers. The old question of theodicy was placed before
the people: 'Why does God permit such evil? Is he not all-powerful? If
God makes it part of a divine plan – the killing of six million of his covenanted group – God is not the good and merciful God whom we know. If
he wants to prevent it, but could not do so, he is not a powerful God,
omnipotent ruler of the world'. But the tradition has not dealt with the
monumental quality of the trauma. It has not given an answer which has
satisfied our contemporaries. The issue can of course be avoided by placing
it into the unknown area of divine action which we may not examine.
Even when disagreeing with Rabbi Richard Rubenstein, I find myself more
challenged by his confrontation than by the traditional evasion. And it arises
out of an American ethos, where one can ask the most impossible questions
and feel the right to expect some kind of answer.

Richard Rubenstein became one of the leading voices in the 'Death of
God' camp of theologians. He did not speak as a Conservative rabbi; he
was not a Reform thinker, despite the Hebrew Union College, or a Reconstructionist despite his participation in Reconstructionist publications and
activities. Rubenstein spoke for himself. Most of his colleagues rejected
him, and for a time he was, rightly, embittered by this. As a university
professor in Florida, and creator and director of a conservative think-tank
in Washington, he went on to develop his own position. More than any
other rabbi, he had developed an awareness for the ultimate evil of the
death camps. He linked this with an understanding of world history and
with an extraordinary awareness of the uses of technology, so much worshipped by the contemporary world, which had become a technology of
death. There are earlier incidences in our century, but society is no longer
constrained from 'getting rid' of excess human lives – by killing. The 'technology of death' now uses a bureaucratic caste to kill humans from a
distance, without feeling compunction, compassion, or guilt. As he rightly
showed, the Nazi system depended upon this pattern. Through this insight,
Rubenstein gave a clearer understanding of what happened during the
Holocaust; it was not the few sadists who killed in the camps, but a whole
society which had accepted this pattern of murder. This insight was also a
criticism of America and its military establishment, whose concepts had led
to the use of the atom bomb over Hiroshima and Nagasaki.

'What does this do to religion?' asked Rubenstein; and that question is
also addressed to the secular religion of America, and to the professing
faiths of the ancient traditions. The Jewish community found various
answers as they came to confront Rubenstein's teachings. Initially, in the

death of God concept one would have to turn to the great 'God of Nothing-ness', an idea grounded in early mystic teachings of the rabbis. The Kabbala and its 'Holy Nothingness' could not replace the old myth with a new one. But Jews could still follow most of the old practices, going to synagogues which might act as a therapy group even if the contents of the prayers were at question. The practices, the sancta, have a healing quality of their own.

There are many positive aspects to the concepts of Rubenstein. Out of it has evolved a passionate adherence to the State of Israel, to the right of Jews to move from powerlessness to the exercise of power. If the doctrine of human immortality is surrendered, there is at least the right to fight for life in this world. One of his gifts to the American scene is the raising of disciples at his university and through his books, and the disciples have become incisive students of the Holocaust. More than anything else, Richard Rubenstein exposes the rationalizations and uncertainties of con-temporary humanity which has begun to live with death and murder as a viable course of action in order to achieve its goals.

The Conservative movement and the Jewish Theological Seminary are opposed to Richard Rubenstein's approach. Throughout the decades, the Jewish Theological Seminary has seen itself more as the preserver of tra-dition, as a bulwark against the radicalism of Reform practices, as a defender of traditional observances. Talmud and Bible (with little 'Higher Criticism' – the Christian 'Modern' approach to the Bible) – were the mainstay at the school located at New York's Broadway and 123rd Street. The school opened itself far more to dialogue during the past thirty years. Professor Ismar Schorsch, the current head, is a fine historian with a German back-ground, and far more involved in the history of Germany, the Holocaust, and new patterns of thought. Once, the Seminary dictated all aspects of the Conservative movement. Now, the voices of the laity have their say, but often, there is an enormous gap between the young rabbi and a congregation which has listened to other teachers addressing them through the media or in the modern American literature where there are many Jewish voices. Auschwitz is remembered by the novelists and poets of America, who need not have been there but who came to understand what the survivors and the historians had to say. Chicago and Los Angeles cannot be ignored but the voices of New York speak a language which is all their own. Here is the place where refugees found the *goldene medinah*, the city of gold, where everything was possible: one could even be oneself. Yiddish is dying out, even though Columbia University inaugurated Yiddish as an academic discipline which keeps attracting students. But the great literature, or the language in the streets, is a thing of the past. Isaac Bashevis Singer won the Nobel Prize for literature because his texts had been translated into English, and made their impact upon the general as well as the Jewish community. This is part of the American scene which has to be appreciated if one searches for the ethos, the direction of contemporary thinking, instruction from poet/prophets. Singer knew all about evil; and this fascinated the American reading public. He brought them glimpses of that old world which the Nazis had destroyed, but it was not filled with nostalgic pictures even when it was read by those wallowing in nostalgia. Singer wrote about demons and evil spirits, about mean-minded people and the suffering they caused, even when he celebrated the human spirit which could rise above the scenes of domestic and general Jewish suffering.

His presentation of the Holocaust was not aligned with any of the theological positions within organized American Jewry. His book *Enemies: a love story* showed his ability to portray the post-Holocaust world as well as those earlier times which he and his older brother I. J. Singer (perhaps an even greater writer) had chronicled. The protagonist of his story, Herman Broder, marries Yadwiga, the Polish woman who had sheltered him during the Holocaust, when he hears of the death of his wife and children. They come to America and live in Brooklyn where he meets his mistress and later wife, Masha. One need not follow the complicated plot where Tamara, the first and reportedly dead wife comes to New York as well. These survivors are shown against an American background where the reality of the Holocaust is not understood, where their religious anguish and struggle with God for meaning lies outside their neighbour's awareness. The old European life, with all of its practices and superstitions, is seen as the truly authentic life: America is a pale copy, at best. And the Jews of America, in a mixture of nostalgia and guilt, wanted to be told that they were inauthentic, that they should either go to Israel where life was lived among Jews including survivors who brought the true memories of *Yiddishkeit* with them.

Alan Berger tries to trace the Covenant – which for him means the Jews' awareness of their destiny linked with God, their religious identity – with the encounter of the Holocaust as it is found in American fiction. Traditional belief, total rejection, acceptance of Jewish fate no matter what rests behind it – are all found in the work of Isaac Bashevis Singer.

There are many writers in America in the generation after the refugee thinkers who give us more of the European image, who write out of an American context. Cynthia Ozyck stands at the top of that list. In her early story 'Bloodshed' (1976), she follows the story of Bleilip, an assimilated Jew who is quite happy to be a contented secularist. He visits a synagogue largely composed of survivors, and hears their rabbi speak about the Biblical image of the goat sent into the wilderness to atone for the sins of the community:

> He hears the *rebbe* contend that post-Auschwitz Jews stand *instead of* the goat whose horns were adorned with a crimson sash. Contemporary Jewish existence is cursed for having to live without the Messianic presence. The *rebbe* laments: 'In the absence of Messiah . . . we are not free, we are only *instead of* . . . instead of choice we have the yoke, instead of looseness we are pointed the way to go, instead of freedom we have the red cord around our throats, we were in villages, they drove us into camps, we were in trains, they drove us into showers of poison.'
>
> Interrupting his discourse, the *rebbe* points an accusing finger at Bleilip as the embodiment of faithlessness . . . and orders him to empty his pockets. Doing as commanded, he reveals that he has two guns, one toy and one real. The *rebbe*, reflecting his experience with euphemism and deception at the hand of the Nazis in Auschwitz ('soap' stones and 'shower' heads) states, 'it is the toy we have to fear'.[3]

Writers can confront the uncertainties of assimilated Americans with the certainties of faith, whether the faith rises out of the European experience or whether it was developed within the enclaves of traditional thought. This does not mean that there were no certainties of faith or acknowledgement of Jewish destiny within the non-Orthodox community. But, somehow, Reform Judaism has not been seen as a secure bastion of faith within the American Jewish literature of that period. Reform Jews, wrestling with some unexpiated guilt, yearned for a rabbi in whom Moses was somehow recapitulated. Erich Segal's *Acts of faith* does more than present the conflict between a rabid Orthodoxy and modern Judaism, when it examines the forces which turn a girl out of a traditional dynasty towards a journey which finally sees her ordained as rabbi. Some of the older themes developed by Chaim Potok in *The chosen* and *The promise* surface here: the scion of the Orthodox rabbinical line who is expected to take over from his father and become the spiritual leader of his community and who rebels, receives full treatment in this novel. The minutiae of synagogue life and politics which turned Harry Kemelmann's *Friday the rabbi slept late, Saturday the rabbi went hungry* into bestseller are absent. Kemelmann's Rabbi David Small was a believable figure of a Conservative, small-minded rabbi with a talent for detective work. Theological issues were raised; but even though Small was shown as rabbi of a middle-of-the-road Conservative small town synagogue, he was generally in line with traditional thinking. In Segal's rebel son we see the influences of traditionalism at war with the environment, and come to a key moment of his education on Christmas Day, when the *Yeshiva* boys are forced to go to school where their teacher, a survivor, addresses them:

In retrospect, I think his severity with us was a personal way of disguising the grief, and perhaps the guilt he felt, at having survived the Holocaust when so many had not.

The Bible passages he had chosen that day all emphasized the otherness of our religion, and as the morning progressed, Rabbi Schumann grew increasingly upset. Finally, he closed his book and with a deep sigh, rose and transfixed us with his hollow, dark-ringed eyes.

This day, this awful, awful day is when they found the fuel for the torches that would burn us everywhere. In the centuries since our expulsion from the Holy Land, has there ever been a country that has not persecuted us in his name? And our own age has witnessed the ultimate horror – the Nazis with their ruthless efficiency – six million of us.

He pulled out his handkerchief and tried to staunch the tears. 'Women, little children', he went on with anguish. 'They all turned into wisps of smoke from the ovens.' His voice grew hoarse. 'I saw this, boys. I saw them kill my wife and children. They wouldn't even do me the kindness of exterminating me. They left me living on the rack of memory.'

No one in the classroom breathed. We were overwhelmed by his speech, not merely for its content but because Rabbi Schumann, normally a stern taskmaster, was now sobbing helplessly.

Then, still weeping, he continued. 'Listen – we are sitting here today to show the Christians that we're still alive. We were here before them, and we shall endure until the Messiah comes'.

He paused, regained his breath, and some of his composure.

'Now let us rise.'

I always dreaded this moment when we had to sing the slender verses chanted by so many of our brethren as they entered the gas chambers:

'I believe with all my heart
In the coming of the Messiah,
And though He may tarry on the way
I nonetheless believe. I still believe.'

The afternoon sky was a grey shroud as I walked home, shaken. Once again, I passed all the Christian lights. But this time what I saw in them were the shining, indestructible atoms of six million souls.[4]

For the traditionalist, Holocaust and the Christians are linked together, and Daniel, the son, has this deeply impressed in his mind.

In the break between Daniel and his father, the Holocaust enters as a muted tone, almost as an additional thought. Yet it stems from the same conviction: the environment tried to destroy the Jew and the precious chain of tradition:

> For a moment he (the father) did not speak. Perhaps no words existed to respond to such a statement.
>
> 'You don't *want* to? You don't want to follow in the footsteps of your father and or his father before him?'
>
> He paused and asked almost pleading, '*Why*, Danny, just tell me why?'
>
> I had come this far – I had to say it all.
>
> 'Because I've lost my faith'.
>
> There was an apocalyptic silence.
>
> 'This is impossible,' he muttered, shaken and disoriented. 'What the Romans couldn't do, the Greeks, Hitler . . .' He did not complete his sentence. We both knew that he was accusing me of murder, of killing off the line of Silczer Rebbes.[5]

What worries me in Segal's book is that neither side in the battle of the tradition against the rebels hears what the other one is saying. They walk their way in almost automatic fashion, and we only catch a sense of the inner fire and conflict in descriptions of certain scenes: the trouble caused by the girl when she sings her prayers at the Western Wall and disturbs the pious men who 'might be enticed away from their prayers'; or the exorcism of a *dybbuk* (the ghostly presence of someone dead who occupies the body of a living person in order to be heard). But perhaps Segal is right. There is little fire today in the 'acts of faith' that are more conformity than self-immolation. And one can understand more about the American Jewish community by reading the novels in which the frustrations and uncertainties of that life are given a name. That large group of American Jewish writers – Saul Bellow, Malamud, Irwin Shaw (and the other war novelists), Hugh Nissenson, Robert Kotlowitz – who deal with the Holocaust and American fractured faith, all increase our awareness of the inner struggle which is evident in American Jewish life, but would not necessarily give us the teachings which lead from darkness towards the light. The moral voices of Arthur Miller in America or of Harold Pinter in London could bring us to the theatre as a modern place of worship; but these writers have moved outside of the Jewish tradition in some ways, although I find them particularly appealing as teacher/prophets of our age.

There is a difference between Jewish and non-Jewish writers, of course. Writing about the Holocaust, the Jewish writer confronted his or her own identity in a way which was not ancillary, but central to the text. In the later days of theology, Irving Greenberg and Eugene Borowitz saw this in terms of the relationship Jews had with God – the Covenant relationship. But the earlier writers, often agnostic or anti-religious, confronted this problem of identity as well. Alongside the 'religious' writers; Elie Wiesel, Cynthia Ozyck, Nissenson, Zvi Kolitz and a host of others, one had the outspoken critics of Judaism or of Jews, who were often just as positive about their Jewish identity and could affirm it in challenges which angered the 'synagogue Jews': Philip Roth, Edward Lewis Wallant, and Bernard Malamud might be cited as examples.

Contemporary Jewish critics often worry about the nature of novels written by non-Jewish writers: how could they feel the critics of identity, or the challenge directed against the God who had forgotten the Covenant, if they wrote from the outside? Nevertheless, there is a long line of dedicated writers, reaching from John Hersey (*The wall*, dealing with the Warsaw Ghetto, and also his short stories!) to William Styron's *Sophie's choice*, which deserve appreciation. They represent a non-Jewish America which had turned to the universal problems of suffering, who saw more than a 'good story'. They felt the anguish of the Jews, and reached out towards their neighbours. When one compares this with the stock image of the Jew as villain or flawed person which has afflicted English letters from the days of Marlowe and Shakespeare to the present, one must at least acknowledge the positive aspects of this literature. In Germany, there arose a 'literature of remorse', in which the sins of the Germans were confessed (the work of Albrecht Goes, for example). The American literature was different; in part, it was a literature of compassion.

One cannot fully analyse the American Jew and American Judaism. It is still vital to make the attempt, since the United States will continue to be one polarity of Jewish existence, set against the community in Israel which has already begun to move away from that dominance – but who cannot survive without America. But what does America teach us today? It is a land where the early certainties have been replaced by doubts; where the extremes in religion grow stronger, and where intermarriage removes half of the next generation before it has begun. And yet there are signs of religious revival which even move the major religious institutions back on stage. The Jewish Theological Seminary and the Hebrew Union College, despite the criticisms which can be levelled against them, have created new voices and thinkers which almost make theology respectable again.

Arthur Cohen belongs in our section of 'Progressive and radical Jewish Thinkers'; but these chapters must not be thought of as water-tight compartments. 'Yitz' Greenberg, while radical, is traditional; the thinkers of the Jewish Theological Seminary were observant in practice. But Arthur Cohen, though he came within a semester of ordination at the Jewish Theological Seminary (and within a semester of his Ph.D at the University of Chicago), escapes from all these categories. His concept of the *tremendum* had become a tool of thinking for all those engaged in the quest for meaning upon that darkling field we call the Holocaust. And he belongs among the novelists for his *almost* Sabbatai Zvi book and for his *almost* Hannah Arendt novel. Here is where we come to recognize something of that special American ambience which breaks out of European ideologies and experiences and addresses a particularly free and open mind to the problems which have come upon the American Jew.

There is, of course, the film world: a mirror of American thinking which has some of the funhouse aspects of a distorting reflection, and a touch of Medusa's mirror enabling us to see horror in an indirect but safe fashion. (One need only think of *The pawnbroker*.) We have to acknowledge that area without entering it. The field is too vast, with too many arid areas; and this also applies to television. There is art: painting, etching, sculpture, and drawing has been particularly challenged in an area where the ultimate horror cannot be seen completely. Auschwitz and Theresienstadt produced much which endures – perhaps more as a witness, a testimony, than as enduring art.

It seems almost paradoxical, then, for me to place so much emphasis upon a popular art form which has not yet been considered *stubenrein* – proper to be introduced into the living room! I refer to comic books, often the crudest representation of the nastiest aspects of the human mind, but, as in this case, a breakthrough in representing human emotions and events.

I first encountered cartoons as a child in Mississippi, in the black and white, absolute depiction of the American ethos that was Dick Tracy and Orphan Annie. And then, in the past two years, I discovered Art Spiegelmann.

Spiegelmann's 1991 lithograph 'Mickey Mouse, Maus, Mouse' links the chronicle *Maus* to an art form which lived under general disapproval but was sold by the million to children (and, of course, to adults): the comic book. *Maus* is a comic book of the Holocaust.

Spiegelmann's *Maus*[6] is something entirely different. And it is totally American. It is the 'alternative' comic book and was actually first published in *Raw*, an experimental 'comix' magazine. It is a highly complex work of art, interweaving the artist's strained relationship to his father with the father's account of the Holocaust and the fate of his family. It is 'a survivor's tale', and does not beautify any aspect of it: the survivors themselves are shown in all their incompleteness, their pettiness and failures as human beings. The Jews are all drawn as mice, and they move from their Eastern Europe habitations – 'Mauschwitz' – to the place of their destruction, Auschwitz. All the figures are drawn as animals – mice, cats, rats – but it is amazing how quickly one accepts the pictorial representation and is drawn into the story which has been told six million times but which is totally new in this representation. The art itself is brilliant and innovative, with the panels of the comic book expanding and spilling over, the past and the present fitting together in a way which makes the Holocaust very much part of the life of the next generation.

It is a comic book which instructs its readers in a way which should make some historians ashamed of the careless writings and vague generalizations found in their work. With all its harsh presentation of the victims and their imperfections, Maus is in the end a celebration of the human spirit, and does as much for the American Jewish scene as it achieves for the Holocaust. The public and personal response to the victims, the attempts of the next generation to come to terms with the *tremendum*, and the fundamental decency which exists between the generations are captured here; and the comic book has come into its own.

The American Jew is not the paradigm for the Jew of today, even though so much of Jewish life takes place within the United States. The answers to life after darkness will vary, but there are constants that can be isolated in America, Europe, and Israel. Religious faith is one such constant, even when it is an uncertain and questing aspect of our identity. In Biblical times, and up to the present, Judaism has been a group experience and the basic teachings are intended for the community even more than for the individual. Covenant theology is central to the Jewish thinkers in the United States. It is another constant in the Jewish quest for the future, since Jews do not walk in isolation. Our identity is a group identity. With Leo Baeck, we can still see the Jews as a revelation in the world – and that means every Jew, the secularists and the rebels, the deeply Orthodox and the uncertain and certain liberal Progressives.

Does the polarity 'American Jewry–Israeli Jewry' still exist? In these days of political conflict, one can not forget that American Jewry ... is American. Israel simply does not understand this, and both the Israelis and their friends in the Diaspora can only despair. For Eugene Borowitz, the leading theologian of Progressive Judaism, the Six Day War was a divine revelation which confirmed his faith for both Diaspora and Israel. But danger is again on the horizon, and one cannot wait for another revelation. For Richard Rubenstein, the Jew who comes to power is the fulfilled identity of a people who will no longer be victims; but power is relative in a world grown unstable since the demise of the Soviet Union. Israel, weaned from the glory of the Six Day War by the uncertainties of the Yom Kippur War, is in danger of moving back into a Holocaust mentality where the world outside its boundaries is a dark threat to survival and it feels that it can only depend on itself.

That, incidentally, has of course affected American thinking. Where it could once point to Israel as 'the bulwark of democracy', and the Jew could see Israel as the role model for young David fighting off all comers, the Galahad without flaws, it can no longer identify itself with, at best, a flawed fighter. American Jewry still needs Israel; wants to identify itself with the land and the people; wants to be its stay and support. The intangible blessings which come with the Diaspora are there as much as ever; but a breach of faith has taken place when the still liberal dreams of American Jewry are mocked by Israel as unrealistic.

Most American Jews today no longer see their future as Jewish leaders in the Promised Land, but as representatives of an American democracy where anti-Semitism has ceased to be a major problem. Of course it is still there: the Messiah has not yet come. Jews have entered the US political arena with confidence; and American Jewry barely sees itself as a minority group in need of protection. American Jews live at peace in a democratic land where Diaspora life is seen as positive and conducive to a Jewish life which will not fear its neighbours; they can cope with the past and share the darkness with their neighbours who are no longer seen as the enemy. For this insight, we have to go beyond the often sheltered academies or the traditional enclaves of religion. The arts, literature, the new liturgies which are both lament for the *Shoah* and a celebration of Jewish life through the millennia – even the brash comics who stand alongside other ethnic groups and make their Jewishness their 'thing'. Many of the non-Orthodox rabbis have become more secular; an appreciable number of them move from the pulpit into the 'caring' societies as psychiatric practitioners or therapists of every possible denomination. More of them enter academic life, now, since this is another pulpit from which to exercise influence upon the next generation of American Jews. The negative aspects of American Jewish life have not caused a failure of nerve.

A symbiosis has taken place, and Jews are Americans. The American reality was big enough, and generous enough. In a world of the 'Declaration of Universal Human Rights', where one does not even know when a boundary in Europe has been crossed, there is a certain danger of rootlessness. Yet American Jewry has its firm and deep roots in the new world, nurtured by a sense of gratitude, but also by the great-grandchildren of those who helped build the United States in the previous centuries. This is an asset for the world Jewish community, a blessing that will in the end help us enter the next century where peace may be found.

NOTES

1. E. Lazarus, *The new colossus*.
2. Selma Stern-Taeubler, *Jews from Germany in the United States*, ed. E. Hirschler (New York, 1955), p. 51.
3. Ozyck, 'Bloodshed' (1976), pp. 49–50.
4. E. Segal, *Acts of faith* (Hutchinson) pp. 35–36.
5. Ibid., p. 235.
6. A. Spiegelmann, *Maus* (Pantheon, 1986, 1991).

# [ 2 ]

# GERMANY

### GUILT AND REUNION

'**D**ENK Ich an Deuschland in der Nacht/werd ich um meinen Schlaf gebracht' wrote Heinrich Heine: 'When I think about Germany at night, I cannot sleep!'
I find it difficult to think about Germany. It is hard to make a rational assessment of a land which is schizophrenic in thought, torn apart by rapid changes and struggling to rid itself of a past which came to an apparent end more than half a century ago, but still refuses to go away. The unresolved guilt of the Nazi period still resides in the land, no matter how often its people celebrate the 'grace of being born after the event', in Chancellor Kohl's often quoted words. There are still traumas in the body politic; the children's teeth are set on edge because the fathers have eaten sour grapes. And then there came the supposed rebirth of Germany. East Germany and its regime fell, and five new states joined the Greater Germany as the Berlin wall came down. The dowry East Germany brought to that marriage was a new guilt. Over 200,000 East Germans had worked for the State Police, had betrayed their friends and family out of fear or out of greed. They had not been the Nazis of the past, had not killed (well . . . not many had gone that far). But the *stasis* – part-time members of the State Police – had kept a corrupt government in power and had themselves been corrupted. At a time when trials for the Nazis are still creaking through the courts, one began to think about trials for the *stasis*, for the leaders who had betrayed them, for the little people who had been little in courage and decency as well.

Can one try a whole country? The argument involves the intellectuals and the pastors as well, even those who appeared to be the leaders of the modest resistance that had taken a stand against the Communist regime. Who is there left to judge? And who is innocent? This will brings back that bleak past of another dictatorship, one that was greater in evil but as persuasive in letting the multitude enter a dark valley in which they ceased to be humans. One of the most positive images in German life is still the faithful German shepherd dog.

## The Dogs of the Berlin Wall

The Berlin Wall had fallen. And all of Germany celebrated. Checkpoint Charlie became the highway for a jubilating stream of East Germans who entered the long forbidden Western paradise. The young men danced on the top of the wall, and all the homes of Berlin opened wide.

And so the East Germans came to West Germany, and received a warm welcome. 'When you go back, tell them how much we love you!' The 'Ossies' (they had already acquired a name to distinguish them from the 'Wessies') looked at their hosts with surprise: 'Who is going back?' they asked; and the welcome became a bit more chilly. There were so many of them! And they wanted jobs! What would happen to the economic miracle of West Germany?

In this fable, one type of Ossie refugee, however, who quickly captured the imagination of the public. Over 5000 jobless dogs applied for work! They had been the guardians of the Berlin wall, had faithfully marched alongside the soldiers protecting the East Germans from the gluttony of the West – and now that job was gone: they had become redundant. Many of them were indeed the pride of German folklore: the noble German shepherd dog. Alsatians and Rottweilers had also been accepted into this special foreign legion for dogs, and a few Dobermans. Others who offered themselves to the West German pet shops were quickly recognized as impostors, even though they insisted that in the good old bad days they had been St Bernards.

At first, there was great demand for these dogs. Ladies from Park Avenue flew in from New York to acquire a truly guaranteed watchdog to protect their valuables. Shady dealers in the dog-fight game appeared to acquire fighters with a long record of victories. And then the shabby truth became known: *all* of the dogs were impostors. Not one dog had killed one escaper throughout the history of the Wall. They had simply relied on their reputation to induce fear in the populace. Their real duty had been to shower affection upon the lonely soldiers walking along the wall. Now, they themselves were deprived and lonely. When burglars entered the homes they were guarding, they were welcomed with yelps of joy and affection (some even claim the dogs pointed out the hiding places of the jewellery!). Germany has its market economy. As thousands of Ossie shepherd dogs glutted the market, the price fell drastically, and that economic sin stamped them as 'evil' in Germany. Their purchasers no longer loved them.

Gradually, the climate of opinion changed. After all, the shepherd dog has a right to affection which few Germans would deny. These dogs had to be retrained, since the lavish new cuisine at first affected their digestion greatly. Now, they have become acclimatized, and sit in front of the luxury food shops, waiting for their masters to provide for them. Other Germans stop as they walk through the doors, look at them, and ask themselves: 'Ossie or Wessie?' Then, they hastily enter the shop, reminding themselves that, in Germany, no-one inquires about the past of anyone they encounter. Who would want to throw the first stone? We all have something in the past we want to hide. And the German shepherd dog, once again, is the guardian of conscience in the reunited land.

The disappearance of the Berlin Wall itself is amazing. Many Berliners have already forgotten where some of the torn-down sections of the Wall stood. The Germans themselves yearn to forget that past, as pieces of the Wall are sold as souvenirs to tourists. In the meantime, I do feel easier about approaching the mystery of German history by looking at man's best friend; after all, Gunter Grass' *Hundejahre* used the same method in trying to probe the German psyche.

In looking for guides, directives, attempts to deal with the problems besetting the Germans, we have had to explore the teachings of the German theologians, and to look into the actual history of Jewish life in Germany after World War II. There, we immediately come to the bifurcation of the land into East and West. The East has been more difficult to explore until recently, because access was basically denied to outsiders. In my own visits to the Jewish community in East Germany, I came to see them as a small minority – less than a thousand – who were almost a protected species. As the head of the Jewish community in Magdeburg told me: 'If I call the mayor of the city and tell him that a stone has fallen out of our cemetery wall, I can observe a whole team of workers the next day, carefully repairing and repainting the whole wall!' Yet the same man had great difficulties in procuring ritual objects for his congregation, and the gift of my *tallit* (prayer shawl) and prayer book was gratefully accepted. The Communist state was firmly against religion; but the few remaining Jews were showpieces used to show the humanity of the state.

It is too early to make a proper evaluation of Jewish life in East Germany before and after the fall of the Wall but some facts are revealing. For example: in 1953, the Jewish community (registered members of the synagogues) officially cut off all links with their coreligionists in the West. It was the summation of the anti-Jewish and anti-Zionist developments in Eastern Europe which included the murder of anti-Fascist Jewish leaders in the USSR, the Slansky trial in Prague (1952), Stalin's attack on the 'conspiracy of the Jewish doctors' in Moscow (autumn 1952), and it was also an answer to the appeal by Rabbi Peter Levinson and community leader Heinz Galinski in West Germany (January, 1935) for the Jews of East Germany to leave and come to West Germany. The West German Jewish approach was rejected. Some East German Jews did leave but the bulk remained; my own observations at that time led me to the conviction that many of the Jews who had returned to the GDR from abroad had done so out of belief in a socialist future. They could have had more material comforts in West Germany, but they believed in a political philosophy which often saw them hounded out of jobs by a West which had a great fear of 'the Communists in our midst'. The GDR recognized that the artists and writers (the Eisler brothers, Arnold Zweig, and others) had returned out of political conviction, and they treated these persons as political assets. But there was also a genuine spirit of cooperation, of wanting to work for a better socialist society, which should not be ignored. Now, when we see the venality of the leaders of the GDR, it is hard to remember that there was a genuine feeling for the disadvantaged members of that society. When the concept of 'sharing' ran through the whole society, there was a feeling of confidence in the ethical values one found in the home. People really did care for one another. It was only after the fall of the government, when people recognized how much those in power had stolen from the powerless, that a deep revulsion set in. Even those who had led the Jewish communities, and for that reason had been members of the state apparatus, were viewed with the deepest suspicion, treated as 'collaborators', were assumed to have been part of the *stasi* machine, and were cast into the wilderness. Many of the best and most decent leaders were suddenly out of office, out of work, out of favour.

Past and present history intermingle at this point. The guilty feelings related to the excesses of the Communist rule and the discovery of the many *stasi* participants had led to a total rejection and suppression of the past, and to trying to prosecute the leaders, as in the attempted Honecker show trial. But one also forgets the difficulties of living under a dictatorship, and the accommodations which minority groups had to make in a police state. At times, the relationship between the Jewish community and the Communist leaders went back to a shared suffering in the Nazi concentration camps. As an exposed minority group, the Jews needed the protection of the state. Looking at Eastern Europe today, where the firm control of the central government has been overthrown, one comes to see anti-Semitism bursting out of a populace where the laws against xenophobic nationalism are no longer in force. But even in the GDR, there were occasions when the Jews depended not only upon the economic help of the government but also upon that government's power to suppress anti-Semitic outbursts. It was the state that helped them avert the overt anti-Semitism which followed after Israel's Six Day War. The small communities (East Berlin, Dresden, Leipzig, Chemnitz, Erfurt, Magdeburg, Halle and Schwerin) had little rabbinical help, though they had an umbrella organization uniting them. Their own periodical, *Nachrichtenblatt des verbandes der Juedischen gemeinden*, although most of the text dealt with the internal affairs of the Jews in the GDR, sounded very much like a party publication; their 'anti-fascist' texts were of no use to the Communist government. Even the 50th anniversary of the *Reichsprogromnacht* (*Kristallnacht*), while expressing the deepest feelings of the Jewish community, could be seen as an attack upon the Nazis 'who were still part of the West German society'.

One comes to see that the environment matters, and that the Jews of East Germany had different attitudes from those held by the Jews of West Germany. They *did* identify themselves with the attitudes of the land in which they lived. State propaganda affects the climate of thought in a country, and the Jews in East Germany did tend to see aspects of fascism in the Bonn government – and did not see the former Nazis who lived in the GDR.

The political situation softened somewhat in 1986: East German Jewish delegates visited the Jewish World Congress in Jerusalem, and East German theologians came to an Old Testament Congress in Jerusalem. By 1988, Erich Honecker could confer with Edgar Bronfman of the World Jewish Congress, on restitution matters, and with Sir Sigmund Sternberg on areas of dialogue between the Jews and their neighbours.

*Brandenburg, Saxony, Saxony-Anhalt, Mecklenberg vor Pommern,
and Thueringen*

When the Wall fell, the Jewish community of East Berlin and of the rest
of what is now called the 'Five New Lands' quickly rejoined the West
German Jewish community. To some extent they were in fact taken over,
and outstanding Jewish leaders, like Peter Kirchner in East Berlin, practi-
cally became 'non-persons' because of the reaction against the role they
had played within the old power structure. Also, the dynamic leadership
from the West swept aside all of the old Eastern structure; the *Zentralrat
der Juden in Deutschland* led by the late Heinz Galinski, took over all the
leadership functions by October 1990. During the continually developing
political changes, the Jews of the Eastern areas had to move quite carefully,
often acknowledging the new political attempts within East Germany to
maintain a semblance of past authority. The last GDR government had
still guaranteed the financial position of the Jewish congregations; but the
internal structure of these congregations has weakened considerably since
that time. Curiously, one sees a parallel development within the churches
of the Five New Lands. Once, they had been the bastions of resistance,
the place where one could speak out freely. Now, when men and women
can say in the streets what was formerly whispered in the churches, the
churches are deemed almost irrelevant. A new religious spirit will have to
develop in the face of the inroads of materialistic thinking; and that is far
more difficult than resisting an oppressive Communist dictatorship.

What shape can such a new religious spirit take? The Church leadership
is largely discredited, even when this is not always justified. A number of
religious leaders who were cautious in public but resisted in private are
deemed unacceptable, and the Church itself – generally a conservative
institution – attracts few liberal spirits. All of the new lands are caught up
in an economic scramble, and the fact that salaries in the East are generally
lower than the payments for the same work in the West has directed most
thinking towards economic survival. East Germany had expected a materialistic heaven through merger with West Germany – and Chancellor Kohl's
election promises had not disabused them of this dream. But the realities
of today's poverty have reached a world reared on the Socialist emphasis
upon this world rather than the next, and materialistic fulfilment cannot
take place for a long time in a declining economy. This may turn the minds
of the people towards those religious values which have often emerged in
difficult times. There will be new leaders, new ways of thinking and, perhaps, a newly structured religious faith.

In Berlin, the new religious life by 1992 was entering a *Kulturkampf* – battle lines had been drawn between the Orthodox Adath Jisroel congregation, which had extended over the years and had basically ended with the triumph of that congregation: they had been granted the properties lost long ago in East Berlin, and were rising in authority. There was also the Jewish *Kulturverein*, founded on 22 January 1990, which united a variety of dissident voices against the older Berlin leadership.

The basic problems of learning to live together in a Berlin – or a Germany – broken into many discrete units still remain. Religious Jews versus secular Jews; the new Russian arrivals – almost a majority – against those who had settled in earlier; and the simple fact that where there are four Jews there are five opinions still make this communal attempt to live in a present which is overshadowed by the past a difficult one. Is there a national identity? A religious one which excludes this? Even, from the outside, there comes the challenge whether or not Jews can be counted as Germans, as the old nationalism grows stronger.

The rise of nationalism in Germany is one of the most disturbing factors to be considered in any prognostication of the future. One cannot rule out right wing developments, a type of nationalistic thinking in Germany, particularly among the youth, which has not yet run its course. I do not feel that history will repeat itself; but it would be foolish to ignore the danger signs emerging in the Germany of today.

The major issues for the Jew living in Germany are the relationship to Israel and, of course, the emergence of a new anti-Semitism, whether open or concealed. In the Five New Lands, the relationship to Israel has changed markedly, and a dialogue has developed which has been enhanced through group journeys from this area to Israel, as well as the recognition of 'righteous gentiles' – those who at great risk or even sacrifice of their life – helped Jews in the Nazi period. Six former GDR citizens were granted recognition as 'righteous gentiles' on 22 January 1990, and their names will be preserved in Jerusalem. And, during the last stages of a separate government in the GDR, the *Volkskammer* confessed the guilt of Germany and gave full recognition to the State of Israel.

But there remains the disturbing effect that East German attitudes exercise upon the new totality of Germany, for a wave of anti-Semitic feelings comes out of that part of Germany. Although the GDR officially made anti-Semitism a crime, there is all of the undigested past to consider. The GDR had found an easy solution to cope with their Nazi past: 'We were the communist opposition against Hitler, the good guys. Look at Erich Honecker: ten years in a Nazi concentration camp! The Nazis all stayed in West Germany and hold offices there. Let them pay compensation to the victims – we had nothing to do with it!' The fact that many good Nazis became good Communists was ignored.

What was also ignored was that West Germany had not only spoken out about the guilt of the past, but had also paid large restitution sums to individuals and to the State of Israel. The GDR had hidden behind the assertion that the crimes were committed by West Germans, and the rightful claims of survivors were ignored.

There were other issues, as well. There were too few Jews to develop an active campaign, although Israel became the favourite enemy. But there were other minority groups, Poles, Romanians – and who needed Jews to be anti-Semitic? The West Germans had at least tried to work out the problems of the past; and had succeeded in many ways. Now, the burden of that first guilt has reappeared, together with a strong nationalism which always encourages xenophobia. Moreover, the new guilt, the *stasi* problem, confronts them with almost the same questions regarding the past: 'should justice be done, or is it better to cover it all up, to forgive and forget? So many East Germans cooperated with their government and spied on their families – but it wasn't quite like the old Nazi days. Why should justice be seen to be done? That black Ossie dog sitting by the supermarket – was he one of the dogs on the Wall? But he was just doing his duty; so were we all, so were we all.'

Undoubtedly, in the darkness of the GDR, there were many who spoke out, whom one might also include in the group which rides out of every darkness towards the morning. There is the novelist Christa Wolf, for example, one of the most gifted German writers of her time. But Christa Wolf has also been accused by now. She spoke out, she showed signs of resistance; but did she do enough? There are miles upon miles of *stasi* files, and there is really no-one whose name might not appear in that huge mountain of papers. But there is also 'disinformation' in those pages, and this thought cannot be discarded automatically. In a world consisting of papers, one can start false paper chases. Even East Germans who escaped early and fought the Communist regime from the outside are sometimes suspected now in that uneasy world where fear of the neighbour has suddenly been reinforced by the fact that everybody seems to have betrayed everybody else!

Having met and talked with Christa Wolf I can only express my conviction that she was not among the betrayers, but a victim of the new wave of intolerance which demands from public figures far more than private persons saw as a duty for themselves. She is a victim of our time.

What *was* needed, and did not emerge during the Communist regime or after it, was an assessment of the relationship between Communism and Fascism. In present day Germany, where right wing and left wing again meet in the streets and fight, the virulence of political extremism becomes far more evident. If we want to understand it, we must go back to the roots, to the foundations of an extremism which will battle to undermine the legal structure of a country (both Communism and the Nazis fought against the Weimar Republic and against all aspects of democracy). This fight against law and morality is also related to the *Shoah*. One must not relativize the Nazi *Shoah* by comparing it to Stalin's actions of genocide and murder; but the contempt for human life and for ways of thinking and living which did not fit into those authoritarian systems shows us complex similarities which become evident in various ways: the use of propaganda, violence, and lies in dealing with one's own population and with other nations.

Something of this way of thinking continued to live within the GDR. It was not only the government which suppressed those who fought the system. The people themselves were suspicious of challenges, and even religious leaders found themselves at odds with their neighbours.

The leaders I saw at that time did not write but act; and, often, these actions were misunderstood. I think of Father Heinrich Pera, a Catholic priest who attempted to develop a hospice movement in the GDR, but had been frustrated by the Communist regime. After the fall of the Wall, he had challenged his congregation which then turned on him: '*You* should have warned us, should have led us!' they argued; and he felt guilty for not having in fact been more courageous. Recently, Heinrich was offered a most important job in Rome. He turned it down, because some of his efforts to create a hospice system in the Five New Lands were now coming to fruition. There were others like him, religious leaders, the pastors of the Sophien Kirche and the Marien Kirche, who preached rather than wrote, and who practised those small steps which led out of the miasma of despotic rule and bureaucratic enslavement.

The Five New Lands are now being exploited in many ways, with carpet-baggers moving in to take a major share of the economic growth which will undoubtedly occur. Most of the charity work done by Jews and non-Jews in Germany centres upon the development of that area, whether in terms of supporting art, religion, or other worthwhile enterprises. Meanwhile even the gigantic profit machine of the German economy has begun to falter as it tries to deal with the tasks which reunion has brought. If and when the economy of Germany triumphs over the large problem of reunification, the economy of Europe will probably recover. We can only watch what happens to the Jews of Eastern Germany and Europe. Now, as ever, they are a barometer of the political climate. The growth of anti-Semitism has always shown the flaws of systems which do not acknowledge the rights of minority groups. To that extent, as George Steiner has shown, the Jews remain the conscience of the world.

The Jews of West Germany have also had a quiet, subdued history since World War II, living their problematic lives in a land which so recently tried to eradicate them from the earth. Until recently, there were about 30,000 Jews in West Germany who had established a *modus vivendi* which avoided publicity whenever possible. Only nine rabbis served their religious needs, and the school that had been established as part of the University of Heidelberg was basically the Judaica department of the university and it did not produce any rabbis.

At some point, the history of this small, imported Jewish community – after 1945, there were very few German Jews; most of the community between 1945–1990 consisted of East European Jews, survivors of the concentration camps and the Displaced Persons Camps – remains to be written. They were, and are, worthy of sympathy and compassion, though some Jewish visitors to Germany during the recent past showed little of this spirit. 'How dare you return to Germany, or to remain in Germany? It's indecent!' was the most common response by tourists or business people who did not hesitate in coming, but used their indignation to salve their own conscience.

Now, suddenly, small communities that have been dormant have revived with the influx of Russian Jewish families whose children fill the religious schools and appear in the synagogue for *barmitzvah* celebrations. A new, more hopeful picture is emerging.

We look for those who gave meaning to a community life in Germany after the Holocaust, among them the rabbis who returned and served with great dedication: 'Abba' Geis, Stephen Schwarzschild, Peter Levinson, Ernst Stein; Orthodox spiritual leaders who often, after retirement, gave service to small communities – Rabbis Posen, Weiss and others. Yet it was not only the rabbis, but more often the laity, and primarily one person, who led the Jewish community of Germany: Heinz Galinski, president of the Berlin Community after 1945 until his death in 1991, was also the head of the Council of German Jewry in recent years. Herr Galinski was a survivor of Auschwitz, and was recognized and honoured as the leader of German Jewry; he received weekly death threats from old and new anti-Semites. But chief among the ways forward has been the work of a dedicated group of Christian and Jewish scholars who present important programmes every two years at the *Kirchentage* of the Protestant Church.

When these *Kirchentage* – the major assemblies of Protestantism – developed, there was at first no notion that Jews should have any share in them. What did Jews have to contribute to Christian meetings? Gradually, it became apparent to the Church after the Holocaust that Auschwitz was the major item on the agenda.

The old, standard answers were inadequate. Could one really say, as some of the old-timers persisted in doing, that God was punishing the People Israel for their sins? Could one claim that the Jews were deicides come to judgement? That this was a way of turning them to Christ? And could one discuss this topic without their presence?

These bi-annual confrontations deal with the Jewish–Christian dialogue, and with the changes which have taken place in German theology after the Holocaust. In part, this was due to the presence of the scholars of the Confessing Church who had preserved a semblance of respect for Christianity and its churches among the people by offering at least some resistance to the Nazis. Great Bible scholars came as well, Rendjorrf and many of the leading pastors of the Protestant community. Their Jewish partners in dialogue were fewer in number but were also recognized for their scholarship and their work. The framework of Germany continues to be important here. It is not that 'the people who have walked in darkness have seen a great light', but that the sharing of that darkness makes each aware of the problems of the other. Sometimes, this is hard.

We live within a Biblical definition which reminds us that we must be kind to those who suffer and are enslaved: 'For ye were slaves in the land of Egypt.' We have had a lot of mileage out of that statement. Clarence Darrow, the great American defence attorney, would remind his staff that it was neglect of duty to a client to challenge a Jew for jury duty in a capital case: Jews were noted for compassion. And, during the early days of the civil rights struggle, Jews were certainly in the majority. Now? In Germany, when suffering confronts suffering, we ourselves often fall into the 'quid pro quo' trap. Jews must retain this compassion, though often it is hard. I have met aggrieved Germans who dwell at length upon the suffering they experienced under the Russian invasion: loss of property, violation of wives and daughters, other acts of cruelty. 'Why should Jews and gypsies receive compensation for their sufferings? *We* didn't get anything!' There is no concept here of the relative and absolute differences between the concentration camps and the suffering endured in the war.

Here, we enter the realm of unatoned guilt, of suppressed history. In what was East Germany, there is sometimes a genuine ignorance – but frequently a disingenuous stance. When there is an emphasis upon the greatness of German history, when Leipzig, Halle, and the Wartburg are cleaned up for tourists to remind them of Germany's greatness as seen in Martin Luther and Bach, we recall the darkness as well as the light. Weimar reassures everyone that Goethe and Schiller, and perhaps even the Weimar Republic, are not forgotten. But, outside the gates of Weimar is Buchenwald, the concentration camp; and there are few who want to remember this. This is not simply a 'guilty' verdict upon the children whose fathers have eaten sour grapes. When I visit Germany, I am aware of the pain and suffering of the innocent, of the passive bystanders, and even of the suffering of the guilty. But I am not in the 'business of granting absolution', I do stress the human capacity of remembering; and it is in that area that progress can be made.

We have spoken of the 'double guilt' which rests heavily upon Germany these days, the inheritance of the *stasis* as well as of the Nazis. And any assessment of intellectual, moral, and philosophical thinking after the darkness must occupy itself with this situation. It is in that context that the dialogue between Jews and Christians, and between Jews and Germans, becomes understandable. It is not the only area where one tries to confront the endemic evil which clings to the matrixes of history. With the break-up of the Soviet Union, and the bitter battle of nationalists reasserting themselves against the minorities and even majorities of the area they occupy, we see that Stalin and his company did sow dragon's teeth which are about to be harvested. And, in the Balkans, one looks at Croatians and Serbs with despair. Again, we are overwhelmed by a situation of suffering far worse than what we see in Germany. When the Serbs invaded Croatia, it was natural to cry out against this blatant disregard of international law; then we heard of massacres on both sides. There are sicknesses of the soul as well as of the body which need to be cured. And where we cannot affect a cure, we must try not to be infected by that madness; we must try to judge, as the Jewish tradition phrases it, *midat harachamim*, with due compassion and we must still condemn the genocide practised by the Serbs, and bring help to the sufferers.

We know so little! Can't we rely on experts? Here, in the area of contemporary history, shouldn't we at least be given guidance by the historians? As a sometime practitioner of the art, I can only utter the warning that historians offer pictures which suit the contemporary mood. Histories are like fashion modes, changing constantly. The Dutch historian Johan Huizinga states: 'History is the intellectual form through which a culture gives an accounting to itself of its past'. Yet one cannot give an image of the past 'as it truly was' – the historian selects a few facts of the million available; and what he or she choses depends on personal mood and the endemic feelings of the environment out of which the historian operates.

The picture of history which West Germany, after World War II, evoked for itself was a most efficient model. It was called 'anti-Communism' and promised security and continuity, and integration after a time of upheaval. The ex-Nazis found room for themselves in this image. They had been *good* anti-Communists, and if they had been wrong on everything else, they were right here; those others who had been passive and had not fought the Nazis could now catch up by fighting Communism. In the 50s this historical construct became a matter of faith, supported by the intellectuals.

The next historical paradigm, the new picture, arose in the 60s when this perspective clearly needed to be corrected. Perhaps Communism, with the social reforms and apparently caring dictatorship of East Germany in evidence, was not that evil. Also, now that time had passed, the crimes of the Holocaust had become more visible: Nazis and Communists shouldn't be compared, viewed as identical. And so the Frankfurt Auschwitz trials began, and an attempt was made to uncover that darkest period of German life. It was an uncomfortable time, but there was a genuine attempt to understand, helped along by the media which could and did show films about the Holocaust.

In the 80s, the historical image changed again. 'It's time to draw a line under the past' showed Helmut Kohl speaking for the general populace. Fragments of the earlier approach reemerged, as Helmut Kohl called Gorbachev a 'Goebbels'; and Bitburg honoured the fallen SS soldiers! But the real battle of the Revisionist historians took place in 1986. Led by the respectable historian Ernst Nolte, it was an attempt to bring the Nazi crimes out of the realm of the demonic by comparing and equating them with the Soviet actions and subsuming them under the normal excesses of war. In the end, the Revisionist historians lost that battle, although they are still very much with us.

Then, East Germany collapsed, and the picture had to be revised again. West Germany became the great united Germany, and the Communist crimes moved to the foreground:

All public thinking now concentrated itself upon the crimes of the GDR. The thought of a tribunal arose, a second Nuremberg. Once again, as in the time of de-Nazification, one had to justify one's past . . . documents were needed . . . whether one should do this exactly as in the past or precisely for that reason differently, the patterns are the same. The

Germans conduct themselves like the Allies cleaning up after 1945. It is almost as if they enjoy, finally, being the victors.

The historical portrait of East Germany is now far darker than it ever was. Erich Honecker, once recognized as a Resistance fighter who served a decade in the concentration camp, has become another Eichmann hunted across Eastern Europe and taken for trial. In Stuttgart, the final process against the SS is drawing to a close – the Court declared its inability to prosecute Nazis; meanwhile, the trial of the guards of the Berlin Wall is moving forward rapidly. The historians and the general populace again fall into the trap of trying to compare two pasts with each other and, in a sense, trivializing the greater crime. By equating *stasi* with Nazi, and East Germany with Hitler Germany, the enormity of the Nazi crimes is again cut down to a normal incident in a time of war. Auschwitz could only happen at such a time – but it surpassed all that has ever happened in a war; and there is no guarantee that Auschwitz cannot happen in a different framework. The world can be brutalized to a point where genocide becomes a way of controlling population growth and of solving economic problems. New theories of government can arise; but the old theories must not be compared in a way which distorts and destroys past realities. Nazism and communism are not the same, although the growth of the far right challenges us to understand current events.

*Stasis* cannot be treated in the same way as Nazis. One cannot ignore them, and I accept that justice at times must be seen to have been done. But everything is not black and white, even if one must differentiate between those who were carried along with the flood, and those who actively participated in evil. We cannot pontificate, but we can watch and see what will happen in terms of the paradigm of history which will now emerge, and in terms of the actions which must take into account the economic and moral sickness which make the Germany of today a land which must be judged carefully.

Where there is crime, there is guilt. Christian theologians often take the stance of speaking for God and of 'forgiving'. Yet the best Christian theologians are very much aware of Bonhoeffer's teaching concerning the 'easy grace' – and those who transgress and sin (the Hebrew concept of *chet*, sin, is a stumbling from the right path) must be given that chance to atone, rather than cashing in on the indulgence of their religion. My own approach is suspicious of systems, of a completely formed theology which gives answers to all the situations; the general rules of the Ten Commandments must be applied by us to individual situations. The teachers whom we find address something within us, and our own intuitions and intellect must then determine our actions.

These actions are more than a response to teachings, though; we live in a world of change, and respond to this with every fibre of our being. A new anti-Semitism, a new xenophobia, is manifesting itself within Germany today. As always, one can detect economic reasons for these outbursts against 'the stranger'. A decline within Germany's prosperity is clearly related to the hasty attempt to absorb what was once East Germany into the *Bundesrepublik*. The massive unemployment within the old Eastern zone has had its effect throughout the land. And the German constitution which welcomed refugees is now questioned by all the German political parties who want to close the boundaries to the new waves of immigration from the Balkans and from Eastern Europe. Franz Schoenhuber's right wing Republican Party is gaining new votes; and it forces the Christian Democrats into a more 'patriotic', right wing stance set against the 'outsiders'.

The Jewish community is not reassured by the positive words and, indeed, actions within today's Germany. There is a new fear abroad, and one cannot easily dismiss the darkness creeping over the land which does emanate from what had been East Germany. At the same time, one must respond positively to the actions of the decent Germans who are in the majority. Recent acts by neo-Nazis have been balanced by counter demonstrations. But one is still afraid there is still cause for fear.

The new realities of a frightened Jewish community and a far more uncertain German populace who saw their economic miracle crumbling had led to great changes in the area of a dialogue between the Germans and the Christians who are ready to confront their past and to talk to the Jewish community who now live in Germany. Anyway, with the passage of time, the discussions between Germans and Jews had to change. The last Nazi trial has probably taken place: the witnesses are dead or no longer capable of testifying to the horrors of the *Shoah*; and the few remaining Nazis (ie., those identified and accused for the crimes committed in the camps, cities and ghettos) are also very old after more than half a century. As in Great Britain, where war crimes trials are still pressed by the government, there are trials which could take place. But: should they, really?

I firmly believe that justice must be seen to be done. Later, I will try to come to terms with the problems of guilt and reconciliation. Here, simply looking at the German situation of today, I can only stress the importance of keeping the matter before the public, of making the communities in Germany realize that this is not a vindictive persecution of a few old men who cannot be denied the possibility of having changed after fifty years.

We are dealing with mass-murder upon which no legal system has placed a time limit. And we are dealing with a country where an honest attempt has been made to recognize the past as it really was, to acknowledge the crimes which really happened. Perhaps, when the last Nazis die, the issue will be clearer: the questions will be addressed to the onlookers, and to the new generations. One does not talk of guilt here, but of responsibility. The last excuse is gone: the old Nazis are dead. But then: why is anti-Semitism still part of a land which has few Jews? Why are the *Sinti-Roma* still persecuted by racist laws? Why are refugee centres burned to the ground? We cannot blame a German government which has a truly democratic system and more than its share of liberal and ethically motivated political leaders (and others as well, of course). Nor, even though I feel that part of the answer I seek rises out of inheritance of intolerance which grew out of East Germany, can I place the growth of intolerance fully into the Five New Lands – the Republican Party developed within West Germany! And I refuse to turn the Germans into a stereotype of xenophobic barbarian. But what is left?

First of all, there is an unacknowledged past. As we have seen, East Germany refused to deal with its guilt of the past, and even of its present. Political and private life, based upon deceit and self-deceit, harbours great weaknesses within itself. An inner sickness, an encapsulated trauma, will eventually burst open and damage the inner and outer world of that community. Since Germany is well on its way to being one of the strong leaders of the European community, the health of that nation matters to all of us. As boundaries begin to fall, other nations and individuals can become involved in the process of Germany finding itself. But, as with individuals, healing must come from within.

Next, dialogue is not simply a rational exchange of ideas. It is an opening of oneself to the other, of revealing attitudes and emotions as much as rational arguments. And dialogue is imperfect. One feels one's own emotions, and listens to the rational arguments of the other without a full understanding of the feeling behind the position that has been taken. In Germany, in particular, there is such a heavy agenda behind each Christian–Jewish confrontation! Not only Israel today, but the Holocaust yesterday. Not only yesterday, but hundreds of years of misunderstanding, of legal oppression, of religious persecution. Out of that, many misunderstandings arise.

Jews do not speak of guilt to the new generation, but of responsibility for the past. But, rightly or wrongly, Germans do feel guilt. And sometimes they seek a role reversal: were their parents the only ones to sin? Can one not accuse the Jews of sinning against the Palestinians? And there is enough truth (and falsehood) in that accusation to create an emotional reaction in the Jewish partner in the discussion which will shatter any hope of a real dialogue emerging.

In general, the dialogue between Jews and Christians takes place with the Christian partner being a member of the clergy or of the university. This tends to make for high intellectual content, but underneath the discussion there is still another dimension: the old confrontation between the Christian faith and Judaism. At the same time, it is my personal conviction that a secular dialogue, particularly along the political lines, contains even greater dangers related to the conflict of ideologies. I still discover the most fruitful areas of dialogue within religion, particularly in a world where the Christians become more aware of the Jewish heritage within their faith. But, in Germany, we keep returning to an environment still filled with fear. And I am also afraid.

A little while ago, walking in London's Hyde Park, I was approached by an elderly couple accompanied by a huge German shepherd dog. I stood and watched, and the dog cocked its head towards me. As a lover of dogs, I dropped my left hand so that he might sniff and examine it. The couple did not interrupt their German conversation, but the man yanked hard at the lead so that the three of them could bypass me without contact or speech. I may have misjudged the situation. Since the dog was on a leash, in an area where many dogs walk freely, its owner was probably trying to protect me from a potential attack. But I still looked at the beautiful animal with longing. Was the darkness in the owner or in the dog? Was this an Ossie or Wessie situation? Might this dog be a pensioner of the Berlin Wall? And then I thought about the fact that where I formerly wondered, during my German visits, what the people I met were doing in the Nazi times (fifty years on, I worry less), now, in the Five New Lands, I look at them and wonder: *stasis*? But one cannot live like this, and there must be trust in first encounters, even if that trust may have to be taken away in the end. When I encounter the dogs, I want to pat all of them – even those who 'were doing their duty'.

# 3

# FRANCE

### RESPONSE AND REWARD

WE cannot divorce ourselves from our environment. The teachers
we seek and find, standing at the edge of the twenty-first century, speak out of the context of a land and a language. Even
when they are in advance of the rest, moving towards the dawn and its
promise, they are the response to the challenges of a world that has experienced a wide 'failure of nerve' in terms of its religions. In England, there
are more than 500 fully documented new religions. Some of them, within
the 'New Age' movement, have picked up the themes of ecology, creation
spirituality, and mysticism, which appeal particularly to the young people
who have come to view the current religious establishments of the major
religions with suspicion. A proper survey of the spiritual quest in our time
should pay more attention to what is happening in those areas. Here, in
what is a subjective search for various ways which lead out of darkness,
one can only make the unfair generalization that most of the new groups
seem to be moving towards darkness rather than light: yet any one person,
in any sect or cult, may yet come to disprove this assertion – and it would
be a gain for all of us. For the moment, though, we will look more at
mainstream teachings and efforts in England and France. Placed into their
cultural context, they are certainly no guarantee that the darkness which is
sweeping over Europe will be dissipated by their efforts.

France is as near to England as the 'Chunnel' now: it will not necessarily
bring the two countries that much closer to one another. Their experience
in this past century has been too different; and the mood and temperaments
are too divergent from one another. France saw itself defeated and occupied

during two world wars; in the last one, the humiliation was complete. England, protected by the channel, could maintain an insularity which created its own kind of xenophobia, cold rather than hot, rejecting rather than persecuting. In France, there was much more passion – and much more suffering, as well. It had its own effect upon its religion, with Archbishop LeFevre a focal point in the Catholic reaction against Rome and against non-Catholics. But how much influence has the Church in France today, a land with over 4,000 registered astrologers! If Nancy Reagan, in the United States, had an astrologer with an impact upon the running of the country, this could influence France. Certainly, the business world has given more employment to these sages than the government: but then, business has a bearing on politics. In the end, the old religions and the old prejudices rule France. The Dreyfus Case, over a hundred years ago, saw a Jew 'railroaded' to Devil's Island as a spy; not because he was guilty, but because he was a Jew. To this day, with his innocence long established, there are many French people who still think Captain Alfred Dreyfus guilty, a traitor to France! The cabal between the Church, the right wing in politics, and the army, prevailed then and has still not completely disappeared. After the war, some members of the Catholic Church helped the Nazis (including Vichy France officials and collaborators) to escape justice by setting up its 'tourist service' to South America, and supporting those who participated in actions against the resistance and in sending Jews to their death.

Enough films, plays, books and actual legal cases have shown the world that there is a public and a private conscience in France which cannot be silenced. The fact that Klaus Barbie, the 'Butcher of Lyon', was actually convicted is an indication that justice does operate in France. Yet this was again questioned in March of 1992, when the courts reached a decision in the case of Paul Touvier, the so-called 'Second Butcher of Lyon'. Three judges ruled that Paul Touvier had 'no case to answer for crimes against humanity'.

The case has to be seen against the background of the growing support for Jean-Marie Le Pen's *Front National* (FN), which surged ahead in the various elections held in France in 1992. In Marseilles Le Pen scored decisive gains against Bernard Tapier, the millionaire glamour personality of the Socialist party. The large number of foreign-born workers in the area was a welcome target for the FN's chauvinism; the decline of the Socialists throughout France gave Le Pen more space in which to develop. It is not so much the changes within French and European politics (the Republican Party also made decisive progress in recent elections in Germany, confirming that right wing xenophobic thinking is on the rise), but the overall attitudes in a land which, after all, had been a leader in proclaiming 'liberty, equality, fraternity' which are unwelcome omens for the future.

Paul Touvier himself could be, and was, identified with the policies of the Vichy party, an ignoble aspect of the French past. The French have many problems in their attitudes to that basically collaborationalist government after the French had been defeated. The choice of Marshal Petain, the hero of France from an earlier time, could not disguise the basic surrender to the Nazis in every area, which included the persecution of the Jews. Yet the French, like the Germans, needed a paradigm in history which would permit them to live with their past. The German paradigm, as we have seen, changed every two decades in response to new situations. The French paradigm did not change, because the past had been too painful. They had lost in every area, including the moral dimension. But they could cling to one reality which could be enlarged to mythic proportions: the Resistance! After the war, it seemed that everyone had been in the Resistance. Of course, the French had a far more proper claim than the Germans who could only point to the few participants of the 20 July group, the Communist resistance, and some outstanding 'righteous among the nations'. The French Resistance was a large movement, and they did fight back. Yet this did not help the Jews who lived in occupied France, or in Vichy France: they were caught in a trap which, ultimately, sent many of them to Drancy and then to Auschwitz. There were notable, noble exceptions: individuals, and even a whole village, to which we will return.

The paradigm of France heroically resisting under German rule was too good to surrender, even if it meant rewriting the history of Vichy France. France had to remain *la belle France* with its Parisian street-chic, that certain *je ne sais quoi* which captivates the visitor and makes him feel boorish in the midst of all this cosmopolitanism, or feel grateful that he has been permitted a house in what will always be 'toujours Provence'. Dare one challenge this image for oneself or for the visitor by admitting that underneath this image, during the war, there had been a different reality, one of accommodation and subservience? And so, when the case of Paul Touvier came to the judges, they felt that they had to defend France in their judgement. Perhaps they miscalculated, and France is ready to turn to a more realistic paradigm of history; certainly, the outcry against the judges seems to indicate this. The actual judgement was a 215-page document which claimed that Marshal Petain's Vichy regime had 'never planned and practised a consistent anti-Semitic ideology' – and therefore none of its representatives could be guilty of crimes against humanity!

One of the great spokespersons of Jewish life in Europe is Simone Vail, a government minister who was deported to Auschwitz at the age of sixteen. After the Touvier acquittal she said:

> There are many people in France, who do not want to face their country's past. Yet we remember how the Vichy regime aided and abetted the Nazis. The French police rounded us up under French racial laws . . . it is an attempt to rewrite history.

Public statements of outrage did, in fact, come from every group, Le Pen's excepted.

The judges rejected five of the six counts against Touvier because of 'insufficient evidence'. This was a remarkable decision, since in this case there were witnesses, not too sick or too old, who took the stand in order to testify that this was indeed the man who arrested them, had tortured them for days, and had then sent them to Germany and to death camps. The judges refused to listen to this testimony as clear evidence of guilt. Instead, they constructed a laborious defence of the Vichy regime, which then enabled them to acquit Touvier as someone who had worked for a Vichy which, the judges concluded, had been 'a constellation of good intentions . . .' In fact, Petain's signature was on all racial laws decreed by Vichy even before the Germans asked for them.

Acquitting Touvier does not whitewash Vichy; and it does not preserve the myth of the French joined together against the evil occupiers of the land by fighting in the Resistance. It is counterproductive, in that it obscures the actual battles against the Nazis which did take place in France, outside the area of the Resistance. Without generalizing too much it can be stated that the French are highly individualistic; that they will not often conform to rules of thought and action laid down by hierarchy; and that, for this and many reasons, there was indeed a spiritual resistance by Catholics which saved many Jewish lives. Church functionaries were also involved in this, and, in the end Yad Vashem has honoured hundreds of French people who helped the Jews at the risk of their own lives.

One of the best examples of spiritual greatness in times of darkness took place within the Protestants of France – perhaps with the memory of their own sufferings (the Huguenots for instance suffered persecution for generations), they could respond without hesitation. Whenever one thinks of France during the war, one should think first of the village of Chambon-sur-Lignon, which organized itself to save over 5,000 Jews, more than half of them children. Their leader was André Trocme, their pastor, who helped them set up an organization which ultimately became the centre of resistance in the region. Often, they managed to get the children of already imprisoned Jews away from the Nazis, provide them with false papers, and with the opportunity to travel to this special haven of refuge. Outside help for this was needed, of course, and it was provided by the CIMADE, Secours Suisse, the Quakers, the Service Social des Etrangers and the DSE. Generally, they were organized into groups of four, set on trains to Chambon, and then assigned to village families. The remarkable part of that story is that so many people knew the 'secret' and could have betrayed rescuers and children; and the secret was kept! This, more than any other story, celebrates a French spirit of concern and decency which rose out of a religious commitment but also out of an atmosphere of secular values which could not be crushed by the Germans or, indeed, by Vichy. Once we have added this dimension to our understanding of France, the discrete elements come together. Resistance against the occupier is natural. A group feeling within those who are oppressed is natural. But there are those whose prejudices and political thinking bring them closer to the enemy, and here we see collaboration.

The Vichy government did, of course, have the preservation of France in mind at the beginning. Yet it was also a haven for opportunists and speedily became tainted through its cooperation with the Nazis whose agency of genocide and its concepts of world power made them a far different type of occupying army than had been experienced before. Vichy itself was bad for the Catholic Church because it in effect bribed the Catholic establishment with concessions which had not existed in pre-war France. The official body of the Catholic Church in France, the Assembly of Cardinals and Bishops, went through various phases in its relationship to Vichy. Looking at the treatment of the Jews in France we can follow the developments from the beginning of the Vichy regime in June 1940 to the summer of 1942; and, the summer and fall of 1942.

First there was the long silence from 1940 to summer of 1942, when the machinery of deporting the Jews was set into place: the 1st and 2nd Jewish Statutes of October 1940 and June 1941; and the establishment of the General Commissariat for Jewish Questions under Xavier Vallat in March 1942. The Church's lack of response may well have arisen out of false hopes that the Vichy government might yet achieve a certain amount of freedom for the French. At a time when morale and even morals were shattered, it was easy to be deluded by hope.

Petain spoke to Catholics of repentance, of the need for France to expiate its sins and to return to traditional moral values. The Church felt itself rehabilitated.

In the summer and fall of 1942, as the deportations gained momentum, the Church did speak out; and Professor Fleishner lists a number of Church notables, starting with the Archbishop of Toulouse, Jules Gerard Saliege, who protested against the inhuman treatment of the Jews through a pastoral letter read in his churches. Others joined him in expressions of protest which, had they been made earlier, might well have made a difference to the treatment of the Jews in France. As it is, we have testimonies from the rescued and from the betrayed, from those who were hidden in monasteries, and evidence that other monasteries also became the 'underground railway' for Nazi criminals after the war.

Was it the Christian texts dealing so negatively with the Jews which caused such faltering? Where the few stood up against both Nazi and French anti-Semitism, Jews and Judaism were seen in a positive light, as an example for all humanity; or simply as human beings, rather than as Jews. But those are all lessons which the Church has not learned fully; once again, we come to the reality of the individual who rises above the group.

The enigmatic varieties of the French response against the darkness can also be seen among the intellectuals, even if there were some who flirted with the Nazis. A study of this, from Sartre to Camus, would take us too far afield; all we can do is to acknowledge it. One member of that group was Claude Lanzmann, whose film *Shoah* summarizes both the anguish and the hidden hatreds which are part of a yet unexplored history of the Holocaust; his film followed Alan Resnais and other French film-makers into this area, where French art and literature have created a special place for themselves.

Some of the writers to whom we have turned for understanding must be mentioned again at this point. We cannot understand the French scene without them, and we cannot fully understand them if we do not see their French dimension.

Elie Wiesel still writes in French, and his wife Marion is his chief translator. Wiesel had come to France in 1946, still a teenager, but after Auschwitz, and received both his education, his language, and his literary support there. He had written his first book in Yiddish (*Un de velt hot geshvign*) ten years later, and it was then published as *La nuit*, in 1958. For Wiesel, this description of a particularly Jewish situation was far more than that: it described humanity in all its anguish. His theme of 'silence' was also part of a French perception, although it was, of course, universal. The French Jewish scholar André Neher later wrote at length about the theme of silence in the Bible. Elie Wiesel was also a witness to a world which did not particularly want to be remembered. Each of his books hammered away at the obdurateness of this world, at the cynicism of the intellectuals, the closed minds of believers, and at the conspiracies to forget.

The mutual enrichment between Elie Wiesel and the French starts at the very beginning, with François Mauriac's introduction to that first book, *Night*. Mauriac's help had been crucial to Wiesel. At the same time, the clash between the devout Catholic whose prejudgements arise in that preface, and the Jew who has suffered for his faith, emerged clearly.

Wiesel's French dimension continues to deepen with each book, with the recognition accorded him by the French community which gave his works major literary prizes: *A beggar in Jerusalem* received the Prix Medicis (1969); *Testament* received the Prix Inter in 1980; and there were other literary awards, including the City of Paris award, alongside the Nobel Peace Prize and his countless international awards. The French Government created him Commander of the Legion of Honour for his contributions to French culture; and his friendship with President Mitterrand and other leaders of France gives him a position of leadership which he has utilized in his quest for peace. The final word of acknowledgement to the French dimension of Elie Wiesel should come from a prince of the Church: Jean-Marie Cardinal Lustiger, who has a Jewish background.

The Cardinal sees Elie Wiesel as one of the great theologians of our time, and expands upon this as follows:

To be a theologian is to acknowledge how incomprehensible God's ways are, and yet never cease to follow them. Is Elie Wiesel a theologian? Yes, in the same way as is any Jew who realizes that he rests in the hand of God, even as he contemplates the history of his people. True theology is a life that is faithful to God. We recognize it in the works of writers like Charles Peguy, in the diaries of St Therese of Lisieux, who spent her life in prayer, the great achievements of Catholic theology in this century.[1]

The Cardinal places the thoughts and teachings of Elie Wiesel into the mainstream of French theological thinking; he is as much concerned with what Wiesel has said as in the experiences of the *Shoah* through which he lived. It is related of course; the experienced suffering becomes paradigmatic for humanity, the mission and the burden to bring this experience to the world is part of an ultimate mystery. Elie Wiesel uses the words which are familiar to the Christian tradition: 'suffering' and 'mystery'. And his view that totalitarian paganism stages an attack on God Himself by striving to annihilate His people may be the defensive statement of a Christian, but one who takes his stand alongside the Jewish community. Catholic and Jew are united as they see the onslaught against God. This is how Lustiger understands the role of the Nazis in history:

> Nazi paganism wanted to proclaim the Aryan race as the only human one and the master of all others. But Israel, the elect of God, is the disturbing witness to the truth that God alone is God and He created all humans in His image and likeness. Thus, Nazi ideology did not find a better way to wrest the divine election and Messianic mission from the Jewish people by stripping Jews of their dignity and depriving them of their humanity.

For Lustiger, Elie Wiesel was the teacher who saw the utmost darkness, the infernal character of this moment in the history of the Jew and the world. And, says Lustiger, Wiesel did not lose his faith or the sense of mission which he had inherited from the earlier Jewish saints, the *Tzadikim*, Hasidim'. The Cardinal links his awareness of Wiesel's writing and his own parental heritage with the Easter concept of Christianity:

> This is why Auschwitz has become a symbolic name for hell. It is a place of silence. A place of silence that allows the dark terror or evil to be made manifest. A place of silence that cries out to heaven, like Abel's spilled blood. A place of silence that must master the beast crouching at the door, eager and waiting to turn man into a murderer like Cain (Gen. 4.7). Because of their vocation, Christians ought to understand what such a silence signifies. The liturgy of the Church makes all the disciples of the Crucified face the emptiness. When all is accomplished on Good Friday and until the end of Holy Saturday, we have to survive in God's obscure silence. How could we fail to understand and accept the fact that the Jewish people fulfil their sacred mission, which is to allow humankind to listen to the silence to which it has condemned the people blessed by God?[2]

One always hesitates when the Christian mystery and Jewish fate are linked together in a matter which almost blends them into one. And yet, unlike other approaches we have observed, it is not that Judaism is here being validated through Christianity. Rather, there is an acknowledgement, as far as Lustiger can go, which in the end sees Christianity being validated by Jewish faith and Jewish experience.

The other French writer who emerged through one text to such power that he is still part of the world of the *galut* and of Israel in a special way is André Schwarz-Bart, the child of Polish immigrants to France, born in Metz and very much part of the literary and activist scene in France. *Le dernier des justes (The last of the just)* (1961) received the Prix Goncourt in 1959 (and the Jerusalem Prize in 1966). From the very opening pages, in a martyrology of such power that it takes every reader along with it into the heart of Jewish experience, this book becomes a revelation of the Holocaust in a totally different way from the writings of Elie Wiesel. Schwarz-Bart's book takes us through all of the past Jewish experience in Europe, the persecutions and the suffering, the agony and the power of the Jewish spirit in the *galut*. The central motif of this text is the history of the Levy family, who are here shown as the hereditary carriers of the role of a *lamed-vavnik*, one of thirty-six people alive in the world to whom a special role is assigned in human history. The basic Jewish tradition is that, as seen in the story of Abraham battling for the evil city of Sodom, God cannot destroy a city or the world if a sufficient number of righteous people – *Tzadikim* – are alive in it. These righteous people do not know that they are part of that select group; they live in anonymity and sustain the world. Schwarz-Bart adapted that tradition for his book, and posited that there was one family, the Levys, which produced one of these righteous, just people in every generation. Ernie Levy, the protagonist of the story, is 'The last of the just'. When he dies, there will not be a sufficient number of *lamed-vavniks* left to sustain the world. The brilliance and sensitivity of the text produces an image of the world as it moves into destruction which is a true mirror of Jewish life at the time of the Holocaust.

The last *lamed-vavnik* dies in the story. André Schwarz-Bart continues to live in this world, to fight injustice and xenophobia in France and in Europe. *The last of the just* makes him a teacher for our time and for tomorrow.

If there is one teacher who represents the best blend of French culture and of authentic Jewish life, one must turn to Emmanuel Levinas, the existentialist philosopher who studied with Husserl and Heidegger and who goes to his own Jewish tradition, somewhat like Buber, when he searches for an 'existent' which arises in the neutral and impersonal 'existence', but which is separate from other human beings, although responsible for them. He is himself aware of human problems which cannot be solved by pious religious instructions.

The concern for human beings and for the existent are linked together in a religion of faith in God. The traditionalist approach of the philosopher here places the Jew under a Law which is, in the end, service to the neighbour. The Law, it must be said, is more the ontological structure, the nature of being itself, which relates us to others. Within that structure the human being has a special meaning which through philosophy or religion moves towards the Creator, God. Once the existent meaning rises out of Creation, human beings cease to be just a result and receive a 'dignity of cause' to the extent that we endure the actions of the cause, which is external *par excellence*, divine action.

Levinas places this perception into his recollection of the war years, the Holocaust, where racial persecution in its absoluteness touches the very innocence of the being recalled to its ultimate identity. In his own experience, encountering the decency of Christian clergy in a German prison camp, he comes to see that there is a common language between Jews, Christians, and Muslims. Yet he does not want vague generalities at this point, but asserts the special character of Jewish monotheism which makes no compromise, but in the end promotes universalism.

It is Levinas the philosopher, the great teacher with disciples, and the human being who reached out to others in a very special dialogue which may be termed the seal of the French experience. It is, as it were, the essence of French thinking which makes us see Husserl and Heidegger's approach as a way through icy crystal caves. French thinking is warmer, and has passion: Sartre and Camus are light years away from the German philosophers. But Levinas, the committed Jew, has even more to teach those who share his premises and who lived in the Bible.

Levinas sees the anguish and self-doubt which besets many Jews living in a world where they are still suspect, in a doubting faith where they assume that the relationship between the Jew and God is liturgical and confined to the synagogue: they have forgotten that Judaism is a total life. And then, in France and throughout post-emancipation Europe, they see that they are still considered outsiders in a secular world which is still permeated by the Christian pattern.

Levinas sees three new factors within Jewish life in France: the creation of the State of Israel with its impact on Jewish consciousness; the appearance of Jewish youth movements; and the renewal of Jewish studies – all of it, a search for new space. He calls upon French Jewry to enter into this difficult freedom.

Within that vision of a future of French Jewry, one must also place the progressive Jewish communities which follow a different pattern but walk the same way: The Union Liberal Israelite De France, and the Mouvement Juif Liberal De France. Their rabbis are the likely inheritors of a

Progressive tradition which does not speak the language of Levinas but shares his goals. It is not only the Riders Towards the Dawn, but the stirrings within the *kehillah*, the community, which give hope for the future.

The paradigm of religious thought, as it arises out of the French scene, contains the politics, the philosophy, the social thinking of its time. In Levinas, one sees so much of the striving towards God and good that it almost compensates for that dark line which extends from Vichy to Le Pen.

The words of a Romanian-French poet whose family had shared the fate of so many French Jewish families, including that of Levinas, can and should serve as the *envoi* to our look at the French scene where so much vision and truth was pronounced by the poets and novelists as well as by the teachers and theologians:

> It is to you that I speak, you men of distant lands,
> I am speaking as a man to other men,
> With the little left in me of Man,
> With the small voice remaining in my throat.
> My blood spills over the roads. Would that it,
> Would that it did not cry for vengeance!
> The bugles blow. The beasts are cornered.
> Let me speak to you with the same words
> We had of old in common:
> There are few you might understand.
>
> The day will surely come, when all our thirst is
> Slaked, and we shall be beyond the land of memory.
> Death will have completed the labours of hate.
> I shall be a handful of nettles beneath your feet.
> Then ... well ... know that I had a face like yours;
> A mouth that prayed like yours ...
>
> Like you I have read all the papers and books,
> And I knew nothing about the world.[3]

## NOTES

1. J. M. Lustiger, 'Night: the absence of God? The presence of God?', p. 190.
2. Ibid., pp. 195–196.
3. RSGB prayer book (London, 1987).

# 4

# BRITAIN

### ON DOVER BEACH

The Sea of Faith
Was once, too, at the full, and round earth's shore
Lay like the folds of a bright girdle furl'd.
But now I can only hear
Its melancholy, long, withdrawing roar,
Retreating, to the breath
Of the night-wind, down the vast edges drear
And naked shingles of the world.

Matthew Arnold

MATTHEW ARNOLD'S 'Dover Beach' was written in another time and place, when the ebb and flow of faith had left those who wander towards light upon a darkling plain of violence and ignorance. England had not then experienced a breakdown of belief that resembles the shattered faith and the necessary self-delusions of the French. Nevertheless, the structure of faith had suffered. Some trace this to the days and nights of World War I, when Haigh and von Falkenheym had confronted one another with the numbers game: 'You only killed 20,000 last night, we killed 25,000. We won, even though no territory changed hands!' As Paul Tillich has said, 'God died in the trenches of the First World War'.

But what about the clergy of our time? Are they still defenders of the faith, proclaiming the morning, the tide coming back to cover the naked shingles? The Queen is still the Head of the Church, and the Church of England is established by law to maintain the Christian faith. Yet there are divisions within the ranks. Curiously, there is a group which names itself 'The Sea of Faith' – related to the poem, but only because a Cambridge scholar, Don Cupitt, named a book challenging Christian dogmas thus.

The Sea of Faith group is made up of clergy who question many of the teachings of the Church. They challenge the Resurrection, the virgin birth, and do not any longer view Christianity as the only revelation. But many would affirm with the Archbishop of Canterbury, 'Belief in the resurrection is not an appendage to the Christian faith – it is the Christian faith!' Among Christian leaders are both open and closed minds: both are representative of their community.

There are many responsible and dedicated clerics in the Church of England who have grappled with the problems of darkness in the past and uncertainties in the future. The pioneering work of Ulrich Simon's *A theology of Auschwitz* (1978), and of the late Alan Ecclestone's *The night sky of the Lord* (1980), represented different approaches in Christian thinking. Ulrich Simon, of King's College, London, has the personal knowledge of his family's suffering, but turns to the traditional teachings of the risen Christ. Alan Ecclestone was more influenced by Elie Wiesel and by George Steiner, and turned to the metaphor of the 'absence of God' in order to stir up a new Christian awareness for the evil that had overtaken Europe. In seeking the meaning behind the metaphor, Alan Ecclestone recognized that Christianity only shed a dim light on the Holocaust, obscuring the reality with the romanticism which Leo Baeck had clearly delineated in his critique of Christianity as a 'romantic religion'. Even the better clerics, said Ecclestone, have lost touch with the realities of life. Christianity in Europe had little to set against the 'messianism of Hitler' which lured millions to his banner.

Ecclestone saw the Jewish question at the heart of the Christian's failing. Anti-Semitism was the denial of the religious role which Israel had played through the ages and which it had to continue to play: not as scapegoat, but as a witness of God and as a teacher of righteousness. But both Christians and Jews had now encountered the darkness of God, and Ecclestone joined Bonhoeffer in mourning how the ground had been cut off under Christian believers. He noted that Bonhoeffer, too, had to turn to the basic Hebrew understanding of God on which Jesus himself depended: Israel's election and meeting with God, its basic experience of exile in the world but nearness to God whose *Shechina* went with them into exile, the prophetic instruction which was transformed into rules for life. Ecclestone accepted Bonhoeffer's critique of a Christianity which had lost its stamina and which no longer grew up in the (Jewish) ancestral household of Christ's faith. Real renewal of faith meant renewal of a sense of purpose, a deep expectation for the future.

Christianity attempts in this period when the Sea of Faith has retreated from the beach to recover God through warm human relationships rather than the coldness of Church dogma. There is a change among some Christian thinkers which has not only brought them back to the Hebrew Bible but also to their Jewish neighbours. The worldliness of the Jew was lacking among Christians, even when both entered into the 'dark night of the soul'.

Christians in Britain must also come to terms with the Holocaust, even though their country had not experienced the full horror of what had happened across the Channel. When the realization of the fate of the Jews dawned, many only saw that darkness as part of a war, placed among the other horrors of war. Some, to this day, accept the Holocaust as a necessary aspect of war which is, after all, only an extension of a failed diplomacy. How, otherwise, can one explain the action of the friends of Air Marshal 'Bomber' Harris, the father of 'saturation bombing' of civilian cities, who dedicated a monument to him on the same date which saw the obliteration of Cologne?

The Christian theologians who deal with the Holocaust and follow the teachings of Bonhoeffer and of Jewish theologians are still very much in the minority in Great Britain. Bishop Richard Harries of Oxford, formerly Dean of King's College in London and a well known broadcaster and writer, is an exception. A brief look at his thoughts of the Holocaust is relevant to our pursuit of those who saw clearly in dark times and who search for the light ahead.

> We tend to be very selective in our memories and this is particularly true of religious traditions . . . we like to defend ourselves by our good memories, by the lives of saints . . . but there are also the tragic memories . . . It is for these reasons that it is important for Christians to remember, liturgically if possible, the Holocaust.[1]

Rightly, Richard Harries points out that the vast majority of Christians today were not alive at the time of the Holocaust – and that soon no one will be left who actually experienced that evil. Christianity has a duty here: to remember. Even if Nazism was an avowedly pagan movement, one which aimed at the destruction of Christianity, it was built upon many centuries of anti-Semitism which were rooted in Church doctrines and Christian attitudes. These attitudes, and Christianity itself, have to change. As Richard Harries indicates:

> . . . a new religious approach is necessary. This does not entail deserting or betraying one's own religious tradition. But it does mean approaching

one's own religious tradition and that of others in a new spirit. In particular we need not only an affirmation or our own religious tradition but a properly critical attitude towards it, i.e., an awareness of when it has gone wrong and reflection on the question of why it has gone wrong.[2]

Self-examination is not a profession of guilt. It is a way of maturing, of moving towards a further stage in religion.

Within the Christian churches in England, this attitude is encountered more and more frequently. It is not confined to the Church of England. In the Catholic Church at least some voices are raised. Cardinal Basil Hume recognizes that the old dogmas of the Church have at least to be examined, particularly after Vatican II. In a preface to 'The six days of destruction' which brings the Holocaust towards the domain of Christian prayer, he wrote:

Together we have to explore the mystery of evil and suffering and what it means to be God's chosen. The Second Vatican Council declared in 1965: 'The Church condemns all persecutions of any men; she remembers her common heritage with the Jews and, acting not from any political motives, but rather from a spiritual and evangelical love, deplores all hatred, persecutions and the manifestations of anti-Semitism, whatever the period and whoever was responsible'.[3]

The Cardinal feels strongly that the world must not be allowed to forget what happened; that this sign of the times had to be studied perpetually so that the mystery of evil would be recognized and confronted properly by the British Catholic community. The Cardinal ended his introduction:

We must retrace the paths of division and hostility along which others once trod. Then Christian and Jew wandered far from each other, and forgot how to recognize family features in each other. For the future those who acknowledge Abraham as their father in faith must witness together God's love and His purposes for mankind.

Something of the Second Vatican Council, of the good Pope John who stretched out his arms to the Jewish community he met in order to declare: 'I am your brother Joseph', comes through the words of the Cardinal. The common kinship is acknowledged, and the common road towards God becomes possible.

Are we again viewing a paradigm of contemporary thinking where the

British background becomes part of a more tolerant interpretation of Church doctrines that are read far differently in Poland or in the newly emerging Christian Russia? Perhaps. Yet the Cardinal is still very conscious of his obligations to Rome as Protector of the Faith. This can be read positively: a traditionalist can let his compassionate spirit gain support from Church doctrine and work within the structure. In England, for good or bad, changes are introduced from the top, approved by the hierarchy, and take the steam out of most of the intellectual revolutions within religion.

A cautiously friendly relationship exists between the (Orthodox) Chief Rabbi and the Progressive movements in Great Britain. The Chief Rabbi's power base rests within the traditional community, and any real liaison with Reform or Liberal could cause damage there. Informal meetings take place with the Progressives where mutual communal problems are discussed – but no public statements are made, nor formal minutes kept. The British scene differs markedly from that of the United States, where the Synagogue Council of America and the New York Board of Rabbis show Orthodox, Conservative, and Reform rabbis working together openly. In the end, the Chief Rabbi's office in the UK is there to protect Orthodoxy and to fight off any inroads of radical thinking.

With the arrival of the new Chief Rabbi, Jonathan Sacks, this situation has not changed although a younger, dynamic style, and personal links with some of the leading Progressive rabbis, give hope for the future. However, the extreme Orthodox have increased their attacks upon the Reform and Liberal groups, and there have also been sharper challenges from Liberal rabbis who want to make it clear to the public that the Chief Rabbi does not speak for all Jews, but only for the group which elected him. On the whole, the non-Jewish British public does not accept this. The old image of the Chief Rabbi as an equivalent to the Archbishop of Canterbury still prevails, and the Chief Rabbi's public pronouncements are assumed to be the voice of British Jewry.

Chief Rabbi Jonathan Sacks is already established as one of the intellectual leaders of religion in Great Britain. He was chosen as the speaker for the highly regarded BBC Reith Lectures in 1990, and this series of lectures was discussed at great length by a British community delighted by his defence of faith. It was the exploration of a British paradigm of thinking in which various disciplines joined together. It was not so much an exploration of theology as a sociological study: how can the religious establishment and the religious person survive in a secular world? Jonathan Sacks acknowledged the moral imperatives built into a democratic society, but felt that these were ultimately derived from the Bible, and that this moral foundation united the various religions in a way which would ensure their survival in a secular world. It was his contention that society had underestimated the persistent faith which remained within the interstices of contemporary life, even if the majority of professing Christians in Great Britain do not go to church.

His teaching was addressed to the contemporary mind, and it made sense to the general public. It did not yet deal with the specific claim of religion, with its possession of revelation. Nevertheless, working out of his framework of Jewish faith, the Chief Rabbi could strike at those concepts within modern society which seemed to him a regression in morality rather than an advance within medicine: abortion and euthanasia. He gave the traditional view which Lord Jakobovits had also espoused and which has had some opposition within the Jewish community. Rejecting autonomous thinking in these areas, Jonathan Sacks made a plea for the recapturing of that world of values which exists beyond the self.

The Chief Rabbi thus suggested that the post-enlightenment freedom of thought, and the insistence upon finding the truth in terms of our own lives, was not a gift of freedom for which one should reach out greedily: it can result in a narrowing of human possibilities. The more we know collectively, the less we know as individuals. Few people understand much of their world, but we still make the choices in our life. These choices, on the whole, are materialistic.

Looking at our materialistic society, Jonathan Sacks nevertheless felt that the people were still identifying themselves in terms of their religion. The Biblical vision might be at the margin of our society, but it has not yet disappeared; the making of moral history is not yet at an end.

The Reith lectures, defending the structure and purpose of the family, pleading for more education, stressing the religious vision, were well received by the general public for which they were intended. The Chief Rabbi had not broached the area of intra-faith, his relation to the non-Orthodox Jew, even though they would be included in his comments;

> Liberal theologies, by conceding too much to passing moral fashion, have lost that sense of timelessness and transcendence which I believe to lie at the heart of the religious experience.

The blinding experiences of transcendence, the anguish and quest for meaning, can be very much part of liberal theology. Sadly, Orthodoxy most often makes its political alliances with the current political Conservatism. One could see this in Berlin at the end of the eighteenth century, and in the London of the 80s. Jonathan Sacks himself admits the unhappy alliance of the extreme Orthodox with the right wing government in Israel, although Lord Jakobovits was far more outspoken in this area. Nevertheless, when Jonathan Sacks states that he cannot believe in the religious value of legislative coercion he addresses the situation in Israel today. He does point to the necessity for revolutionary changes in Christianity if a dialogue with other religions is to commence; something of that insight still needs to be transferred to the Orthodox Jewish community. But he is hopeful: faith has not had its day; its history has barely begun!

Rabbi Sacks still had to address himself to that part of the Jewish community which is not part of his domain, especially as he does want to be seen as the spokesperson for all of Jewish life in the United Kingdom. In many Jewish issues there is a disagreement between Orthodoxy and Reform. Halachah (Jewish Law) and ritual observances certainly separate them; but there is also the understanding of the Holocaust. All Jews feel the same anguish. All of us know that we are both too far from it and too close to it to do much more than Aaron, whose response at the death of his sons was *va-yidom Aharon* – 'and Aaron was silent'. All Jews – all humanity, to assert the complete truth – also have to remember. We must make new theological assertions which refuse to see the traditional answers: acceptance, admission of guilt, bowing to the divine plan, recognizing chastisement as a way of purification, to be valid in our time and place.

Basically, Jonathan Sacks follows the approach of Michael Wyschogrod – an enlightened, intellectual Orthodoxy which feels the answers of the past are sufficient for the evil of our time. In 'The Holocaust in Jewish theology',[4] he reviews the various approaches by Jewish scholars. Against Fackenheim's stress on the uniqueness of the Holocaust, he follows the argument that such a perspective is not relevant to faith. God does not intervene in acts of human freedom: we can do evil or good. God is powerful precisely through his self-restraint: the central religious paradox is that God leaves the arena of history to human freedom, and therein lies his greatness.[5] The Nazis attempted to destroy the true witness of God – and the miracle of our time is Israel's creation which removed hopelessness from the Jewish soul. This does not explain the Holocaust, but it gives us faith despite the Holocaust. That, again, is why the Chief Rabbi is not enamoured of *Yom Ha-Shoah*, of a special memorial day and special prayers, when the old ones suffice. Rabbi Sacks writes:

One writer about the Holocaust records that he met a rabbi who had been through the camps and who, miraculously, seemed unscarred. He could still laugh. 'How,' he asked him, 'could you see what you saw and still have faith? Did you have no questions?' The rabbi replied: 'Of course I had questions. But I said to myself: If you ever ask those questions, they are such good questions that the Almighty will send you a personal invitation to heaven to give you the answers. And I preferred to be here on earth with the questions than up in heaven with the answers.' This, too, is a kind of theology.[6]

Perhaps I read this story differently from Jonathan Sacks: it seems to me to be one of the most bitter comments I have heard about the Holocaust. And perhaps Jonathan agrees with me – but still feels that these questions are asked by the tradition in a way which reassures him. I still prefer the challenges of a Richard Rubenstein when he dons the mantle of Elisha Abuya, or of Emil Fackenheim whose faith is renewed through autonomous reason, the Israel experience, and the awareness that theology has travelled and moved forward into as yet uncharted territories.

In a just published book, written for the Littman Library which I helped edit, Jonathan Sacks tries to arrive at a formula which can include the Progressive Jewish community within his constituency. It is an unselfish quest, rising out of his desire to avoid the prophecy of Yeshayahu Leibowitz: 'Perhaps we will reluctantly arrive at a separation into two nations, each going its historic way imbued by intense hatred (of the other).'[7] Professor Leibowitz spoke out of an Israeli context, on the conflict between the 'religious' and the 'secular'; but it does apply to the conflict between Orthodox and Reform. This, according to Rabbi Sacks, is mainly a problem in the Diaspora where Orthodoxy and Reform confront one another. There is also the fracture between Israel and the Diaspora. Different aspects of Israeli life unite in sh'lilat had-golah (negation of the Diaspora), where a Jew outside of Israel is seen, at best, as an impotent Jew. Outside of Israel, some (but not many), view Israel as a threat to their own national identity as Americans, French, or British. Nevertheless, in these difficult times, Diaspora and Israel draw closer together. And Rabbi Sacks is basically concerned with achieving unity for all Jews:

> . . . given that Jewish unity is a value for many Jews, what sort of value is it? Not, surely, a unity of culture . . . Nor is it a political unity . . . Unity is, as it always was, a religious value: a fact of Covenant, a mutual commitment and faith.[8]

This cannot be achieved by any act of rejection; and the Chief Rabbi here carefully traces the 'rejection of rejection' from Biblical times to the great philosophers. It must be clear that God's choice of a person or a people is not a rejection of other persons or people, as he shows convincingly. Nor is the Covenant ever terminated by rejection. Even in exile, God and Israel are bound together in a marriage bond that cannot be dissolved. Jews survive, either as an accidental remnant or a chosen remnant (both teachings exist in Jewish thought). Maimonides' *Epistle to Yemen* of 1172 stresses the 'chosen remnant': 'As it is impossible for God to cease to exist, so is our destruction and disappearance from the world unthinkable.' The saints and the pious who resist forced conversion will remain within the fold. And Rabbi Sacks calls this 'theological Darwinism: the survival of the religiously fit.' Nevertheless, another Letter of Maimonides, the *Epistle on martyrdom* is a powerful inclusivist document. There, he declared the *conversos* (those forced to become Christians, often called *Marranos*) to be true Jews. 'The religious deeds they did in secret would be double rewarded.' In one case, he addressed those who had not converted. In the other, those who had converted but could still be part of Israel.

In our time, there is a crisis of faith. Viewing the Jewish community caught up in the snares of modernity, Martin Buber questioned the wholeness of the Jewish people. Rabbi Sacks accepts that the concept of the Jewish people as one entity standing before God is problematic.

He sees the conflicts among Jews as an illness which one must combat for at least four reasons: 1. After the Holocaust, and after the attack on Israel, Jewish anti-Semitism is as bad as Christian anti-Semitism. 2. Jewish Darwinism is sociologically unrealistic – no major grouping of Jews will disappear. 3. This internecine warfare is historically blind, ignoring the battles of the past which tore Jewish life apart. 4. Above all, 'the idea of "one people" forms the very core of Jewish faith in the Covenant between God and a chosen nation.' The idea of 'one people' can only be seen as a religious commitment. And this leads the Chief Rabbi to a position which is less tolerant than he surmises, but more tolerant than what may be expected of a staunch 'Defender of the Faith'.

Rabbi Sacks begins by repeating the basic stance of an uncompromising Orthodoxy. The Jewish pluralism which he sees in Progressive Judaism cannot be accepted: a *de jure* acknowledgement of different 'denominations' is ruled out by the classic term of (his) Judaism. Halachah, the Law, is central. It turns the chaos of individual choices in the field of ethics into a shared code of righteousness:

A pluralism that would formally recognize the obsolescence of Halachah (Jewish secularism) or its subjection to the autonomous self (Reform) or the local ethic of time and place (Conservative) would not be a proposal to unite Jewry but, instead, announce its dissolution.[9]

The argument rests, of course, upon the notion that only the Orthodox view of Judaism has any validity. Within that stance, Rabbi Sacks would still argue against excluding other Jewish groups from *K'llal Yisrael* (even though he would exclude their ideas). He feels that one *cannot* exclude other Jews who stand under the Covenant of Sinai. It is like a marriage contract, 'where God will hide his face'.[10] The problem here, as I see it, is that too many traditionalists build a cause-and-effect formula into this proposition, which again gives an excuse for exclusivism. I do understand and appreciate the Chief Rabbi's point that 'Inclusivism is the belief that the Covenant was made with a people, not with righteous individuals alone', even though both conversion and apostasy exist. Traditionally, Jewry was kept together through family, through the *kehillah* (community) and through a process of education which began in the home and continued through the synagogue and the system of Jewish schools. This had to be accommodated within the modern society and its emphasis upon the individual and the state. According to Rabbi Sacks, Judaism cannot live within the new structure. Reform Judaism may opt for the individual, and Zionism will choose the state – neither, he thinks, can be the formula for the 'one people'. And the Chief Rabbi mourns this escape into secularism. Reform Jews and Zionist Jews are more to be pitied than censured, and he will not consider them wicked. Wrong, yes – but their redemption is always possible. In his doctrine of inclusivism one can love them, but one must not agree with them.

It does not surprise the Chief Rabbi that his concept of inclusivism will not be acceptable to modern Orthodoxy which is, after all, an ideology. What Rabbi Sacks presents in inclusivism is seen by him as a statement of Jewish ecology. Jewish life is a world of varying approaches, and he can only see the validity of Orthodoxy; even there, many variants exist. But all of Jewish life possesses a deep love of Jews and is reluctant to divide the Jewish people.

His inclusivism advocates a sensitive language when one addresses other Jews; it does not want to use coercive means to return Jews 'to the fold'; it will stress education; it wants to apply Halachah to its widest possible constituency, but rejects corrective change as suggested by Eliezer Berkovits, for example. It seeks what the Chief Rabbi calls 'a nuanced understanding of secular and liberal Jews [and] refuses a dualism that

divides the Jewry into unmixed categories of good and evil'.[11] The inclusivist
also sees that secular Zionists and Israelis fulfil the command of 'settling
the land' (which Nachmanides records as 'equal to all the other commands
combined).[12] The inclusivist attaches positive significance to the fact that
liberal Judaism has played its part in keeping alive for many Jews the values
of Jewish identity; and he strives to recognize the positive consequences of
Jewish liberalism and secularism even as he refuses to recognize their truth
or ultimate viability. He will demand secular and liberal Jewish leaders to
act responsibly in the context of the totality of Judaism and the Jewish
people. The Chief Rabbi's inclusivism will respect much of what he sees
in Reform Judaism and in the secular Israeli stances. But he claims that
within Reform the laxity of conversions, the decision of patrilineal descent,
the endorsement of homosexuality, premarital sex and abortion on demand,
are fateful breaks with the letter and spirit of the Jewish law. Rabbi Sacks
knows that he is being patronizing in all of this, but pleads for Reform
understanding that he is acting out of love, out of the logic of his position,
and that this position does not give him other options. His opponents
should not only understand him, but must also have sympathy for exclusivist
Orthodoxy. He believes what they believe, even if they reject his inclusivism.
But, perhaps, all Jews can come to respect the sanctity of the Jewish people,
collectively and individually. Every Jew who remains part of Jewish life and
has children after the Holocaust makes a momentous decision and must
not be dishonoured. And, as all Jews should respect all Jews, so must all
of them hear and heed the divine call in history. Then, even if we stay
divided, we are travelling towards the same goal – the promised union of
Torah, the Jewish people, the land of Israel, and God.

It is an impassioned, decent, ethical plea which one can only respect.
This does not prevent me from registering my dissent. I cannot ask the
Chief Rabbi to abandon his personal belief in the one truth of Orthodoxy,
or to abandon his task of strengthening the traditional Jewish community
and defending it against what by his light appears as heresy. Like Beruriah
(the wife of Rabbi Meir and a great teacher), he hates the sin but not the
sinners. Jonathan Sacks approaches the liberal Jew as a person whom he
loves and respects in many ways. As it happens, I am not an amorphous
person, but a rabbi who represents the Progressive Jewish community
through a variety of official responsibilities placed upon me by my peers –
Liberal, Reform, Conservative and Reconstructionist rabbis. We grant more
to Orthodoxy than Orthodoxy grants us. At times, I feel that there is a guilt
feeling in traditional Jews which credits us with greater animus against
them than is present in us. The weakness of the liberal Jew is always the

readiness to concede truth to the other side. But my stance of uncertain truth belonging to both of us is not acceptable where only one supreme revealed truth is recognized. The Chief Rabbi agrees to dialogue with the Christians, but rejects shared prayers. He applies the same ruling to non-Orthodox Jews: they may pray with him, he cannot pray in their synagogues. He wants Christians to 'accept the validity of non-Christian paths to religious truths'. We should not ask him to apply this to Progressive Judaism: it is the rigourist's way of creating sects outside the Orthodoxy. The one people he seeks must live and pray together, and recognize each other's validity. But that, I am afraid, will not come for a long time. In the meantime, liberal Jews will be inclusivists, and will view Orthodoxy to be on a right path, part of *K'llal Yisrael*. And I, personally, welcome Rabbi Sacks as a teacher and friend who strives to unite Jewry.

I could not leave the subject of Britain without a word on George Steiner, arguably one of the great thinkers of our time, a professor of English at Cambridge and in Geneva. Some of the fiction he has written is linked with the so-called 'weightier' texts. George Steiner's novel about Hitler, *The portage to San Cristobal of A.H.*, became the centre of a storm of protest when Christopher Hampton adapted it as a play for the London stage. But behind that book stood a solid body of work, notably the brilliant lecture series published as *In Bluebeard's castle* and a much earlier volume of stories about the year 1941–1942, *Anno Domini*. There is also his great *Language and silence*.

I would prefer to start with a gentler, lighter text: George Steiner's recent (1992) *Proofs and three parables*. The protagonist of *Proofs* could have stepped out of many books of contemporary literature. He is the typical intellectual, a member of the proletariat, an expelled Communist who has his own little fringe group. Steiner captures the arid but impassioned discussions at their meetings; but it is the debate between the lapsed Communist and a lapsed priest which carry forward the ideas which do not come out of textbooks but out of life:

[The proof-reader speaks] I don't know much about Jews. I was young when it was done to them. But I have my own theory. That business about being a chosen people, the covenant with history. I believe in it. But not in the way they tell it, Father Carlo: it is the wretched who are chosen. It is those who are born into hunger, into AIDS . . . almost the whole cused lot of us. The numberless tribe of the losers. They are the chosen people of despair. But also of hope, Carlo . . .

George Steiner here looks at the secular Messianism which was contained in the vision of Karl Marx, the 'God that failed'. Nevertheless, Steiner's proof-reader in the end returns to the Party – he sees no alternative! He needs a system of laws, and has to find them within humanity. And Father Carlo replies to him with the reminder of the twenty-five million Stalin starved, froze, and tortured to death. He is as much aware of the Jew-hatred created by the Church, of the suffering caused by religion. And he compares religion's yearning for God's eternity, in which he can still believe, with the Communist lie of a classless brotherhood in this world, that monstrous perversion.

In the on-going, unresolved dialogue which is at the centre of this cautionary tale, Steiner brings us into the world after the Holocaust, into the human situation where we will be propelled into that world after the dawn whose dimensions we cannot foretell.

The burdens we carry with us into that future are both memory and language. George Steiner sees the limitations of language, where our ability within religion to speak *with* God and perhaps even *about* God, is no longer possible after what has happened: 'The problem as to whether there is a human form of language adequate to the conceptualization of Auschwitz.' But, beyond eloquence, is there even a rationality which can be applied to the *Shoah*? In the end, Steiner turns back to the position he has espoused over the decades: silence. It might be suicidal, might be impossible to keep – but it is the place of authenticity. I think of this as Job's silence – that span of time which precedes his outbreak into rebellion against the meaninglessness of human suffering which must have *some* explanation.

Steiner brings us back into the present-day world of genocide, where humanity can be defined as murderous and murdering primates. This does not destroy the uniqueness of the *Shoah* and its defining Jewish identity. Steiner has indicated how the Jewish refusal to recognize Jesus as the Christ has postponed human salvation in Christian terms. In our time, as Steiner notes, the Church has seen a new possibility: self-examination. There, the process of salvation may depend upon the Jew entering freely into the Church and becoming the fulfillment of the Church.

But the thesis of Steiner's *In Bluebeard's castle* is that the Jews will not be forgiven for forcing humanity to believe in God and a moral code:

Three times, Judaism has confronted Western man with the merciless claims and exactions of the ideal. Three times – in its invention of monotheism, in the message of the radical Jesus, in Marxism and messianic-socialism – Israel has asked of ordinary men and women more than human nature wishes to give. Nothing is more cruel than the blackmail of perfection.

Jews are not loathed for killing God – they are hated for inventing him. The Jews as the moral conscience of the world will always find themselves persecuted. Placed into the matrix of Western civilization, this hypothesis (Steiner does not claim it as proven) gives a modicum of explanation to Auschwitz which still remains beyond explanations. And this may be related in the same way to the inexplicable miracle of Jewish survival. Why did Cain not succeed in killing Abel? How, when the Nazis acted out their hidden dream did this people still manage to fulfill its ancient function of being a witness for God and a conscience for the world?

The thrust of Steiner's work, in the exploration of language, in his fiction, in his essays, never moves him far from his role as a 'remembrancer' of the *Shoah*. He honours the scholars who sort the debris of history to make us more aware of what the Nazis actually managed to do, and which gives us a greater awareness of the nobility of human beings put under intolerable conditions, inside and outside the camps. He still wants answers to questions which have no answers. If we cannot hear George Steiner, we cannot hear anyone. If we listen to him, we have found our Rider Towards the Dawn in the world of English letters.

NOTES

1. E. Wiesel and A. Friedlander, *The six days of destruction* (Oxford, Pergamon Press, 1988), p. 9.
2. Ibid., p. 10.
3. Nostra Aetate 4, ibid., p. 8.
4. J. Sacks, 'The Holocaust in Jewish theology', *Tradition in an untraditional age* (London, Vallentine, Mitchell, 1990).
5. Ibid., p. 152.
6. Ibid., p. 153.
7. Quoted in U. Huppert, *Back to the ghetto* (New York, 1988), p. 40.
8. Ibid., pp. 212–213.
9. Ibid., p. 228.
10. Ibid., p. 229.
11. Ibid., p. 234.
12. Ibid., p. 235.

# [ 5 ]

# ITALY

'Kennst du das Land ...'

Goethe

## SHADOWS AND SUNSHINE

EVER since Goethe journeyed through Italy and placed this experience in the heart of his writings and into German literature, Germans have yearned for the land 'where the citrons bloom, where oranges glow golden amidst the leaves'. Today, some Germans refer to Italy as the *Bundesreiseland*, the place where Germans go on holiday. Nevertheless, the shadows of the past hang heavily over any relationship between the two lands. The history of the Axis, with its supposedly friendly relationship between Hitler and Mussolini, is difficult to forget. Hitler had learned much from Mussolini in the early days, and patterned his own brand of fascism on that of his teacher. They shared certain aims for the betterment of their own people at the expense of other countries. Yet there was something totally alien to the Italian people and its leaders in the Nazi system with its view of people as subhuman and its burning zeal to exterminate the Jews. We have learned by now that it is not possible to fashion a stereotype which is then used to define a person and a people, but generalizations which allow for exceptions are still permitted; and the image of the Italian as warm hearted and generous is realized in countless instances which justify this as a general comment upon Italy: even when it is applied to the Italians' relationship to the Jews during the time of fascism. A certain uneasiness remains: Mussolini's granddaughter has, after all, been elected to the national assembly. Had she been elected as a liberal or socialist candidate, Jews might have looked on with positive feelings, mindful that the sins of the fathers are not visited upon the children. But the spectres of the past are all around us. And that past is not easily assimilated or understood, even by the historians.

Questions arise at this point. How much cooperation did Mussolini give to Hitler? How much cooperation did the Italian army give to the Germans in helping with the 'Final Solution'? Was the Pope silent – and if so, why? Scholars have worked in this field, and have often disagreed in their answers to these questions, sometimes admitting their inability to give a convincing answer. I also do not think that one can find an 'Italian paradigm' of religious, philosophic, or historical thinking which will satisfy our quest; but there are at least cryptic, intermediate answers we can give which will bring us closer to a world which also saw sunset and sunrise.

Scholars agree that there was little anti-Semitism in Italy's fascism before Italy and Germany became linked together, which would suggest that it was Hitler's emphasis and insistence on an anti-Jewish policy which made Mussolini participate in this crime. In fact documents of that time show that Hitler had not pushed Mussolini to act against the Jews in 1938. Mussolini did this on his own, as a calculated act to bring Germany and Italy closer together. It was more a token, although there were always some officials who tried to enforce the anti-Jewish laws.

The fortunes of war changed. Italy was invaded, and Mussolini fell. On 11 September 1943, Field Marshal Kesselring declared that all the Italian territory which was under German control would henceforth be under German military and civilian leadership. Once one of the most rabid henchmen of Hitler was placed in charge (a certain Theodor Danneker), the real pogrom could begin: the Black Sabbath, 16 October 1943. All the Jews in Rome were arrested and while the Germans complained that the Italian police were uncooperative, the Jews were assembled for transport to the death camps. In the end, over 1,000 Jews from Rome were sent to their deaths.

But, on the whole, Italian Jewry had enough protection to be saved from mass deportation; to the fury of the Germans the Italians, regardless of their feelings about Jews, wanted to resist the impact of Germans upon Italy. This was true of the army as well as of the civilians.

In France the Vichy government had cooperated fully with the Germans. In Italy, although the Fascist Party Congress in Verona, on 14 November 1943 declared all Jews to be 'foreigners' (*stranieri*), this happened after Marshal Badoglio's surrender to the Allies in September 1943, when he and the king, Victor Emmanuel III, had fled to Brindisi and Italy had become a German 'colony'. Long consideration was also given as to whether to invade and occupy the Vatican City. To the fury of the group around Hitler, there were enough diplomatic reasons to respect the Vatican. Undoubtedly, this saved many Jewish lives.

Within the Church, there were countless examples of priests and nuns who went to great lengths to help Jews, even when their superiors ordered them to comply with the German demands.

So in contrast with other countries, four-fifths of Italian Jewry escaped death, mainly because of help from the Italians, though some who were captured suffered because of Italian complicity. Certainly, the hatred which Italians felt for the Germans, who now showed themselves as an occupying force rather than as partners in the quest to achieve a national destiny bound up with the teachings of fascism, was instrumental in creating a partisan army which now fought against the Germans. Their political orientation, more often than not, was Communist; and the political history of the postwar period was predictable from these beginnings. Yet the partisan battle was, in a sense, pro-Jewish.

Mussolini's government behaved quite differently towards those Jews who had come into Italy from other countries. There, much more co-operation with the German demands was shown:

> The Italian government ordered the arrest of thousands of Jewish refu-gees living in Italy . . . about 3,500 refugees were sent to concentration camps in southern Italy. Another 5,000 refugees were assigned to live in a state of semi-confinement in small towns throughout Italy.
>
> Paradoxically, while the fascist government was mistreating refugees at home, it was rescuing them overseas. During the occupations of France and Yugoslavia, the Italian army steadfastly refused to give in to German demands that they hand over the Jews in their control.[1]

The actions of those within the Church were understandable. Inside a Christian structure there must always be a special awareness of the Biblical imperative to 'love your neighbour' and to strive for a better world in opposition to evil. But the Italian army was an organization dedicated to quite other aims. Waging war, going into battle, killing in order not to be killed leaves far less room for acts of benevolence.

The Italian soldiers had shown themselves capable of great cruelty in their treatment of Ethiopians and Arabs. Why didn't they hand over the Jews to the Germans? Why did they say 'no' to the Croatians who were willing to participate in Hitler's Holocaust by turning over thousands of

Jewish Croatians – in the hands of the Italians – for transport to the death camps? The Italian army refused to do this, and eventually followed the same pattern in Italian-occupied Greece and in southern France.

Jonathan Steinberg's compassionate and deeply informed study of these events shows the essential difference between the Italian community and the German state. There existed a sense of honour in Italy which seemed dormant at times, but which emerged in this time of crisis: the Italians simply did not want to be part of that momentous crime, even where individual units within that society followed the multitude to do evil. But this is too simple an explanation. There were too many victims of the Italian fascist regime who had suffered brutal persecution, and the Mussolini puppet state after 1943 had its Jew-hunters, its real concentration camps (Fossoli) and all the dark aspects of a totalitarian dictatorship. Dr Steinberg finds the path within a structure where an understanding of the ethical dimension is present. Steinberg sifted through a vast number of German letters and bureaucratic documents without ever finding a German expression of sympathy for the approach of the Italians to the Jews. The word 'ethical' was absent. Italian documents, on the other hand, almost always contained an ethical vocabulary when they had to deal with the anguish of the Jews. Once again, we confront the reality of paradigms of thought and action which emerge out of the stream of history.

A full understanding of what happened in Italy, with its dark and golden pages in the annals of humanity, requires, at the very least, careful study; but we are also dealing with human beings who cannot be catalogued, or seen as reflections of a stereotype.

Jonathan Steinberg saw Primo Levi as a witness who came out of that darkness and who turns to his Italian inheritance in order to make some sense of suffering to his fellow prisoner, a young French Jew. He wants:

... to remember and to interpret for his French comrade the great passage in Dante's *Inferno* which stands for the whole human quest, the final journey of Ulysses:

'"It's late, it's late, we're already at the kitchen, I have to finish:

> Tre volte il fe'girar con tutte l'acque,
> Alla quarta levar la poppa in suso
> E la prora ire in giu, come altri piacque."

I hold Pikolo back, it's absolutely necessary and urgent that he listen, that he understand that *come altri piacque*, before it's too late. Tomorrow he or I could be dead, or never see each other again. I have to say it, explain the Middle Ages, the anachronism so human and so necessary and so utterly unexpected and much more, something gigantic which I have only now seen, in the intuition of a second, perhaps the why of our destiny, of our being here today.'[2]

Levi remembers Dante in the dark night of his suffering; and he saves his own humanity, he shares the vision of Dante with his friend. Ulysses' ship, beyond the Pillars of Hercules, is all of human audacity which finally moves beyond its capacity. In the end, the ship's bow and stern plunge into the deep, *come altri piacque*, in accordance with the divine will. The prisoner in the concentration camp sees himself in his own final quest, still able to celebrate an inner strength which has set itself against the dark storm surrounding him, still affirming the ultimate meaning which god gives to life. And Primo Levi, riding towards the dawn, expresses the life of the Italian Jew within the context of a society in which, despite its flaws, there is the dimension of the ethical and the knowledge of a past which was old when the Caesars were young. He found an affirmation of life in the ancient classic texts.

Primo Levi (1919–1987) had been an outstanding chemist who had worked in Milan until, after the Germans had taken over from Mussolini, he fled into the Aosta mountains. Captured that December (1943) he had experienced the reality of the Fossoli camp, and then the unreality of the camp outside the world: Auschwitz. In order to extract some use from this unit in the death camp, the 'masters' transferred him to the laboratory of a rubber factory, where his scientific mind observed everything and forgot nothing. Some literary critics have compared him with Dante: and both covered the same subject: the Inferno. Primo Levi had not abandoned hope when he entered his hell; but he had discovered demons and total evil. He had also discovered the inner dimension of humans put to the absolute test, men and women who were dehumanized and made to participate in their own destruction. With scientific clarity, he isolated the factors in the human psyche which enabled humans to endure, if not to survive – survival was too often due to fortune, to chance. Yet reason and self-awareness could at least give support to a prisoner who might die any way, but not as the sub-human being his tormentors wanted him to become. Scientific training and a classical education came together in him, into the domain where human powers failed. At the very end, when the books had been published and the poetry had been written, he took his departure from the world. It was suicide, and it was part of a totality of life which has to be understood in the context of his recorded teachings, as the final page of his writings.

Primo Levi's *The sixth day* is one of the last of the canon of his works in English translation (it was translated in 1990 from texts written in 1966 and 1977). The stories in the book are more in the nature of glosses, the application of scientific knowledge and thought to the absurdities of human existence. When they are seen as part of the total work of one of the Riders Towards the Dawn, there is a connection between these science fiction tales and the awe inspiring *If this is a man* (first published in 1947) in which humanity in all of its anguish and its internal battle between good and evil comes to be seen in the report from the innermost circle of hell. *The sixth day* shows a committee of scientists at work who have been entrusted with the creation of man. Experts from all fields, ranging from thermodynamics to chemistry, anatomy, and psychology have been earnestly engaged for aeons ('. . . please hurry: the fourth glacial age is about to begin'), in this project of creating a new species: a human being. The chairman of the project is Arimane, and his chief opposition comes from Ormuz (the Persian gods of darkness and light). As the argument between them develops, some of the difficulties which will face humanity in its development are clearly put forward. Finally, in this ironic tale, Ormuz can proudly proclaim that the final design can now be approved: man will be a bird, a flying bird. At that moment, word comes from a higher authority: man has already been created. The details given to them are taken from the Book of Genesis; and the committee sadly closes its books and departs from the scene.

In the Midrash, the rabbinical homiletical exposition of the Bible, there is a similar text. The angels argue among themselves, and with God, whether or not Man should be created. They list all the evil qualities which will manifest themselves in human life: sin and rebellion, imperfection, an unworthiness to fulfil the basic teachings of the Pentateuch which should be given to them, the angels, rather than to unworthy humanity. Finally, God stops their arguments: 'Why do you argue? Man is already created!' That, too, is the reality already confronting Primo Levi. In these fanciful tales, he tries to show how science could transform the world: machines could duplicate anything, including human beings; hunger could be eliminated through machinery which could distribute to starving human beings throughout the world; but, ultimately, failure is inevitable where human beings are in control . . . And yet there were times when Levi believed in science and humanity. Anthony Rudolf's study points out that:

Chemistry itself is anti-fascist, according to this Jewish chemist, because it can tolerate impurities, life-giving impurities such as carbon, by supplying a literal, metaphorical and conceptual framework for containing impurities, unlike the Nazis who wanted to destroy the allegedly impure people known as Jews. And who is not impure? 'I am the impurity that makes the zinc react, I am the grain of salt or mustard,' Levi writes in *The periodic table*.[3]

Salt and mustard are also religious, New Testament concepts. And we come to see the richness of Levi's concepts of life by placing him into the concept of a civilized world where Rome and Jerusalem comingle. What must also be stressed is the fact that science became an armour for him when he entered the concentration camp – not only in providing him a task which at least made survival a vague possibility (without luck, none could or did survive), but also because an inner armour came to surround his personality, the knowledge of other values which would not accept a hell governed by evil as the norm upon which one based one's actions.

Often, these values and the need to remain a human being were taught to him by other prisoners who made him aware that one could not surrender to a system which tried to dehumanize every human being caught in the trap. The simple task of washing, of keeping clean, was difficult and apparently senseless. Yet it was part of the mechanism of survival. And always, there was the knowledge that survival was often not the decision between right and wrong, but between greater and lesser evils. One did not remain untouched by evil. Rabbinic tradition always emphasized that every human being contained within the soul the *yetzer ha-tov*, the good inclination, as well as the *yetzer ha-ra*, the inclination to do evil – and both were necessary to life. In one of his books (*The drowned and the saved*, in English 1988), Levi recounts the harrowing experience of finding a saving source of water, drip after drip of life, which could sustain him and perhaps one other person – but there were three of them in the work party! In the end, he shared with one of his two comrades, and they kept the secret of the water from the other comrade. That man also survived and, years later, confronted Levi with the knowledge which he had had even in that time. Levi's guilt and anguish is described in the text together with his awareness that a decision had to be made by him which could not be avoided. In the Talmud we find the classic example of two men in the wilderness, with one man possessing a flask of water sufficient to guarantee life for only one of them. Should he drink it himself, or give the water to his friend?

Altruism and decency urge him to give the water to his friend. Or: should they share? But then, both would die. The majority of rabbinic scholars insist that he should drink – for is not his blood as red as his comrade's? Suicide is also a sin. But a significant minority (a late contemporary teacher, Steven Schwarzschild, prominent in our time) brought valid arguments why one should give the water to the neighbour. In our time, Jews do not easily live with the guilt of turning away from the neighbour, of surviving with a heavy guilt and an undying remembrance. But there is the injunction to live! Primo Levi heard it, and his life proclaims the anguish and the necessity of living after the *Shoah* – until the darkness overwhelmed him.

Primo Levi was made a Jew as much by the laws of the enemy as by his inheritance; but then he lived his Jewish fate, with its need to 'bear witness . . . to live in order to tell'. There his gentleness was sometimes joined with melancholy humour. One interviewer asked him whether, on his visits to Poland after the war, he had witnessed any anti-Semitism. He replied: 'No, not any more', then, with an ironic smile, he added, 'for lack of material'.[4] Reason continued to control emotion, and his most telling impact upon his contemporaries arose out of this quiet, firm celebration of the human mind which could confront absolute evil and, in the end, continue to hope in humanity. A genuine absence of hatred against the enemy can be observed in all of his writings even if, under the surface, one senses the boiling emotions which had to be kept under control. The same interviewer asked Primo Levi whether he could explain the absence of hatred. He replied:

> In fact, I have many times been praised for my lack of animosity towards the Germans. It's not a philosophic virtue. It's a habit of having my second reactions before my first. So before heating myself to a fit of anger, I begin reasoning. And generally the reason prevails.[5]

Primo Levi was more than a man of science. He was also a man of action, as his participation in the resistance shows. The English text of one of his works, *If not now, when?*, again reflects a rabbinic teaching which is not an inaccurate assessment of this remarkable person. The text of the ancient rabbi Hillel from which the title is taken is: 'If I am not for myself, who will be for me? But if I am for myself alone, what am I? And if not now, when?' The fact is that Primo Levi knew himself for what he was: a witness, a remembrancer, one who could and who would not escape out of that darkness. The point is not that Primo Levi died, but that he lived and taught and remembered until he could be reasonably certain that his work was going to endure; then, quietly, his anguish reached out to a public which would mourn a light which had been extinguished. One final glimpse may be caught of him in one of his later poems, even if it is only one more facet of the man. The poem is called 'The survivor':

> *Dopo di allora, ad ora incerta,*
> Since then, at an uncertain hour,
> That agony returns:
> And till my ghastly tale is told,
> This heart within me burns.
>
> Once more he sees his companions' faces
> Livid in the first faint light,
> Grey with cement dust,
> Nebulous in the mist,
> Tinged with death in their uneasy sleep.
> At night, under the heavy burden
> Of their dreams, their jaws move,
> Chewing a non-existent turnip.
> 'Stand back, leave me alone, submerged people,
> Go away. I haven't dispossessed anyone,
> Haven't usurped anyone's bread.
> No one died in my place. No one.
> Go back into your mist.
> It's not my fault if I live and breathe,
> Eat, drink, sleep and put on clothes.'[6]

But he was a survivor, who had to talk to the shades, to the spectres of his comrades who died in the camps. And, we have to speak Primo Levi's language when we act as remembrancers. And then, too, alongside of him, we might say to the shades: 'Go back into your mist. It's not my fault if I live and breathe . . .' But can we say that to Primo Levi who came out of the mist to talk to us?

One did not have to come out of the innermost circle of the inferno to give testimony. The Italian system of support for the Nazi programme was of limited value to the Germans, as we have seen. Their mills of injustice stuttered at times, and anti-fascist and resistance fighters often received prison sentences: eight, seven, or fifteen years. Others were sent *al confino*, to a kind of house arrest in southern Italy – a device the fascists used to keep political enemies out of circulation. The device worked only imperfectly; one thinks of Carlo Levi who used his time of exile in a malaria-stricken town to write *Christ stopped at Eboli*. There exists an ample literature of testimony, of reassessment, of reports on the ethical actions which stand out alongside of the evil that was done. Unlike both Germanies, the Italians do not have to carry the guilt of that time as a nation, even if there were a great many individuals whose active and passive guilt continues to live with them.

In that elegant and civilized world that was and remains Italy, one can turn to other thinkers and teachers whose lives and works reach out to us.

Italian Jewry – this must be stated very clearly – played a unique role within Jewish history. Almost 2,000 years of a very special symbiosis, often under difficult circumstances, define its character. Some scholars actually claim that this uniqueness was a weakness, consisting of the lack of a clear self-identity: it was too much absorbed by its surroundings. Yet Italian Jewry always had its links with the Jewries of Europe, and was rooted upon the past traditions of Palestine and of Babylonia. Its very openness to its host country not only made its special contributions to the Renaissance, but contributed to all of the eras of Italian Jewish life linked to its neighbours. And there was a special sparkle, an openness to dialogue, a genius of listening and answering to the outside culture, which was unmatched by Jewish life elsewhere in the world.

Writing about the acclimatization of his own family, Primo Levi characterized Italian Jewry in this manner:

Our fathers, and above all our mothers, daily and with great naturalness, used Judeo-Piedmontese; it was the language of the family and the home. They were nevertheless conscious of its intrinsic cosmic charge, which sprang from the contrast between the fabric of the discourse, which was the rustic and laconic Piedmontese dialect, and the Hebrew inlay, drawn from the language of the patriarchs, remote but enlivened every day by public and private prayer and the reading of the books, polished by the millennia like the bed of a glacier. But this contrast mirrored another, the essential contrast of Judaism dispersed amidst the 'peoples', the *gentes (gentiles*, precisely), torn between divine vocation and the quotidian misery, and it mirrored yet another, much vaster contrast, that intrinsic to the human condition, since man is twofold, an *impasto* of *celestias afflatus* and earthly dust. After the Diaspora the Jewish people have dolorously lived this conflict and have drawn from it, together with their wisdom, also their laughter, which in fact is absent in the Bible and the Prophets.[7]

Has the Holocaust split the Jews apart from their neighbours in Italy? As we have seen, there was much generosity and decency between these two groups even in the dark times. Now, only 35,000 Jews live in Italy (mainly in Rome, Milan and Turin); and there is less laughter and openness. Clashes between young Jews and neo-fascists have taken place recently and Italy has recorded a rise in its nationalist groups not unrelated to the world around it. Mussolini's grand-daughter won a place in its Parliament, representing the extreme right, and recent surveys have shown an upsurge in Italian anti-Semitism. In L'Espresso magazine, 10.5 percent of the respondents thought Jews should leave Italy, and 9.5 percent believed the Holocaust was a myth. Over a third thought that the 35,000 Italian Jews were not Italian after all, and more than half thought that Jews 'had a special relationship to money'.[8] Against this, there is also an outburst of pro-Jewish statements from Italian leaders which mirror the pro-Jewish statements in recent days led by Chancellor Richard von Weizsaecker in Germany: we utilize outside criteria here: even a judgement on the guilty and innocent does not enter into the psyche of a nation. And the selection of great thinkers to guide us certainly depends upon our own subjective response. This said, I happily turn to an Italian Jewish scholar whom many would see in the context of his American and British teaching experience, but who must also be considered the product of all Italian history, as already signalled by his name: Arnaldo Dante Momigliano.

A child called Dante, born into a strictly traditional family, must somehow become aware of a dual heritage, or of one which has absorbed both the inner and outer aspects of its surroundings. Shortly before his death, Arnaldo Dante Momigliano wrote an affectionate memoir about his family home and its Orthodox character. The domestic routine was governed by Jewish ritual requirements. This traditional Jewish family, living in some isolation in Caraglio, came to the attention of anti-Semites; one text written in 1938 and attacking the Jewish dietary laws, commented concerning ritual slaughter that 'this cruel practice had now fallen into disuse among Italian Jews, the only exception being a certain "rich Italian Jew in Caraglio"'.

Momigliano held professorships in Rome, Turin (he shared its atmosphere with Primo Levi), Pisa, London, and Chicago; and his dominant influence left its impact in all these places of learning. By the time he was twenty-five, he already had a reputation in three distinct fields of ancient history; and his work in the area of Roman history invites comparison with that of Eugen Taeubler, one of the great Jewish scholars of our time. On our way into the future, we always need the historians and the roots they give us in a past which has anticipated most of the situations in which we find ourselves. Momigliano was an authority on the Second Temple period and on the Maccabees, eras of particular significance to the Jewish community living in Israel as well as in the Diaspora.

In his own life, too, he placed Jewish life into the framework of Europe, and particularly into the Italian scene. Pagan, Jewish, and Christian (read Greek, Jewish and Roman, out of which Christianity had emerged), he characterized in three major works between 1930 and 1934. There was his book on the Maccabees; on the emperor Claudius; and his works on Philip of Macedon and on Judea between 63 BC and 40 CE. This is the last paragraph of his work on the Maccabees:

> One may legitimately conclude that inasmuch as the history of the Maccabees is the history of religious and moral life, it is continued in the history of their own tradition ... and in our attempt to make a critical study of the Maccabeen tradition and bearing in mind the spiritual force it established, we prolong that history.[9]

We deal here with Momigliano's awareness that the Jews, throughout history, refused to assimilate to the outside world, and the questions this raised for him in his own time. Living in the fascist era, he moved into the fourth century and captured the image of freedom as it existed in Greek society. And, when Momigliano studies Josephus, he enters into the world of Jewish apologetics, where one's own identity is defended against the defamations which emanate from the outside world. Some defence against anti-Semitism and against the attempts to swallow up the Jew within the majority culture *has* to take place within the world of scholarship. There are battles which have to be fought here, particularly when the attitudes of the public are based upon the work of suborned scholars – one need only look at the treason of German scholarship during the Nazi period. This, too, is far less noticeable on the Italian scene. Scholars were often aware of the patronage of noble houses and of the Popes – but there was a sense of honour, again, which kept them from the actual crimes committed by European scholars who falsified the texts in order to attack the Jews. The integrity of the scholar finally depends upon individuals – there were always exceptions – and Momigliano emphasizes this pattern when he defends, for example, Josephus who was viewed as an assimilationalist by most Jewish historians. In fact Josephus, in his defence of the Jews had to modify his style to appeal to a Greek audience. Some of the literary works of German-Jewish self-defence during the Hitler period also sound too assimilatory, but were attempts to reach a populace which had already been brainwashed.

Momigliano does fault Josephus – but only because Josephus omits the religious dimensions of Jewish life in his defence of his people. In his own work, Momigliano achieved a masterly understanding of the symbiotic relationship between Judaism and Greco-Roman culture – often not acknowledged by the outside world – where one could see both absorption and rejection on both sides, and where both were changed.

Cultures can learn to live together, like individuals. Any forward moves on our part are taken in unison with the world in which we live. The paradigms of thought for which we search rely on multiple sources, and the academic area is not the least of these. Unless there are those who still search for the integrity of the texts upon which the next generation always builds we will falter in our quest. And a scholar of the depth and wisdom of Arnaldo Momigliano is indispensable among our Riders Towards the Dawn. In Momigliano one also finds the dimension of a religious faith – which is established out of the deepest possible understanding of Hebrew texts in their historical setting, and is of extreme importance to our understanding of this scholar. For Momigliano the word *emunah* in the rabbinic texts had an earlier meaning than the concept of faith found within Christianity; thus he restored to Jewish life a form of expression which links it to an earlier time and asserts an identity of the Jew, badly needed in an outside world where religion has faltered and lost its way.

In all the lands of Europe, there is no place where the golden glow of antiquity still shines out of the hills and valleys and out of the lives of its inhabitants as in Italy. 'Civilization' is a word which needs constant redefinition, and its component parts cannot be confined to one area of human life. Nevertheless, we cannot begin to think of Europe without realizing that the historical events associated with Italian landscape, art, literature, and the religious strivings which are the foundation of modern thought, even the anguish of the immediate past, must be assimilated into the future. More than one Jewish writer has written about 'Rome and Jerusalem'. The one city was the place of the secular law which bound the ancient world together under the *Pax Romana*. Jerusalem had a different law; the Revelation of Sinai. Yet they were people who reached towards one another. When the Maccabees had won their freedom in their fight against Syria, they were happy to establish a non-aggression pact with Rome. In darker times, when Christianity began to emerge, differences arose. But like was still calling to like. The history of the Holocaust has to bring back sad memories, but the appreciation of what the Italians did in terms of their Jews is a very real one. And the muted tragedy will also continue. One of the finest records of shared memory is probably the book and the film: 'In the gardens of the Finzi-Continis'. At the tragic end of the film, a voice is heard; the cantor, chanting the prayers; the last one – *El mole rachamim!* Sometimes, history is connected with seamless patterns which unite all of Europe. The cantor in the film was Estrongo Nachama, the cantor of East and West Berlin, from a Sephardi background. He had a noble voice, and that was a noble song. That sad nobility, too, is Italy, which will again move from sadness to joy.

NOTES

1. In A. Stille, *Benevolence and betrayal: five Italian families under Fascism* (London, Jonathan Cape, 1992), p. 231.
2. J. Steinberg, *All or nothing*, p. 11, citing Primo Levi's, *Se quest e un uomo la tregua* (Turin, 1963), p. 103.
3. A. Rudolf, *At an uncertain hour: Primo Levi's war against oblivion* (Menard Press, London, 1990), p. 2.
4. Gabriel Motola in 'Primo Levi: his life and death', *European Judaism*, vol. 41, p. 42.
5. Ibid., p. 43.
6. From P. Levi, *Collected poems*.
7. P. Levi, in *Gardens and ghettos*, the art of Jewish life in Italy, catalogue for exhibition, ed. V. B. Mann (New York, 1989).
8. *International Herald Tribune*, 7–8 November 1992, p. 2.
9. *A Momigliano Prime linee di storia della tradizione maccabaica* (Rome, 1930), p. 5.

# [ 6 ]

# ISRAEL

WHERE JOY AND ANGUISH MEET

I T is difficult to come to terms with Israel if one lives outside the land; it is not a problem if one has settled there – which seems to prove that existence precedes essence. For many Jews, Israel is still the paradigm of Jewish life. It is the ancient dream recognized in the prayers of centuries; and it seemed to be the escape from a Europe devastated by the Holocaust. Jews have always been in the Holy Land, even if there were long stretches when it was no more than a statutory presence, a maintenance of the old right by Jews who came to pray and to die there, accepting all kinds of restriction as long as they could gaze upon the holy walls of Jerusalem. There is the mistaken notion that Jews only arrived after the Holocaust, which ignores the whole history of the Zionist movement. There is also some acceptance of the glib assertion that 'Zionism is racism', once incorporated into the resolutions of UNO, then removed.

One of the major problems of understanding Israel is that it is viewed almost exclusively within the realm of politics. In earlier times, the world marvelled at the social experiments of the kibbutz, or saw the return of the Jew through the eyes of Orthodox Christians, as a basic stage of the coming of the Messiah. Now, there are many in the non-Jewish world (and in the Jewish world as well), who concentrate upon the mistakes of Israeli politicians in handling the relationship between the Jewish state and the Palestinians.

The dreams and hopes of the early period were too high: Israel was not the golden place where a truly ethical society was established, where those who had been persecuted would never persecute others. The trauma of the Holocaust, xenophobia, paranoid thinking influenced the actions of Israeli politicians; 'just because we are paranoid doesn't mean that they are not out to get us' is a sad joke which became reality. Israel is still important as a land of refuge for Russian Jews, Jews from Ethiopia and various Arab countries; but the outside world sees this as an infringement upon Palestinian rights. An enormous amount of support flows to Israel from the outside Jewish community; in political terms this is a new provocation against its neighbours. While much of Israel's economic support, particularly from the USA, is indeed political and is tied to conditions which relate to possible solutions for the 'Middle East problem', Jews all over the world are also deeply concerned, and show their concern, with the poverty which exists in Israel, a state which spends most of its income on defence, and where social problems abound for the immigrants, whether they are Yemenite or Russian, for the Holocaust survivors, for the elderly Jews who came to die in their Holy Land.

Yet Israel has made some conciliatory gestures. The reality of Palestinian suffering demands an accommodation on the part of Israel. It also demands a rejection of populist leaders and the fanatical rabbis who support the extreme right. Often, the democratic and just structure of the State of Israel challenges the wrong decisions of politicians and generals. And the Arab community should keep in mind the genuine desire for peace and the deep compassion which exists at the core of the Jewish state: if it did not exist, there would be no hope.

What does Israel think about the outside world? Again, the endemic fears created by anti-Semitism over the centuries and by the Holocaust in our time is at the heart of the Israeli view of their near and far neighbours. There is the 'fortress mentality', and there is the often expressed 'Never Again' attitude which stereotypes the neighbour as the enemy. It is a fear which extends to every dimension of life: literature and the arts are not excluded from this. In December of 1991, Daniel Barenboim hoped to have the Israeli Symphony Orchestra perform music by Richard Wagner. The public reaction was so negative that the proposal was dropped. Many Germans, particularly Christian clergy, come to Israel in acts of reconciliation; a hard task. The Israeli attitude was most clearly expressed when the President of Israel, Chaim Herzog, came to Germany in 1987 as the first President of that state to visit Germany. Standing at the memorial site of the former Bergen Belsen concentration camp, he said:

My pain is with me forever. I do not bring forgiveness with me, nor forgetfulness. The only ones who can forgive are the dead. The living have no right to forgive. Thus I will surely remember, with all my heart . . .

The young people, in particular, often want to avoid special knowledge of the Holocaust. They acquire it, by osmosis, through the social and political structures, through the presence of Yad Vashem, the Holocaust Memorial Institute in Jerusalem, kibbutzim named Yad Mordecai or Lochame ha-ghettaot founded by survivors and dedicated to the task of remembering. There is the language itself and the literature; and there is a continuing discussion, inside and outside of Israel, which insists upon linking the creation of the State of Israel with the Holocaust itself. It is an almost obscene thought, an attempt to create a 'silver lining' around that dark cloud of destruction. Often, it is built upon heavy traditional thinking which cannot come to terms with an omnipotent Deity who permitted the Holocaust. There must have been a reason humans can discern – and the only reason they could see was the emergence of the State of Israel. To declare that Israeli life is built upon the sacrifice of six million dead is still a betrayal. The attempt, within Israel, to ignore the past and the *galut*, the Diaspora, is related to this. *Sh'lilat ha-galut* – 'Negating the outer world of exile' – is a negation of Jewish life because it also cuts off that generation from its parental roots, the rich Jewish life of the Diaspora which is needed for the stability and future of Jewish identity in the land of Israel.

For that reason, it is important to look at Jewish Israeli writers, in order to see how they came to terms with the Holocaust and gained a certain understanding of the past upon which to build their present-day life. The philosophers, the poets, the theologians – perhaps even the politicians – can help us to draw an accurate picture of the Israeli approach to the Holocaust and the way to live after it and separate oneself from it.

The philosopher Emil Fackenheim was born in Germany, where he was ordained a Progressive rabbi in the Berlin school at the time of the Holocaust. His main area of teaching was in North America – Canada and the United States – as well as Europe. Now he has made *aliyah* (settled in Israel) and has placed Israel centrally in his thinking in an almost obsessive manner. The teacher of the 614th Mitzvah: 'The Jew is commanded to survive the Holocaust – that is the revelation of Auschwitz' links Israel and the *Shoah*:

The Midrash has it that when the Egyptians pursued and the Dead Sea split, the people hesitated, until Nachshon the son of Amminadav jumped into the waves. Not accidentally are Israelis fond of naming their sons Nachshon, for they have learned the stern truth that there are no miracles without human action. The Jewish people itself became a modern Nach-shon when it responded to the Nazi Holocaust not with despair or escapism, but with the founding of a Jewish state – the modern Nachshon had not time to wait for miracles. He had only two choices. One was to die. The other was to jump into the waves, not knowing whether the sea would split and, if not, whether he would have strength enough to swim through the raging waters, if necessary, alone.[1]

The myth of Israel which has become part of Israeli civil religion perhaps turned Emil's judgement. But he does live in Israel; I do not. Most of his books, over the past years, have instructed at least two generations of the Diaspora in the creative life which must be lived in a world torn apart by the evil of the Holocaust which still swirls about us in the poisoned atmosphere of Europe and the other continents. One of the recurring themes in the Fackenheim books is the concept of *tikkun*, of rebuilding the world in partnership with God: 'To mend the world', as one of his books is named. Emil Fackenheim served his apprenticeship in the concentration camp Sachsenhausen. His own life as well as his work is his testimony. He came to Israel recently when it was under siege. After his retirement as a professor of philosophy, he began to teach at the Hebrew University in Jerusalem; and he has made new disciples for himself. His celebration of Israel moves into areas where I cannot follow; but I must respect him. I think of Jehuda Halevi and his Zionist passion which took him out of a golden age of Jewish creativity in Spain to the land of Israel, to a concept of Jewish uniqueness as a people who could be prophets. *Eretz Yisrael* is fortunate to have Emil Fackenheim as its advocate.

Israel has great scholars who were born and nurtured in the land. As a new nation, it also has many who came to it from Europe and brought the traditions of the Diaspora with them. Emil Fackenheim is one of them. In the field of literature, there is a vast array of great writers who belong to that category. I turn to those teachers and poet/prophets who have taught me most and who, as it happens, can be viewed as comrades to the poets we encountered in the previous section. Paul Celan, Nelly Sachs, and Erich Fried speak the same language as Aharon Appelfeld, Dan Pagis, and Yehuda Amichai; and this is not surprising. Amichai was born in Wurzburg and was 13-years-old when his family moved to Israel. Nevertheless, the German language and European culture are very much present in his texts. Dan Pagis came from the Bukovina, as did Paul Celan, and arrived in Israel after several years in a concentration camp. Aharon Appelfeld was also part of that vast group of Jewish thinkers and writers who came from Bukovina, one of the 'wise men' of that centre of Jewish creativity. All, then, are a continuation of the European poets who represent European thought clarified by the experience of Israel – and changed.

Paul Celan had been the neighbour of Appelfeld in Czernowitz, although it was in the transit camp that Appelfeld came to know him better. Celan was captured, but Aharon escaped . . . into the forest.

The child learned that the human environment contained death and danger; humans were to be avoided. In time, he made contact with those 'beyond the pale', the horse-thieves, prostitutes, farmers forced off the land and drifting around the edges of the land. The war came to an end. His wanderings were continued: to Yugoslavia and then, in 1946, to Israel.

In a sense, Aharon stayed an outsider, particularly when it came to an evaluation of the *Shoah*, the Holocaust. At that point, Aharon would not talk much about it. It was typical of his generation, of the new arrivals, to stay quiet and to feel somewhat ashamed. As he points out, in Israel there were other models, heroic models, the *Palmach*, the *Haganah*, and individual heroes praised as much as European Jewry was condemned. 'They went like sheep to the slaughter'. But Aharon's generation did not stay 'shamed' forever. As he pointed out, the two million Europeans who came, established themselves in Israel, fought for Israel, in fact became its new heroes! Nevertheless Aharon is writing of victims, not heroes. It is sometimes felt that victims should be 'nice'; their surviving relatives, and the world, demand it. In Aharon's books, they are certainly not nice; and this makes his work stronger, more honest, more of a true requiem.

Aharon Appelfeld also spent two years in the opposite forest, in Harvard. And he is still sifting through that experience, bemused: 'Most of them were Jewish – and they were so un-Jewish!'

The forest . . . Harvard . . . the desert. In Israel, Aharon Appelfeld teaches Jewish literature, a course moving from Heine to Kafka but also to the modern Americans: Roth, Malamud, Singer, Elie Wiesel.

Arguably among the great writers of Israeli fiction and poetry, he brings the experience of Europe, of the camps and the forest, of good and evil; and he applies this to his function in life. As a teacher, as a friend.

The life is here, not necessarily the writing. When we read the novels, we come back into a world which is clearly the world of the Holocaust; but it is concealed rather than revealed by his language. Appelfeld in Israel is less and far more than he was in Europe. He remains a stranger; he pushes against the world he creates in a desperate effort to get out of that world. The novel *Badenheim 1939* may give us a clear sequence of events which seem familiar, which bring us to the quiet horror of a place where nothing happens but one can see all that will happen – the goldfish bowl with its trapped fish remains a central symbol in this text in which Jewish life is mirrored.

The plot is quite simple. The Jews have come to a resort which they often frequented, and try to pretend that everything is normal. Years ago, I passed through such a resort at the edge of the Black Forest in Germany. Everything looked orderly and beautiful. The tulips stood there in military precision; the ducks in the pond kept in formation; and we were stopped by the police because we dared drive our car between 12 and 3 p.m., 'a time of rest for guests'. Once, the town had been almost a Jewish resort; and one of the waiters in the *Kursaal* pointed out to me the former 'Jewish' and 'kosher' hotels. 'There are no Jews here, any more,' he said. At the end of Badenheim, the one Jew who had refused to go with them is brought to the train station by two policemen, and the rest placidly accept this. Things change about them, danger becomes an aspect of their life, the very air seems to alter – and all this is ignored or absorbed. The reader wants to cry out at the blindness, wants to enter into the book and shake these doomed Jews awake – but they live in a language and world that we cannot enter. They were not protected or informed, for there were set patterns to which they had to conform. And they did not turn to each other as Jews to gain strength: their Jewishness had already been defined as their misfortune. Pappenheim, in some ways a leader, can only guess that the filthy train awaiting them is a good sign – it must mean that they will not be travelling a long distance! Appelfeld's novel is more frightening, more disturbing, because we are permitted, indeed commanded, to put all horror into the text which is only hinted at, a dark secret for which we know that answer.

Aharon Appelfeld returns to the theme in various ways. There is also the survivor, *The immortal Bartfuss*, who is isolated and alone in the world after the Holocaust.

Bartfuss represents the survivor who internalizes the events of his life. Even when he talks, he remains a silent witness.

A writer always lives in exile, occupying a no-man's-land between the outer and inner landscape, carrying a passport not recognized by those who view this other world as 'imaginary', unattainable. A writer who is physically in exile, attempting a new language, stamped by the horror and beauty of the past, is permanently alienated. The poets and novelists are colporteurs of a special Bible which only rarely exercises its authority upon the reader who will not let go of the certainties of his own language and of the limitations to which imagination is exposed in one's 'real world'. The writers we are encountering have moved from one language to another, from one landscape to another. In Israel, they are enjoined to create a new and vital culture; and the images of the past which accompany them carry guilt and angst along with them. Nevertheless, they succeed in the task they set themselves – or which their society demands from them – and they can carry it beyond boundaries, even into the future.

Dan Pagis is another key writer. In an intriguing story, the author is permitted to visit the Elysian Fields. He is shown around the place by the club secretary and observes Byron, Tennyson, and other notables at play. Then a thought occurs to him: 'How did you become club secretary?' he asks his guide. 'Which notable poet are you?' 'No-one important', is the reply. 'I only wrote one noteworthy line of poetry, and that gave me the job'. The line was 'a rose-red city, half as old as time'.[2] It is a comforting thought to aspiring writers that one moment of perfection can bring fulfilment.

This is an unfair introduction to Dan Pagis and his substantial writings. Yet there is one short poem by him, reprinted many times, in which he says more about the Holocaust than almost any other writer:

> here in this carloaq
> I eve
> with abel my son
> if you can see my other son
> cain son of man
> tell him I
>
> 'Written in pencil
> in the sealed railway car'

An unending silence stretches around that sentence, and all the anguish of the world reverberates in it. The whole breakdown of the human family, the introduction of the crime of murder into the world, and the mother still reaching out for that son: the sparseness of the poem encompasses all of this and more. The images of the Holocaust are present in the railway car and in the sudden death; but there is no framework of history, of time, even of standard poetic forms. If there had only been this poem by Dan Pagis, he would not be forgotten.

Dan Pagis was born in Radantz, Bukovina, in 1930. By the time he was a teenage boy, he had been swallowed up by the Nazi machine and spent several years in a concentration camp. He survived, and went to Israel to go through similar experiences as Aharon Appelfeld: learning Hebrew, learning to live in another world, learning how to live with his past. Dan

Pagis became an educator and scholar, on a way which led through a teacher's job in a primary school (in Kibbutz *Gat*) and which eventually brought him to the Hebrew University in Jerusalem, where he taught until his death. It is strange to think of these men and women from Bukovina who mastered the language which became their enemy and who wrote epitaphs for a broken culture which fell into evil – and who could then achieve the mastery of Hebrew which characterizes Appelfeld, Dan Pagis, and Yehuda Amichai.

Dan Pagis entered the Hebrew language in a very special way: he became the scholar, the examiner of the text through the centuries, specializing in medieval Hebrew.

The sparseness of his poems can communicate the experience of the Holocaust and of the Jewish people in history, even if this is private memory, linked to the texts in Genesis of human beginnings explored again, in a poem called 'Autobiography':

> I died with the first blow and was buried
> among the rocks of the field.
> The raven taught my parents
> what to do with me.
>
> If my family is famous,
> not a little of the credit goes to me.
> My brother invented murder,
> my parents invented grief,
> I invented silence.
>
> When Cain began to multiply on the face of the earth,
> I began to multiply in the belly of the earth,
> and my strength has long been greater than his.
> His legions desert him and go over to me,
> and even this is only half a revenge.

It is not surprising that Cain and Abel have been central to so many Jewish texts, for the Jews see themselves hunted by their brothers; Erich Fried and Dan Pagis here explore the same area. In Fried, Cain and Abel exchanged roles. Dan Pagis seeks self-effacement in the paradigm of the murdered brother who even in death finds no individuality. The legions who join him are not only those murdered in the camps, but those who have died since time began.

All right, gentlemen who cry blue murder as always,
nagging miracle makers,
quiet!
Everything will be returned to its place,
paragraph after paragraph.
The scream back into the throat.
The gold teeth back to the gums.
The terror.
The smoke back to the chimney and further on and inside
back to the hollow of the bones,
and already you will be covered with skin and sinews and you
will live,
look, you will have your lives back,
sit in the living room, read the evening paper.
Here you are. Nothing is too late.
As to the yellow star:
it will be torn from your chest
immediately
and will emigrate
to the sky.

'Draft of reparations agreement'

The text can be set alongside Ezekiel's vision of the valley of bones, but Pagis has distanced himself from the visionary prophet who promises a future. Within Israeli thought, 'reparations' was always a dirty word, particularly since Israel was aware that the flood of German money was important in establishing and defending a new home. Nothing was forgotten or forgiven. Pagis has to fight against the language of today, in the same manner as Aharon Appelfeld. 'Reparations' is a nonsense word, as the text makes clear, particularly in the image of 'paragraph after paragraph' – on paper, things can be made good again (*wiedergutmachung*). And the reel of the film, after it has already gone to the very end of the story, with the concentration camps hastily covered up, can be run in reverse. Those who watch will see something as terrifying as what they witnessed the first time: smoke back into chimney into bodies . . . gold teeth back into the gums – skin covering bones. Rebirth is as terrifying as death; that is why, according to the rabbis, an angel places a finger upon the mouth of a new-born child (that little indentation upon the lips) so that it will have no memory of past lives lived.

The Holocaust cannot be taken out of the bones of our people and buried in a history book.

Perhaps we expect more in a book of poetry where we demand much – too much – from those who have escaped out of a whirlwind and are now condemned to be witnesses. Pagis is so much the poet of the land of Israel, refashioning the language, digging down to its roots, struggling against the insufficiency of any language. His fight against chaos was very much part of a vision where the experienced past could not be exorcised nor excised from his mind or from his world: ahead of him, he saw the end of creation, and behind him, a world had already ended. Not only was there the memory of the concentration camps from which he had escaped, but also the guilt for *having* escaped! We have seen this as an aspect of life in an Israel built upon the memories of the Holocaust, hurried into life by that very darkness. The new generation, and the vast group of Sephardi Jews coming out of Arab countries, did not have as complicated a memory or as clear a vision of the Holocaust as the Jews of Europe: Appelfeld, Pagis, and Yehuda Amichai differ from the poets born in Israel, from the poets who came before the Nazi period. Yet, precisely for that reason, those writers carried the specified burden from the past into the future. Pagis knows he is different from those who did not survive, who surround him as reverers with whom he shares something, but not everything.

One has to let go of the past, and one has to affirm the future, or at least the human right to hope for a future whatever the past has held. Dan Pagis' poems do not always deal directly with the Holocaust; many celebrate life. Our generation seems cursed to sift through the bones, to read the runes, and to find more death than life, but the poets also want us to live. Beyond the tragic apocalyptic vision of Dan Pagis stands a comforter who affirms life. Poems can fail us; but they are still clues to life in a new land, after the escape from darkness.

Pagis was an Israeli scholar and teacher, and a master of language. He was also a child of Europe, bringing the *Bukovina* along with him across his shoulders; he was one of the remembrancers.

In speaking of Jewish life after the Holocaust, we must begin with the recognition that this is to some extent the definition of Israel. The State only came into being after the end of World War II. If there is a strain of paranoia in those living within that beleaguered land, this could be normal: Jews living among Jews, as a majority rather than minority, armed to the teeth and ready to repel any attack by near or distant neighbours. This self-awareness expresses itself in every aspect of Jewish life and culture and is, of course, reflected in its literature. The European poets, who came out of the time of the Holocaust or as the next generation, are one aspect of the land of Israel, that mother stretching out her arms to her children living in exile, telling them to come home. Even if there are troubles to be faced, is it not better to be surrounded by family? Yet the European poets, who are part of that family chorus, bring the memory of the darkness into the family house. A Jew remembers. And if that member of the Jewish family is a poet, the Holocaust is certain to break through his lines in a way that is hidden or open.

Yehuda Amichai had the same problem of language as the other poets we had met. Perhaps more. Coming from Würzburg, in the heart of Bavaria, he had not only learned the language of those who destroyed him, but he had grown up in a landscape of rare beauty which had folded around the child even when the neighbours turned ugly. Traditional patterns of faith and practice had secured his Jewish identity for him, but as a 12-year-old child, fleeing from Germany to Palestine (in 1936), he had discovered much of the darkness which exists in the soul of those around and in oneself. His pattern of conformity to the tradition did not change initially – he moved from an Orthodox school in Würzburg to an Orthodox school in Jerusalem. He lived in a world at war. He served in the Jewish Brigade and then in the *Palmach* (in 1948). And he discovered that he was a poet.

There were greater opportunities to come to terms with language. Arabic was spoken around him; English became part of his education, opening his mind to new ways of writing and thinking. When he had acquired Hebrew, he could feel freer to change it and move it towards new directions in his poetry. He was a poet of the 1950s and 1960s – and for every decade, of course – experiencing a life in Israel that could be a life of ideals, but also of disappointments. Old, traditional patterns of Jewish writings and of Jewish life also emerged: he could write of Jerusalem, or become a voyager – not quite, but another Jewish 'Benjamin of Tudela'. He could look back on the road from Germany to Israel, he could examine those who travelled alongside him, and could thus paint a sometimes highly critical picture of our century of brutality in which much beauty could still be found. Like Pagis, Amichai also felt at home in the groves of Academe. He was visiting professor and poet-in-residence at many American universities; and, as a poet, he received more recognition than many of his colleagues, particularly, an ironic twist, in the world of the *galut*. However, he has also been honoured in Israel.

Amichai wants to be secure in his land, where he can celebrate the traditions, where the harvest festivals unite one with the soil:

And that's the way to remember this land,
In which childhoods are far away from people
Like times before the destruction of the Temple.

Hebrew means more to him than the language of his childhood in Germany.
And still its problems plague him. The landscape means much to him,
and he can celebrate every stone and hill. He uses Hebrew in subtle
ways; he can be gently sarcastic and wickedly sensuous. Yet he cries
out at:

This tired language
Blinded, it lurches from mouth to mouth,
The language which described God and the Miracles,
Says:
Motor car, bomb, God.[3]

There is a displacement here, a movement from childhood scenes to another
reality. Once, in a German and then Palestinian Jewish school, he encountered the tradition which still fills the poetry, but much of it is the impending
Holocaust; some of it was confronted when he fought the Germans, and
more when he had to fight the Arabs. The cruelty of one war pressed down
other cruelties of other times.

The question of God abandoning His children is born out of the poisoned
atmosphere left us after the Holocaust; and yet, Amichai's questions about
God seem to belong more to the particular period in which he lives. There
is again the recognition of the landscape in which Amichai lives, but his
writing is filled with a sad and terrible beauty:

God's fate
Is now
The fate of trees rocks sun and moon,
The ones they stopped worshipping
When they began to believe in God.

But He's forced to remain with us
As are the trees, as are the rocks
sun moon and stars.

'God's fate'

Amichai is part of that land where the rocks were worshipped, are perhaps worshipped still where Israelis are unwilling to swap them for peace:

> It's sad
> To be the Mayor of Jerusalem
> It is terrible
> How can any man be the mayor of a city like that?
>
> What can he do with her?
> He will build, and build, and build.
>
> And at night
> The stones of the hills round about
> Will crawl down
> Towards the stone houses,
> Likes wolves coming
> To howl at the dogs
> Who have become men's slaves.

'Mayor'

The land is still alive, and Amichai knows this; but he has doubts about the vitality of God in a land where the language is no longer holy, where a sacred and maimed people no longer want to remember, and where warfare often seems the most viable option. And yet, of all the poets in that land who speak to the Diaspora, Yehuda Amichai seems to me the rare poet who has moved beyond the darkness and into love, and who can take us along with him. He does not always proclaim joy, but he points towards a task, as in 'To summon witnesses':

> When did I last weep?
> The time has come to summon witnesses.
> Of those who last saw me weep
> Some are dead.
>
> I wash my eyes with a lot of water
> So as to see the world once more
> Through the wet and the hurt
>
> I must find witnesses.

Amichai is his own witness, and speaks through a life where the memory and knowledge of the Diaspora is mediated through his life as an Israeli. Würzburg is part of his language – a Hebrew enriched by the patterns of Europe. And the events of the Holocaust are also an invisible presence. His great novel *Not of this time, not of this place* (New York, 1967) with its sense of irony and feeling of displacements, brings these parts of his life together with its awareness of the destruction which befell the Jews of Europe. The novel is set into the landscapes of Bavaria and of Israel: its structure of chapters alternating between the first and third person show Yehuda Amichai in this movement of the Jew who is always marked, branded, by the past experience of Europe – and who achieves his identity in Israel. Amichai is a Jew of our time.

We demand of our poets that they give consistency to our vision; they are the guilty conscience of our time. In Israel, where happiness covers the unhappiness and guilt of being inheritors of darkness, it is more important to proclaim guilt. In this manner, the memorizing of those who died in the camps has been built into the institutions and public awareness of that land. We can only acknowledge our awareness of a special way in which Jewish life has come to terms – imperfectly – with the caesura which cut apart the continuity of Jewish writers in that land, these prophets of our time who give us guidance.

Abba Kovner was more than a poet and novelist (he won the Israel Prize in Literature in 1970): he was one of the leaders of the Jewish community in its most testing hour. Born in Sebastopol in 1918, he grew up in Vilna, Lithuania, where he took command of the United Partisan Organization after the invasion of the Nazis. The fate of every Jew, and of every Jewish community is unique, each has its own story to tell. In Lithuania, where the Nazis moved closer to the 'Final Solution', most of the killing of the Jews was done by the Lithuanians themselves, who joyfully participated in the Nazi plan to rid their land of Jews. Whatever one might want to say about them, the Lithuanians were the victims of a system which had removed all restrictions upon the dark aspects of their behaviour. Yet Abba Kovner did not only see evil around himself. He had come to Vilna as an 8-year-old boy who immersed himself in his Jewish studies, a left-wing Jewish ideology, and learned at an early age to assert his poetic abilities. But he was sheltered in a Dominican convent when war started, as is reflected in a major poetical work of his, 'My little sister'. He became a leader of the resistance in the Vilna ghetto. One of the few to survive, he fled into the forests and led a group of Jewish partisans there. After the war he organized the movement of illegal Jewish immigrants to Palestine and, after imprisonment by the

British in Cairo, settled in Israel in time to fight for his new land in its War of Independence.

All of these experiences become part of his poetry and prose: he has said 'When I write, I am like a man praying'. His poems are prayers, a threnody, in which we hear echoes of the Book of Lamentations:

> How mourn a city
> whose people are dead and whose dead are alive
> in the heart.[4]

From a mass grave at Ponar, a half-dead, half-crazed girl had fled to bear witness to a total destruction which the world had not known previously. All of Kovner's life (he died in 1988) was filled with the encounter with that ghost, a little sister of his people who accompanied him throughout his life. The poems echo the terrible pain which the Nazis inflicted upon the soul of the young partisan leader who knew that, by the Nazi doctrine of collective responsibility, each act of defiance, and each escape during the black days of the Vilna Ghetto's destruction, was punished a hundred-fold. The choices he had to make in those days should not have been forced upon a young man, or, indeed, any human being. Abba Kovner's Jewish faith, with its stress upon the goodness of human beings, was tested against the utter evil of those who persecuted him in Lithuania and, later, in the difficult situation of fighting against those who were basically good and had helped crush the Nazis – the British – but who now stood between his comrades and his own attempts and the land of promise to which he was determined to lead his people.

We can and must see Kovner as a poet of his time, speaking out of the experience of Europe, out of the life of Israel. If silence is the ultimate tribute to the world, then one can sense the silence beyond his words, the teaching that the incomprehensible must be assimilated together with all that can and must be remembered. And Kovner also remembers the compassion of the nuns who give shelter, whose Christian faith reaches out to Jewish sufferers:

> Night after night
> the Sisters breathe hard in their beds
> as if raised on a ladder.
> Their bodies shake.
> And on this night, too, heavy with longing,
> the gowns on their skins are burning.

In this high place,
quiet as a tree alone,
he stands.
And light of the mother and the father
trickles down from his face.

Then his bright body breaks out
of a golden frame.
Lord! He comes down
on a ladder of thorns.
His blood is not running.

He swings
in his thin limbs.

The anguish and suffering of the Christian mystery which Kovner encountered in the convent hiding place come to the foreground here, intertwined with the suffering of his people. If we could see with Abba Kovner's eyes, survey all that Israel has lost, all he saw in Vilna and in the forest, and then go into the Judean hills with him and to the sands of a land again drenched with the blood of his people, we might begin to understand his outcry.

Looking for other voices out of that vast chorus of Israeli writers, one is tempted to stay with those who brought the experience of the Holocaust with them and served as focal points between Diaspora and Eretz. But some of the most sensitive poets of Israel are the next generation, those who respond to the past. Uri Greenberg (1896–1982) and Natan Alterman (1910–1970) moved back and forth from the Diaspora to Palestine. Greenberg edited a Yiddish newspaper in Warsaw from 1937 to 1939; and Alterman studied in France between 1928 and 1932.

Greenberg was the master of Yiddish, one of the great voices and creative artists of a European culture which brought him into contact with many of its writers; but he abandoned all this once he had established himself in Israel, and became a major influence in Hebrew literature. He had known warfare and slaughter in World War I; had seen his fellow Jews suffer long before the Holocaust and had absorbed this into his writings. His experience made him the militant Jew who joined the Revisionists and the Irgun in Palestine; the enraged lion who laments for his family could become a total challenge to the outside world. His 'The streets of the river' is considered one of the greatest products of the literature in which the

Holocaust is confronted. Here a prose translation brings us into an imagery and content which stands between traditional and modern poetry:

Like Abraham and Sarah by the terebinths of Mamre
before the precious tidings,
and like David and Bethsheba, in the king's palace,
in the tenderness of their first night –
my martyred father and mother rise in the West over the sea
with all the aureoles of God upon them.
Weighed down by their beauty they sink, slowly.
Above their heads flows the mighty ocean,
beneath it is their deep home.

This home has no walls on any side,
it is built water within water.
The drowned of Israel come swimming from all the corners of the sea,
each with a star in its mouth.
And what they speak of there, the poem does not know;
only they know who are in the sea.

Greenberg had lost so many relatives – like so many others that his lament for the people could and did become very personal. Solidly rooted in the tradition, he brought the ancient and present heritage of the land to bear upon an event which could not be comprehended, but had to be experienced in grief. When one reflects upon his combatative life, the poetry becomes part of a passionate whole which affirms his people.

Natan Alterman was just as important as Greenberg in the next generation. He came to Tel Aviv at the age of fifteen, in 1925. He brought a talent to his work which made him one of the most influential poets of his time, in the 'imagist' mould. There was a satiric humour in his work which also marked him as a rare, brilliant messenger who could challenge all the pretensions he saw around him. Perhaps his French training as agronomist and engineer gave him roots within the new Jewish society emerging in Palestine. He was of that world, challenging in his newspaper columns, writing 'subversive' texts banned by the British, finally centring upon the tensions of his time between the polarities of life and death which inevitably brought him to the Holocaust. In 'The joys of the poor,' considered one of the great modern creations of Israeli literature, he touched upon the darkness of his time; but in oblique ways. He was, in the end, more concerned with affirming life, giving hope – and criticizing mercilessly! His critique of Israeli politicians and Zionism was one of his lasting contributions to Israel, but he was just as harsh in condemning the Jews in the Diaspora for their failures.

Alterman felt that the Jews in the Diaspora were too weak and too accommodating. European Jewry, as well as their relatives in Israel, blocked out the memory of the suffering and the shame; their cowardice, their foolishness in not recognizing the nature of the Nazi evil, their lack of leadership. In the end, Alterman felt that the greatest Jewish sin, in Israel as in Europe, was their attempt to forget; for forgetting is collaboration with evil. Israel Ben Josef points to those sections of 'The joys of the poor' where Alterman challenges the Jews of the Holocaust period:

> Much of Alterman's most challenging work appeared in his *The seventh column* which challenged the issues of the day, including Jewish responses to the Holocaust. And one still goes back to 'The joys of the poor', where the critique is opaque and unspecific, but can be found and related to the experience of the darkness and where the interpretation becomes part of the reading experience. There is the section 'ger ba la-ir' (a stranger comes to the city) which Ruth Finer Mintz in her translation calls 'A convert' – one who has been converted from the religion of life to the religion of death:

> > I will bring you the very last crust.
> > Your name I shall call out, the first.
> > The water jug to your broken mouth I guide,
> > I the elder, I who provide.
> >
> > For, behold, the living shall not save the living.
> > To cover you with love like water, I come.
> > It is strange to my brothers, this love unforgiving,
> > Revealed like the rapine at noon.
> >
> > And By God you shall swear to me
> > To draw strength from catastrophe,
> > To cry out as it reaches your soul,
> > To me the last one of all.[5]

The soul of Israeli life cannot be constructed with scattered fragments of poetry. Yet it is there, in the reaching beyond words, that something appears which is more than a political, sociological, or psychological appraisal of the Israeli community and its relationship to the Holocaust. The intensive prophecies of the poets are augmented by the everyday experience of the journalists who do not have that specialized gift of seeing beyond the veil, but strive to make sense of the world within Israeli life. Our last 'witness' is such a person: the journalist Uri Avneri.

When Uri Avneri met publicly with Yasser Arafat in July 1982, he was considered a traitor by many Israelis who had already viewed his strivings for peace and for accommodation with the Arabs with the deepest suspicion. Yet his life, curiously resembling that of the poets we have discussed, was not dissimilar to theirs. He was born in Beckum, Westphalia, in 1923, and came to Palestine in 1933. There, he became a member of the Irgun in 1938, fought as a member of the *Haganah* in 1948, and was wounded in that year. In 1950 he became the publisher and chief editor of *Haolam Hazeh* ('This World'), an active member of various peace organizations, a member of the *Knesset* for some years and, always, a Socratic gadfly challenging Israel's conscience. He retired from *Haolam Hazeh* in 1990 and works as an independent journalist. His most recent book published outside Israel is *Wir tragen das Nessos Gewand: Israel und der frieden im Nahen Osten*[5] ('We wear the Nessus Garment: Israel and the peace in the Near East') which sums up his basic peace concerns. The 'Nessus Garment' goes back to the Greek tale where the centaur Nessus gives Hercules a magic shirt drenched, supposedly, with a love-potion but actually with a deadly poison; it is impossible to take off the shirt. Avneri defines it as the areas annexed by Israel: the Golan Heights, Gaza, and the West Bank – and desperately wants Israel to trade this territory for peace. There are negative reactions to his efforts; it is not wholly unrelated to the shadow of the Holocaust which hangs over the land. Avneri is almost isolated these days. What he has to say is unpopular, unacceptable. As he says:

In Israel, it is very difficult 'to dance with wolves'. Every true confrontation with the Palestinians would bring up questions which would be too painful. Was Zionism only a movement to attain freedom? Have Jewish needs and the Holocaust rendered us blind to the sufferings of other peoples? Is our right to *Eretz Yisrael* absolute and exclusive?[6]

The questions already reveal what the answers of the Israeli community would be. Even those who would say 'Let us make a new beginning' do not want to face the (apparently) insoluble problems of the past, though we could argue that Avneri is as intractable as the others. At least he brings the problems into the open.

In 1986, when Elie Wiesel won the Nobel Peace Prize, Uri Avneri professed himself to be highly outraged by this. In an open letter to Wiesel he indicated that he was amazed:

> I was surprised because I see no real connection between peace in this unhappy world of 1986 and your remarkable writings about the Holocaust.

Of course, adds Avneri, Wiesel was only an Israeli for a short time and then moved to New York where it is far easier to be a good Zionist and Jewish patriot! There, indicates Avneri, one can sit and think about the Holocaust rather than the exploitations and tortures of the present:

> I do agree: nothing in the present approaches the monstrousness of the Holocaust. It is therefore almost a profanity to compare the Holocaust with any other crime of this century. But neither you nor I nor the Nobel Committee are in the situation to call even one sacrificed victim back to life, or to undo a single deed among the horrors of the Holocaust.

Why, then, does Elie Wiesel not work against present evil? Grudgingly, Avneri admits that Wiesel has worked against the persecution of Indians in Nicaragua, spoken out for the *Bahai* in Iraq, for the Jews in Syria and particularly in the Soviet Union; he accounts all of this as nothing since Elie Wiesel has not taken up the cause of peace with the Palestinians. This is what has to be achieved.

Today, Avneri continues to be one of the few voices for peace left. It is not only hard to move constantly against the stream of public opinion; it is also difficult to maintain confidence and hope in the neighbour in a time when the land seems threatened and under siege. But Uri Avneri persists in his dreams despite the new problems of a changing society – the many Russians who come are on the whole committed to the radical left and feel a special pride in standing up and confronting the enemy.

Can we assess Israel's relationship to the Holocaust, and its possible teachings about how life should be lived now, through a gathering of poets and writers? Looking at the past, one is always confronted with the silent majority who have not expressed their feelings, their attitudes.

The poets, prophets and writers are often well in advance of their lands; but they are needed to give vision to their people. Israel is a very special land, in any event. Built on a vision which includes survival, it has generated its own impetus. The Holocaust is not a separate event here, to be studied in history classes or assessed in philosophy. It was part of the creation of the land, and the number of survivors who have helped to shape all aspects of the state is larger, in proportion, to those of any other community in the world. In the present we can see something of these attitudes which permeate the atmosphere and shape the very contours of the land. New communities placed into occupied areas defy common sense as well as the United Nations, but express a new determination to survive. And there are also some very specific ways in which the memory of the Holocaust is present here: in the institutional preservation of private and public commemoration.

Some of these institutions deserve a closer look:

## LOCHAMEI HAGETAOT

When I last visited Israel, I went to Lochamei Hagetaot, a museum for ghetto fighters, in the North of Israel, on the way towards Rosh Hanikrah, and found an impressive settlement created upon a former swamp which had been brought into rich and fruitful life. The kibbutz had been founded in April of 1948 on land purchased by the Jewish Agency in what had been mainly an Arab area. The nearby villages are still Arab, and the Jewish settlers are aware of the need to reach out towards each other. Just as another kibbutz, Yad Mordecai, carries the name of a ghetto leader (and a statue) as its centre, so Lochamei Hagetaot was founded by leaders of the uprising in Warsaw: Itzak Zukermann and Livia Lubetkin. The community is centred upon awareness of the Holocaust; here, as throughout Israel, the term *Shoah* is employed; a more fitting word than Holocaust, which does not encompass the full tragedy.

Each Holocaust museum has some unique aspects to it. In Lochamei Hagetaot it is the model of the Treblinka Camp, built, from memory, by Yossele Wianek who had been an inmate in that place of death. Together with Belzec and Sobibor, it was set up for one specific task which it performed for fourteen months: to kill Jews. Those who greet the visitors – and one must understand that it is not just the tourists from abroad who come here: this is a place of education for Israelis, too – are given details of the *Shoah* by survivors with a full knowledge of all the details. These still find it difficult to speak of that time; but they need to talk; it is one of the main reasons why the kibbutz was established. The new life was to overcome the old one; memories of the past had to be shared. It is so unlike Europe, where many want to run away from that dark knowledge. In Israel, it is acknowledged as part of life. It is bearable, because it is the past, in the *galut*, and they are in the present, in their own land. The second and third generation who come to Lochamei Hagetaot in order to be instructed do not come to condemn. The old statement 'We went like sheep to the slaughter' still exists where there is no knowledge; but the visitors who come to these museums acquire that knowledge. They do not feel that without the *Shoah* there might not have been the State of Israel, but they do accept that aspects of that European experience motivated the founder generation and cannot be forgotten by the grandchildren.

Amos Oz, writing about 'the perfect peace' in 1987, suggests that there is a break now between the generations. The founders were confident that they had justice and morality on their side when they established Israel. And the soldiers, in the early years, could still think of the 'purity of weapons' used only in defence. This is no longer true for a present generation confronted with far more ambiguous moral questions, uncertain at times whether it is in the right or in the wrong. Yet the memory of the *Shoah*, linked to their elders' experience of it, keeps them more united than Amos Oz assumes. Generations meet in this museum which is more and less than a museum: it is a moral instruction to the young Israelis who feel that such a reminder belongs to the hills and valleys of the land. It reminds them of courage as much as of death; and, for that reason, it gives us more of an insight into the national experience of the Jews in their own land than many books that have been written.

Yad Vashem has a worldwide importance which underscores the fact that Israel is achieving something which is of the highest significance for Jews and Christians after the Holocaust. Here, in that museum, the world is educated. One cannot walk through it without walking into the Holocaust. Its streets of the Righteous Gentiles are as important; here trees are planted in memory of those who did not abandon their humanity but helped Jews at their own risk, often giving their lives freely in order to redeem the human image in a time of shame. Nor must one ignore the library and the research facilities of Yad Vashem, where the scholars of our time meet to explore the unexplorable.

Some years ago, I took the youth group of my Westminster Synagogue to Israel. We came with two special gifts. My Synagogue also has a museum, the Memorial Scrolls Centre, which has almost 1600 Torah Scrolls saved from destruction by the Nazis themselves in a macabre plan to set up a museum in Prague for the 'Vanished People' – how else would the world learn who and what the Jews had been after the last Jew was dead? The rabbis and scholars who catalogued and sorted out the scrolls taken from all the synagogues of Prague, Bohemia and Moldavia were sent to Auschwitz when the task was over. The scrolls remained, stored in a cellar, until the Westminster Synagogue ransomed them from the Czechs (through the generosity of Ralph Yablon) and brought them to London to be reawakened from their sleep and to serve new communities. Acting against Orthodox doctrine, we did not bury those scrolls which were too badly damaged to be repaired: they became Memorial Scrolls, used by communities throughout the world to remember the Holocaust and to instruct the next generation.

Our group came to Yad Vashem with two of the Torah scrolls. One was in perfect order, and was taken by Yad Vashem and placed into the synagogue where daily services were conducted. The other scroll, damaged, tattered, torn, was placed into the exhibition and became part of their presentation of the *Shoah*. The children came back to London with a far deeper understanding of the *Shoah* than if they had listened to a two hour lecture in the synagogue. Israel, and Yad Vashem, accomplishes this pedagogic task for the Diaspora. Israelis sense that this is part of their national task, even if the lessons they teach are often not appreciated by the Diaspora Jewish community; and even when the lessons they teach are not always correct. The whole concept of *Shoah*, as we shall see, has grown up within that land through its times of triumph and failure, and has developed into a far different teaching than what was assumed initially to be the central message: 'Outside Israel, Jews live as a persecuted minority and under threat of annihilation. In Israel, as a majority, Jews will have a secure existence in which they fulfil themselves in the only way possible!'

Earlier, Israelis had accepted the teaching of the first Zionists: Jews will only be safe in their own land, where they are the majority. Diaspora Jews will always be persecuted and will always be in danger. Now one sees the complexities in Jewish life, and learns that Israel is not a safe land, even if it is a sane land. The *Shoah* is not just the trauma of the destruction of European Jewry: one also sees the heroism of those who opposed the Nazis, and the museums tend to stress the cultural heritage, and to deal as much with the heroism as with the destruction.

The Holocaust studies which have developed at Yad Vashem have been models of objectivity and sound research. There is another function to Yad Vashem; it serves a political purpose. No world leader will visit Israel without the mandatory visit to Yad Vashem, where he or she can be photographed in the presence of Israeli dignitaries, and pay tribute to the message of 'Never Again' and 'The world will not forget'. Yad Vashem cannot and must not change its identity or develop in directions which do not concern themselves with Hitler's war against the Jews. Sculpture, paintings, cinematography, and Holocaust literature are developed there, but all add to the impact of the total teaching of the *Shoah*. And the Israelis who go there are reinforced in their feeling of a Jewish identity in which the pain of losing their ancestors is balanced by the pride of achieving a Jewish community which is no longer powerless – despite the dangers of the Near East conflict which to the outsiders seems so near and therefore so frightening. With all their disunity, the Israelis are united as a people who have seen the worst and expect the best in the course of time.

Israel as a teaching community, with its best face displayed to the visitors, is seen in total clarity in the Museum of the Diaspora, a place which recognizes that the full course of Jewish history has found its climax in the State of Israel. It is an educational institution, a 'place for happenings' where the tourist is expected to find himself and herself. The central idea is the portrayal of past Jewish communities, their rise, glory, and ultimate destruction. Aware of the American passion for nostalgia, it has perhaps placed an undue emphasis on Eastern Europe, the *haim* (homeland) for so many Western Jews, scattered throughout America and Western Europe, who still have faint memories of what their grandparents, their *bubbes* and *zaides* taught them. Recently, with the new emphasis upon Sephardic Jewish life and the commemoration of the Exodus from Spain in 1492, more emphasis is placed upon *Sepharad*.

The *Shoah* is also there – but hidden. It reveals itself more in the sudden awareness that this or that segment of Jewish life came to an end. Perhaps there is too much emphasis on the greatness of Jewish life and not the agony; the museum gives a picture of history which does not look at the individuality of that past but at its resemblance to the future. But it does give a reminder of that Europe which was a continuity, and an assurance that the essence of Jewish life endures in every Jew of today.

How did the *Shoah*, the Holocaust, affect this land? First there is a period preceding the reaction after 1945 which must not be ignored. Germany and the *Shoah* are bound together within Israeli consciousness; from 1945 until about 1960, 'German' and 'Nazi' were considered the same word but that attitude has changed; there are now many cultural exchanges with Germany. From the beginning, the build-up and development of Jewish life in Palestine was marked by a distinct German Jewish presence. There were the ideologues whose books were written and read in German, from Moses Hess to Theodor Herzl and Max Nordau. The influx of German Jews before the advent of Hitler had left its mark upon Jewish life in the land and had provided the academics, civil servants, scientists and politicians for a growing and changing community. Then, after 1933, there was the flow of Jews from Germany, those who were able to escape. These were no longer just the convinced Zionists, and the wry joke of that period was 'do you come out of Germany or out of conviction?' The *jeckes* (German Jews) were viewed with a mixture of amusement and slight animosity by the Eastern European Jews who had been the most stalwart, convinced pioneers of the earlier period; but all could and did live together. The challenge and very real achievements of that time united them in a community which had also brought much of its culture and shared experience from Europe: the writers from Bukovina and from Berlin spoke the same language. And the tragic events which then overwhelmed Europe united them in an anguish where they mourned a lost world as well as their lost family.

After 1945, when the full extent of the Nazi crimes became known, there was a clear change in Israel's relationship to Europe. They now knew that they had been right; Europe was the killing ground from which they had escaped. Israel now entered into its own life with an intensity which had no room left for Europe. All Jews should leave Europe, or America, or any other place, and make *aliyah* – settle in the new State. Jews who preferred the Diaspora clearly had a 'guilt mentality' quite inferior to those who had come to 'redeem the land and were redeemed by it' in the words of an old Zionist pioneer song.

The Holocaust was blocked out of Israeli thinking. The European Jews had lived amidst their enemies who wanted to kill them – and had not left. Even worse: they had submitted meekly, they could be pitied but not praised. The few exceptions, the heroes, were those who had fought, on occasions, particularly the Jews of the Warsaw Ghetto. Abba Kovner was a paradigm of these rare heroes; the bulk of European Jews were willing victims, or, worse, collaborators. And the many survivors who had come to Israel were given the cruel grace of having their experiences ignored. The Holocaust was not discussed. One Israeli scholar reports:

Looking at the time span from 1948–1961, I searched through the issues of one of the biggest Israeli children's magazine. And in all those years I found only eleven mentions of the Holocaust. This means: 700 magazines mentioned the Holocaust only eleven times! One of those, for example, was the announcement of the publication of the *Diary of Anne Frank*, in Hebrew. Another mentioned *Yom Ha-Shoah*, the 'Memorial Day for the Holocaust'.[7]

Many of the children's books of that time had a similar plot; little Jossele comes to Israel, pale, weak and frightened. A few months later, in the Kibbutz, he has been transformed into a healthy, tanned child who has rejected the Diaspora name Jossele for the Israeli Joshke. In this fable the sick memory of Holocaust has been cured by the land which renews the Jew. The attitude was clear: 'Let us finally begin to build up the land: that is far more important than to remember that past!'[8] Europe was still recalled as the land where Jews were persecuted; there was the image of Russian pogroms in the previous century. But the citizens of Israel refused to place it into their full awareness.

Why did 1961 become a watershed, a time when public opinion turned around totally in relation to the Holocaust? It was the year of the Eichmann trial; there were daily reports in the world's press. In Israel there was full radio and press coverage. The witnesses came: survivors, to whom no one had listened before. They stood there in all their dignity – no longer dishevelled wrecks, but firm and clear-minded accusers who could be respected by the neighbours who finally listened to their stories. The atmosphere had been transformed.

A new period had begun, which lasted from perhaps 1961 until 1973; and it was a time of deep soul-searching. The poets now spoke for self-examination of a people who had previously sealed off that chamber of their heart containing the anguish of a people who had gone through hell. Documents and studies appeared, diaries were published, and the Holocaust became far more of a public issue. And there were conflicts between Israelis. The West German government accepted the claims by refugees for loss of property, suffering in the camps, interruption of education, etc. The Jewish community then pressed for at least an acknowledgement for the murdered Jews, and the state of Israel became the recipient of millions paid, not as 'full' compensation but in acknowledgement of the *Shoah*.

> Everything will be returned to its place,
> paragraph after paragraph.
> The scream back into the throat.
> The gold teeth back to the gums.
> The terror.

The matter went beyond elderly Jews getting a pension. The State of Israel had become the logical inheritor to the claims which could be made on behalf of the dead six million. There is no such thing as 'reparation' for the death of one child, let alone a million people; every person is unique and irreplaceable. Then were the murderers to inherit the possessions of the slaughtered Jews as well? argued those who favoured the vital payments which were the life-blood for the new and struggling Israel. But that argument was flawed, and its opponents did not want to accept one penny from the murderers, did not want them to get off, as it were, by paying a fine. Neither side could yet understand that they were not dealing with the actual murderers, but with the next generation. Then this argument was brushed aside: there was collective guilt, and inherited guilt! It was all too easy to ignore the Biblical injunction that 'The guilt of the parents must not be inflicted upon the children – each soul, each generation, each individual stands for itself; it is the soul which sins which will die!' But, throughout the argument, one fact had become clear: the Holocaust was to be remembered and not forgotten. The survivors with their tattooed arms were no longer ghosts; they had become neighbours and they were listened to, invited to schools to speak to their children, used as guides to the past: we recognized ourselves in them.

1973. In our synagogue in London, on Yom Kippur, we were hermetically sealed off from the rest of the world (although in most synagogues the news marched in and out with the visitors and family rushing to the sanctuary). We did not know that the Yom Kippur War had started. For us, it was a significant day because our youngest daughter Noam Ilana was born the next morning. And, by then, we were engaged in various activities – from giving blood to sending money to lobbying for the threatened state. In Israel, 1973 was the year in which everything changed again. Already, there had been the Munich massacre of the Israeli Olympic team. The Holocaust seemed closer than it had been at any previous time since 1945. Perceptions changed again, particularly when the early attacks by the enemy proved more successful than ever before: the legend of Israelis as super-warriors had been shattered. Many deaths . . . uncertainties about the fate of prisoners . . . questions about the nature of heroism in this world. After the war, Israelis also looked at the problems of the *Shoah* with a new awareness. Was heroism really only a matter of valour on the battlefield? Israeli soldiers in captivity were still heroes; but then, so were the Jews in the concentration camps who had shared a crust of bread. And those who had prayed in times of darkness – was that not another way of resistance? A photo from a death camp, many photos, came to be re-evaluated. How do we now interpret that picture of the young boy, hands raised high, with a storm-trooper and gun facing him? Or the old man leading the child into the ovens, talking to him, one hand pointed to heaven?

A re-evaluation began. In 1974, one questioned for the first time the name given to Holocaust Memorial Day (*Yom Ha-Shoah*): '*Yom Ha-Shoah V'Ha-Geverah*' (the Day of the Holocaust and of Courage). This had referred to the Warsaw Ghetto fight and made it the paramount aspect of that period. But were there not other acts of courage, secular, religious, pacifist? Even compromises were now viewed with more sympathy, those apparent collaborations which saved lives. The older attitudes still persist, but it is respectable to differ from them. And the complexities of a land once built upon European memories and now dominated by the Sephardi influx from Arab countries have not been resolved adequately. Most Jews from Arab lands have no organized or real memories of the Holocaust, although Europe has begun to appreciate how much destruction was caused among the Sephardi communities in the days of the *Shoah*. But the emphasis has also begun to swing back to an attitude of strength and of military actions. Living among the Arabs, assimilating many of their attitudes, Sephardi Israelis tend to accept straightforward military solutions proposed by right wing politicians and extremists. In a curious way, this again leads back to the earlier attitudes towards the Holocaust. This time, its memories are rejected because it is less central to the Sephardi thinking. It again becomes encapsulated, an enclave, a hidden trauma within the body politic which will explode within the tested Jewish soul which lives in a land of promise and pain.

Israel is the youngest and oldest state, the youngest and oldest Jew in the world. It lives on its ancient soil, part of that land for more than 3,000 years. It wants to be the mother of all other Jewish communities and individuals, reaching out its arms and calling to all of them to come home. The Holocaust, as we have suggested, is an encapsulated trauma in its soul, and cannot be resolved by us or by Israel in the near future. Israelis felt that all Jews must love Israel, since Israel needs that love. Much of its self-confidence has disappeared, its own citizens note that not all its actions are righteous, that many of its political decisions are wrong, and that it lives under constant criticism. But that criticism, Israelis think, comes from those who were responsible for killing the Jews in the Diaspora. Therefore, it is seen as inimical. Wrongly, it is ignored. I feel that Israel finds it cannot abide criticism by its friends, and particularly by its Jewish supporters. The old answer, from Ben Gurion to the most recent immigrant, is given to criticism from abroad: 'If you want to criticize, come to Israel. Then, you have the right to speak!' That was the answer which Avneri gave and gives to the prophetic moral messages of Elie Wiesel, which all Israel gives to those who support Shalom Achshav from the outside. But is that not, too, part of the unassimilated destruction caused by the Holocaust to a land built upon the need to survive? And will it survive?

Leo Baeck's image of Jewish history is in the form of an ellipse, with two focal points: one is Israel, the other one is the Diaspora. The two always interact upon one another, and the Jewish community in the *Golah*, the Diaspora, is always tested by Israel's perception of it, and by the demands Israel makes upon it: both moral and ethical, and demands for full support of Israel in a time of desperate uncertainty. In many ways, Israel feels reassured by the writings of the Jewish scholars who live far away, but are linked to Israel through family and through ideology. Thus, Dow Marmur's basic concept in his *The star of return* is an Israeli commitment; it picks up the old question of the Holocaust and its role in creating the State, but, for this thinker, there is the new beginning:

> The Holocaust was not the cause of the creation of the Jewish state but the tragic end of the old paradigm of exile . . . the beginning of something new, which at the same time also evokes the very old, namely, Biblical time.[9]

From this vantage-point of the American continent, Rabbi Marmur sees the past, present, and future in this land. It is more the land of the first generations, it is also the world of the Bible where the ethical teachings of the prophets can be realized. The problem which arises then, amidst the less than perfect actions of the people, and particularly the politicians, is whether the darkness does not invalidate the bright dream.

One of the more radical challengers of the Jewish establishment, working with the Christian proponents of the 'theology of liberation', is Marc Ellis, who does not hesitate to attack this Diaspora understanding of the State of Israel and, of course, the State itself, in the sharpest terms:

> The Holocaust thus served as motive and justification for the formation of Israel. Yet this formation caused – and some will claim required – the creation of a stateless mass of Palestinian Arabs. The satisfaction of the claims of justice of the Jews resulted in a great injustice done to Palestinians . . .[10]

The reminder of wrong-doing within the land, the pain of the Palestinians, and the injustice which is done to them can be found in so many writings of Israelis – from Amos Oz to the *Jerusalem Post*. These writings are the work of those who live with the dangers and the pain of everyday Israeli life; there is the feeling that outside criticisms should be curtailed.

Marc Ellis goes far beyond a comment about the creation of Israel and the immorality he sees in the very creation. He wants to change all Diaspora thinking as well. A Holocaust liturgy of destruction must include the suffering of the Palestinians who would then see the significance of the Holocaust in their own lives. Here, Marc Ellis comes to the central theme of his liberation theology; he wants to unite all the poor and disenfranchised, all the powerless who suffer in this world. Israel, at this point, seems to him one example among many. Universal justice has become his goal.

Part of this text was written in Jerusalem, the sacred city which maintains its sacredness despite the noises of traffic and of building. Looking at the community of Israel, with all its anxieties and visions, at the poets and philosophers, listening to the babble of languages, one can see that the ravages which came out of the Tower of Babel are being repaired as the diverse elements of that society are welded together by Hebrew, the land and the language. The Russian Jew is a new element in the shaping of Israel, with all the disappointments and destroyed illusions burning like a bonfire on Lag Ba-Omer. I see the American students redefining themselves within the cultural and religious streams which surge around them, and come back to the conclusion that there is no answer, no one guide to lead us. One cannot walk through Rechavia, the old German part of Jerusalem, without being reminded of the impact made by German Jewry before and during the Holocaust. And one cannot walk anywhere in Jerusalem without meeting Orthodoxy in all its strength. There are many who think that in one of those *Yeshivot* – or in any of them – the ultimate truth is now being proclaimed. The Lubavitch movement sees messianic stirrings in the air, even when they guard against false hope. Sephardi and Ashkenazi traditions unite with Arab and Druse customs. Simple humanity, and the knowledge of living under the threat of attack makes life more intense. Here are so many subterranean streams which move through the life of this land. From the early days of Judah Magnes and Martin Buber to the great German scholars whose impact has not faded completely, we begin to discern the special atmosphere of the land; when all is said and done, and I have listened to the profound thinkers and rabbis and scientists, I can only give my confidence to the people itself, and not to any one leader and Dawn-Rider.

On this last day I prayed at the Wall and in a congregation which described itself as 'Hasidic-Reform'. I ate at the YMCA and at the King David Hotel; and went to a salon – that old, great tradition of a hostess assembling at an open house guests who are under the obligation to be interesting. Walking through one of the small side streets, I saw a regal woman clad in black turning the corner ahead of me. Time stood still for a moment, and I thought of that tragic, half-demented German prophetess who came to Jerusalem where she starved to death: Else Lasker-Schueler. Perhaps our last glimpse at this rich scene should be one of her poems which I translated thirty years ago:

> I dissolve
> In anguished heart's blossoming
> Chaff blown into space
> Into time
> And eternity,
> And my soul's glow dies in the evening colours
> Of Jerusalem.

That is where she did die: in Jerusalem. Over the centuries, many pious Jews took that pilgrimage late in life, since they wanted to die in Zion. Now, a people with all its complexities wants to live there, after the Holocaust; no easy thing, for the neighbour and for the Jew.

## NOTES

1. In 'Holocaust and genocide studies', ed. Y. Bauer (Oxford Pergamon, 1986), vol. 1, no. 1, p. 117.
2. From The Newdigate Prize poem, 'Petra', by John Burgon.
3. From 'National thoughts'.
4. From 'My little sister'.
5. R. F. Mintz, ed., *Modern Hebrew poetry* (LA, University of California Press, 1966), pp. 219–220.
6. U. Avneri, *Wir tragen das Nessos Gewand*, p. 84.
7. Rachel Meir, 'Schoa als schuldiger lernprozess' in *Identitaet und erinnerung* (ed. Kiesl and Karpf), p. 66.
8. Ibid., p. 67.
9. In *The star of return: Judaism after the Holocaust* (New York, Greenwood Press), p. 10.
10. Marc Ellis, *Beyond innocence and redemption: confronting the Holocaust and Israel's power* (San Francisco, Harper Rowe, 1990).

# A DIFFERENT LANGUAGE

## THE WORLD OF THE POETS

*Paul Celan*

W E do not fully understand this world in which we live – the world after the Holocaust, moving towards the dark uncertainties of the twenty-first century. Various disciplines try to organize our thoughts for us. The historians present the past as an orderly sequence of events which march towards us with all the inevitability of a dialectical process which in the end swallows us up and dictates our future actions. Once their predictions are seen to be less than perfect, they become irrelevant as prophets and suspect as interpreters of the past. There are, of course, the theologians who begin with a revelation which we are required to accept. Since we live in a post-theological age where both scientific thought and the realities of daily life contradict many religious dogmas, the truths of theology are at least suspect. Faith may still be our best option, and the religious vision will enlarge life; but it is not necessarily the vision of the ministers appointed by religious institutions to support the old structure. We look for the truth which will burn in our souls like a living flame, and find these disciplines arid and cold.

Are there other sources of inspiration? Clearer visions to which we respond with inner affirmation? In almost every age, questing minds have turned towards the poets of their times. Homer and Virgil, Milton and Dante, or the wilder tones of poets who gave us religious visions whose anguish led to greater understanding. In the Bible, we hear more in Job and the Psalmists than in the structured ordinances of the law-givers.

In our time, too, there are the poets who speak in a different language and live in an adjacent world which reflects our own reality. When they talk to us about darkness, they are not bound by the evidence of historians or by the logic of theologians. They may see 'through a glass, darkly', or they may see with a terrible clarity which breaks through the defences which our mind has set against the onslaught of the truths. They teach us of the darkest night, and at the same time catch a glimpse of the dawn ahead of us. In a world where logic and faith have broken down, they become guides who help us discover an inner strength of which we were unaware, of enduring powers of the human soul which survived in the innermost circle of hell.

Paul Celan was such a guide. The Holocaust is the dark background for all his work. Paul Celan was born in Czernowitz, the capital of the Romanian Bukovina in 1910. Many Jews are born in places where languages and cultures are a maelstrom of civilization which swallows them up and twists and shapes them in curious ways before spitting them out again into the world. Different influences then wrestle within them; in Paul's case, the Hebrew of a children's school which nevertheless brought a precocious boy towards the glimpse of a half-understood mysticism; the German language which became a blessing and curse – his one way of expression even if he had to reshape it from a distance; the Romanian language of daily life, in which he even wrote some poems; and the French of his scholarship and eventually his livelihood when he worked as a translator in Paris.

Paul's parents were killed by the Nazis in autumn of 1942; autumn became the cruel season in his writings. Paul was sent to a work-camp; the stones, the debris, the rock, ice and cruelty of those landscapes is visible in his poetry. The death of his parents, the tragedy of his people, his wandering through various countries and languages – all of this made him a witness of the past to the present; and that past killed him in the end.

There are occasions when one needs to know a great deal about the language and its images; and there are times when one needs to know the past and present situation of the poet in order to be instructed by the text. Since Paul Celan was arguably one of the greatest poets of the twentieth century, anyone who loves poetry will be shaken and enriched by most of the Celan poems encountered by chance or by design. What we *can* do, if our premise – the poet as prophet – has validity, is to approach at least one aspect of his poetry with a certain amount of preparation. Scholars may argue about every line or word, and we need not argue with them. There is, I am certain, a way of coming to his teachings which acknowledges our own limitations but also insists that Celan's genius breaks through the fences created around him and permits us to learn and to love the word he carries through the barriers of darkness.

We should begin with the *golem*, an image which may be helpful to us in our explorations. The 139th Psalm refers to the unshaped substance of our body fashioned by God ('Thine eyes did see my *golem*); this relates to the Creation where the body of clay is infused with the divine. We may also move on to Shelley's Frankenstein, Capek's 'RUR' – the first robots; or the *golem* created according to legend in Prague by the High Rabbi Loew. So this is also an image of our time. Gershom Scholem's writings on 'The golem of Prague and the golem of Rehovoth' recognize the relationship between a computer-governed society and the absence of the spirit which makes these fearful servants of their fashioners a caricature of humanity. And Paul Celan, writing about Rabbi Loew, about Prague, about the dark forces standing upon the threshold of our lives, brings us to an understanding of a world where the individual is subsumed to the state, to society, to the corporation, even to synagogue or church, with the implication that one must be obedient and follow instructions instead of thinking for oneself.

We are responsible for the world in which we live. When we see it in all of its imperfections and cruelties, a defence mechanism tends to take over which relieves us of responsibility. We hypostasize evil as Satan; we look for dark forces which operate outside humanity. The popularity of the Jekyll and Hyde story is a way of splitting the evil from the good, of looking for 'doppelgängers' – and this too fits into the golem legend. The golem of the Prague legends represents brute, unthinking force which can be utilized for good by the rabbi; to that extent, it is part of the Jewish people.

In one of his poems Celan saw that figure:

> One who stood before the door, one
> evening:
> to him
> I opened my word –:

In the poem, Celan appeals to Rabbi Loew to control that figure, to circumcise its word, to place nothingness into its brain and, finally, also

> slam shut the evening door, rabbi,
> . . .
> tear open the morning door, ra –

Evenings and mornings are the limits of creation. *Va-y'hi erev, va-y'hi voker*: 'and it was evening, and it was morning, a first day' is the rhythm of the Creation story in the first lines of the Torah – the Messianic age will move through the evening gate, into the darkness of wars of Gog and Magog, and then the morning gate will open for the Messiah. First is the darkness, the golem with the power of the word that is given him (the tradition varies: sometimes the word *Emet* (Truth), sometimes the divine name for God placed into his mouth gives life to the golem). Man controls him through the word. In one legend, the golem has grown too strong and tall. The rabbi still has some power, and asks him to tie his shoelace, bringing his forehead with the world *Emet* into the reach of the rabbi, who wipes out the first letter. *Emet* is changed to *Met* (dead) and the golem crumbles into dust.

In a variant, the rabbi tears the parchment with the divine name out of his mouth with the same result. Does the rabbi die with his creation, as he cuts the name, as he opens the morning door? The cutting short of the name: 'ra–' suggests this; and in much of the traditional represent-ation of good versus evil the good has to make this sacrifice. In the Jewish story the good Rabbi Loew and the golem servant are always closely connected.

In Prague, I heard the story that the 'Altneuschul', the synagogue which according to the tradition still contains the ashes of the golem in its attic, was not destroyed by the Nazis because the golem protected it. And the stone I placed upon the grave of Rabbi Loew joined the many stones and petitionary parchments placed upon that grave by Jews and non-Jews who still believed in the saving powers of the great rabbi and his great servant. Yet Celan's poem 'In Prague' is more concerned with that ultimate darkness where evil has grown strong, where the 'Hebrew bones, ground to sperm, ran through the sand clock . . .' And yet, before the awareness of the Holocaust, one catches a glimpse of the golem:

> That half-death,
> suckled big with our life,
> lay around us, true as an ashen image –
>
> we too
> still drank, soul-crossed, two daggers,
> sewn on to stones of the sky, born of word blood
> in the night bed,

bigger and bigger
we grew interlaced, there was
no longer a name for
that which drove us (one of the how many
and thirty
was my live shadow
that climbed the delusory steps towards you?),

a tower
the halved one built for himself into where
a *Hradshin*
made of pure gold-makers No,

bone-Hebrew
ground into sperm
ran through the hourglass
through which we swam, two dreams now, chiming
against time, in the squares.[1]

We are in Prague here, with the Hebrew clock on the square, golden
Hebrew letters directed against the Jews on the bridge leading towards the
castle, and the half-dead golem, half alive through us, our doppelgänger,
brooding against the sky. Interlaced with him are those who died and who
are part of us, buried in the sky. There are questions and answers here,
addressed to Jewish fate; but there is also a universality here which wants
to define the human being who continues to be created after chaos. At that
point, the image of the golem is once more addressed to all of human
nature and goes back to the original Creation. That is why Celan's 'Psalm'
has at least the shadow of the golem behind the challenge addressed to us:

No one moulds us again out of earth and clay,
no one conjures our dust.
No one.

Praised be your name, no one.
For your sake
we shall flower.
Towards
you.

A nothing
we were, are, shall
remain, flowering;
the nothing –, the
no one's rose.

With our pistil soul-bright
with our stamen heaven-ravaged
our corolla red
with the crimson word which we sang
over, o over
the thorn.[2]

To be 'conjured out of earth and clay' is more golem than Creation. Yet this is a psalm, a religious prayer, addressed to the 'Great Nothingness', the *en sof* known to the Kabbalists and radical Jewish theologians where the non-meaning of our suffering ultimately does become meaning again. The 'we' of this poem could be the voice of the dead; but the dead are part of us. And the 'Nothing' comes to life again, just as the golem was put to rest on the Sabbath, and was awakened again. In Ezekiel's vision of the 'Valley of Dry Bones', the prophet is asked: 'Can these bones live again?' and he replies, in affirmation: 'Thou knowest, O Lord' as the bones knit themselves together and arise out of the dust to reaffirm the rebirth of the Jewish people. Celan's psalm is therefore a true prayer; but it moves into dimensions which the closed traditionalist cannot understand. 'Nothingness' in our time depicts the limit of our understanding of the infinite, and our own condition of non-belief.

There is a tortured dialogue in which we engage ourselves before we turn towards God. In Celan there is the attempt to see the paradox between Kingship and 'Nothingness' which confronts humanity in its encounters with the divine, and even with the uncertainty (but hope) of a new Creation.

Celan confronted another Jewish vision and hope which had separated itself from traditional teaching and liturgy and had often clothed itself in cabbalistic texts. In a letter-poem addressed to Nelly Sachs the Nobel Prize winner he recalled their meeting in Zurich. Celan approaches their shared but conflicting visions:

Of too much was our talk, of
too little. Of the You
and You-again, of
low clarity troubles, of

Jewishness, of
your God

of
that.
On the day of an ascension, the
Minster stood over there, it sent
some gold across the water.

Of your God was our talk, I spoke
against him, I
let the heart that I had
hope;
for
his highest, death-rattled, his
quarrelling word –

your eye looked on, looked away,
your mouth
spoke its way to the eve and I heard:

We
don't know, you know,
we
don't know, do we?
what
counts.[3]

Some interpreters, overstating the Ascension Day reference, turn this text
into a Christian declaration. It may pick up the theme of a Messianic death
but the basic theme is set out clearly. Celan has his lover's quarrel with
God, and Nelly Sachs responds with gentle mysticism which turns insecurity
into conviction: we don't know, do we, what counts? The tension between
the polarities moves towards a hope which falters so often in Paul Celan.

   In the end, we can only begin to understand the particular role Paul
Celan performs for us in the world after Auschwitz if we turn to the two
poems which deal most specifically with the Holocaust: the 'Death fugue'
and 'The straightening'. 'Death fugue' has suffered many attacks at the
hands of those who felt that Auschwitz could not be treated in an aesthetic
way; that Celan was somehow 'profiting' from this theme.

There is a difference in the way German and English scholars approach it. Many Germans still seem to suffer from the poem's statement that 'death is a master from Germany'. English interpreters, notably Michael Hamburger, were immediately aware of the greatness of this poem with its outcry of pain. More than a fugue, it was a choral lament and a proof that the scientific disciplines had less to convey about the heart of the Holocaust experience than the poets.

> Black milk of dawn we drink it at even
> we drink it at noon and mornings we drink it at night
> we drink and we drink
> we are digging a grave in the skies there one lies uncrowded.
>
> A man lives in the house he plays with the serpents he writes
> he writes when the dark comes to Germany your golden hair
> Margarete
> he writes it and steps from the house and the stars flash he
> whistles up his dogs
> he whistles out his Jews let a grave be dug in the earth
> he commands us now play for the dance.
>
> Black milk of dawn we drink you at night
> we drink you mornings and noon we drink you at even
> we drink and we drink.
>
> A man lives in the house he plays with the serpents he writes
> he writes when the dark comes to Germany your golden hair
> Margarete
> your ashen hair Shulamith we are digging a grave in the
> skies there one lies uncrowded.
> He calls stab deeper into the earth you there you others sing
> and play
> he reaches for the iron in his belt he swings it his eyes are
> blue
> stab deeper your spades you there you others play on for the
> dance.
>
> Black milk of dawn we drink you at night
> we drink you noon and mornings we drink you at even
> we drink and we drink

a man lives in the house your golden hair Margarete
your ashen hair Shulamith he plays with the serpents.

He calls play sweeter of death death is a master from
Germany
he calls stroke darker the violins then you will climb as smoke
into the sky
then you will have a grave in the clouds there one lies
uncrowded.

Black milk of dawn we drink you at night
we drink you at noon death is a master from Germany
we drink you at even and mornings we drink and we drink
death is a master from Germany his eye is blue
he hits you with a lead bullet his aim is true
a man lives in the house your golden hair Margarete
he sets his dogs upon us he gives us a grave in the sky
he plays with the serpents and dreams death is a master
from Germany
your golden hair Margarete
your ashen hair Shulamith.[4]

The uniqueness of his talent, and the particular impact of 'Death fugue'
make this poem one of the great achievements of Celan's early period
(c. 1945?). The camp experience of Tirgu Jiu, the Biblical Shulamith and
Faust's blond Gretchen are voices in that chorus of pain. More than a
metaphor of Jewish suffering, it is a description of actual events where the
victims are forced to make music and join the *danse macabre* of their own
death by their torturers. The 'black milk' drunk constantly is not the actual
gas of the chambers; it is the atmosphere of the concentration camp which
carries death within itself. The 'grave in the sky' is the smoke from the
chimneys. In this way we see it also through the eyes of death, 'the master
from Germany' who views and who binds the victim into grim complicity
with himself. Death appears as the average German, innocuous, writing
letters to his girlfriend in distant Germany. But he writes when it gets dark,
and he plays with snakes: the demonic element quickly becomes apparent.
'His' Jews and dogs are all the same to him as he whistles for them to
perform the death dance.

The role of the dogs in the camps has been described all too often.
Blue-eyed death, the master from Germany, confronts the whole nation

with its victim, a confrontation which contrasts the golden-haired Margarete with the ashen hair of Shulamith. There are still churches and cathedrals where the women figures of the Church triumphant confront the broken and blinded Synagogue; it is not surprising that many German critics want to push the 'Death fugue' into a realm where it can be moved beyond any reality. But it is *not* a 'beautification of the Holocaust', *not* an elegy *about* death; it describes that death as it was and permits us to stand alongside the victims. Celan's major works are distinct from the 'Death fugue' but they cannot be understood without it.

There is a second poem, written much later, which is the counterpart of his 'Death fugue'; it is a piece of music caught in the special rhythm and structure of a poetry that wants to be prophecy – prophecy which looks at the past before it can look at a future. The poem 'The straightening' (or *stretta*). In music, it is that part of the composition where voices are united, placed upon one another shortly before the end of the fugue. It is one of Celan's longest poems; I shall only quote the beginning and end of it, although a reading of the full text is almost mandatory:

> Driven into the
> terrain
> with the unmistakable track;
>
> grass, written asunder. The stones, white,
> with the shadow of grassblades:
> Do not read any more – look!
> Do not look any more – go!
>
> Go, your hour
> has no sisters, you are –
> are at home. A wheel, slow,
> rolls out of itself, the spokes
> climb,
> climb on a blackish field, the night
> needs no stars, nowhere
> does anyone ask after you.
>
> &ast;  &ast;  &ast;
>
> Nowhere
> does anyone ask after you –

The place where they lay, it has
a name – it has
none. They did not lie there. Something
lay between them. They
did not see through it.

Did not see, none
spoke of
words. None
awoke,
sleep came over them.

*  *  *

It is I, I,
I lay between you, I was
open, was
audible, ticked at you, your breathing
obeyed, it is
I still, but then
you are asleep.

*  *  *

. . . . . . [closing   section:]

ascends and

    joins in –

At owl's flight, near
the petrified scabs,
near
our fled hands, in
the latest rejection,
above
the rifle-range near
the buried wall:

visible, once
more: the grooves, the

264

choirs, at that time, the
psalms. Ho, ho,
sannah.
So
there are temples yet. A
star
probably still has light.
Nothing,
nothing is lost.

Ho–
sannah.

At owl's flight, here,
the conversations, day-grey,
of the water-level traces.

\* \* \*

day-grey,
    of
        the water level traces –
Driven into the
terrain
with
the unmistakable
track:

Grass,
grass,
written asunder.

'The straightening'

'Death fugue' had been a cry of martyrdom in which there was no hope for redemption. It is written out of reality. 'The straightening' is a text of remembering, written out of a future from which one looks back at the event.

The opening stanza of 'The straightening' gives us a scene of desolation, with the white stones of death strewn across the landscape. Here it is not so much a reality of a known place; we are remote from it, reading a text 'written asunder', where the shadow of grassblades become letters which we read – only to be enjoined to stop reading and to look, to stop looking and to go.

Go where? Into the time of death. The text becomes a gateway to a landscape which is highly surreal: the rolling wheel could come out of a picture by Klee, Magritte, or even Dali. It pulls us along with it, into the field of night. We listen for something – and there are no words. Is it the sleep of death?

But then, there is awakening; something is still left, something lies there, and 'it is I, I/I lay between you . . .' in the past tense. Is the 'I' time itself ticking away and by its entry into the field of desolation also restoring life? Is it language, the poem itself? In the end the poem becomes an affirmation.

Finally, there is some recognition of a word that has managed to reach us, the mourners, the weeping eyes. 'At owl's flight' is twilight when the owls take to the air, that area between night and day. Celan must have thought of Hegel's word, that 'the ōwl of Minerva flies only when it gets dark' – the intellect assesses events only after they have happened, recreating them from a perspective where they have already lost reality. Fleeing from the past, passing the bullet marks in the wall which recall the deaths of our people, we can reject that suffering for ourselves, but the events again become visible in the grooves of the stones; they become audible, in the psalms sung at that time. Religion is reborn through the recognition that suffering humanity responded to ultimate evil with the good dormant within it. The ho, ho, sanna sung by the chorus was a broken sound; but it was sounded. And it *still* mattered that the choirs sang and that people prayed, that they were not frozen into the total silence of night.

> So
> there are temples yet. A
> star
> probably still has light.
> Nothing,
> nothing is lost.

The hope is limited by the qualification that a star 'probably' has light left. Yet the Hosannah is repeated, asserts a Jewish hope where light conquers darkness. The opening verse then closes this *stretta*. It is placed into parentheses, as an affirmation rather than a negation. It reminds us of the beginning, gives it back its own identity and yet breaks through as a link with the psalms once recited. The ground water underneath rises and gives life to the grass.

Celan has to be read rather than interpreted; but can this prophet and poet address us in a post-Auschwitz world and bring forth inner qualities of our being where we need not flee from that past but recognize it within the world and in ourselves? We must be 'remembrancers'; we must recall what actually happened, and then hold it fast in our life through acts of remembrance. The Hebrew word for this, the ritual in which we recall those who have died: *Yizkor*: a religious act, yet close to secular life.

Paul Celan's 'The sluice' can clarify the use of the word *Yizkor* for us:

> Above all this your
> mourning: no
> second heaven.
>
> . . .
>
> In a mouth
> to which it was a thousand words,
> I lost —
> I lost a word,
> which had been left to me:
> Sister.
>
> To idolatry
> I lost a word which searched for me:
> Kaddish.
>
> Through
> the sluice I had to go,
> the word put back into the salt-flood,
> to be salvaged out of it and beyond it:
> *Yizkor*.

It is not that Paul Celan cannot remember the sister; she lives in him and is part of him. He does not need to mention his parents: their deaths are the evening-door and morning-door of his daily existence. But what has been lost and what has to be regained is the act of remembrancing: *Kaddish* and *Yizkor* are rituals through which the Jew renews himself. Water is an element of the Creation. The ground water moved through the opening and closing of 'The straightening'; and salt water moistens the eye in the ritual of remembrance which becomes more than ritual. So, in this text as in so many others, the private grief can become an observance in which the reader can participate. Without *Yizkor*, one has no right to approach the past; but one cannot live without the past. Those without memories are robots, are golems from which the truth can be separated; we cannot live without the name of God in the mouth.

## Nelly Sachs

I met Nelly Sachs in her home, a small flat inside an asylum for the mentally-ill. The many fears which surrounded her throughout her life had broken through her defensive barriers. The expert care and kindness with which she had been treated had been effective, and she could have returned to her flat. For the present, at least, she decided to stay in the hospital. 'Why should I leave?' she said to me. 'I am still afraid in a world of much anti-Semitism. As a Nobel Prize winner, I am a marked person.' The darkness lurked at the threshold. She was still frail, would always remain frail, even if the image which the critics and readers had built around her overstressed this weakness.

She had won the Nobel Prize in October 1966. Now, in the spring of 1968, Nelly Sachs was clearly frail, but not shy or silent. We spent most of the day together, and it became one of the *sternstunden* – decisive occasions – of my life. As a child of assimilated parents, she had had little contact with the formal structures of Judaism in Berlin. One belonged to the congregation but did not become involved in it. Her father had been a factory owner in Berlin, and the cultured, humanistic atmosphere of her home meant she was brought up on Goethe and Beethoven rather than on the Jewish tradition. That came later; much later.

The yearning and longing which was so central to her style was that of a German poet with a romantic vision of the Middle Ages: her first book, in 1921, *Legenden und erzählungen* was dedicated to the Swedish writer Selma Lagerlöf 'from a young German' (*einer jungen Deutschen*). If we now view her within the framework of the poet/prophet guides to life after the Holocaust, we cannot transport her into the synagogue pulpit or into the dialogues among rabbis, even though the *Zohar* becomes central to many of her poems. It is important to see her as she was, with all the sensitivity of a great poet, with all the anguish of a Jewish refugee – but also as a German writer in exile. The fact that she did publish poetry in *Der Morgen*, a Jewish periodical, between 1936 and 1938, only reflects the changes which took place for everyone born Jewish in the Germany of Hitler after 1933.

Germany had rejected her then. Her father had died in 1930, when she was 40, and her life had become interwoven with her mother's existence. The next twenty years (the mother died in 1950) were totally dedicated to the task of helping and then nursing her mother. Nelly Sachs, through the help of Selma Lagerlöf and the royal family of Sweden, came to Stockholm on 16 May 1940; but it was still a life of privation, poverty, and suffering.

It was Nelly Sachs's fate as a Jewish woman to experience a tragedy which did not place her into a concentration camp. There were different types of victims in that night without stars. Nelly Sachs experienced the brutalities perpetrated upon those who lived at the edge of the abyss. She was not tortured or imprisoned – although living in that Germany had already been a type of imprisonment and torture. Her total sensitivity to the evil perpetrated at that time meant that she passed through a caesura of time, a break which separated her from what she had been and wanted to be. How could she be a *German* writer now? All the post-war prizes, the frantic attempts to reclaim her, were of little avail. No attempts to claim not only Nelly Sachs, but the German Jew for that cultural domain, will be successfully completed in this century.

Nelly Sachs was surrounded by the love and appreciation of the Swedish people who welcomed her – eventually – and whom she rewarded in her work as a translator who bridged the cultures. She remained the tragic suffering figure of the bereft mother: Rachel mourning her children. The incidents of her life were reshaped accordingly; a young girl's friendship for a boy who died in the camps became the 'mourning for the lost bridegroom'. And all of the longing and yearning which were so central to her work became part of a threnody which is the chief characteristic of her 'Jewish' writing – the large body of her major writings exhibited that same dark sound. Yet her words often danced – as she had danced to her father's music – and reached out towards light and joy.

The great contribution Nelly Sachs gives to us is that she teaches us to mourn. This may seem strange to Jewish ears, to a religious culture where the language of mourning and the ability to remember loved ones is so central to our heritage. The fact remains that, in the last decade of this brutal century, many have forgotten *who* and *what* is to be mourned. We live too much in an outer world where the Holocaust has been covered up by new events, where Jews are challenged and criticized for remembering the six million when new hundreds of millions have been the victims of new genocides. Reading Nelly Sachs, we regain the knowledge of what has been lost.

The great illness afflicting post-war Germany was the inability to mourn. A people tried to deal with an unacceptable past by closing its mind to the crimes, by removing the Hitler era out of history. Nelly Sachs has been of help to the German psyche, for, in trying to reclaim this Nobel Prize winner for themselves, they were forced to read the 'Jewish' poems along with the rest of the work. Nelly Sachs, more approachable than Paul Celan, taught Germans to mourn.

But Nelly Sachs is not merely a poet who recreates horror for us, or who shows us a Holocaust in the framework of beautiful poetry which somehow diminishes the terror. Nelly Sachs speaks for the dead and the living victims who still lie down in loneliness. She evokes compassion but also kinship. Her great choruses also demand a response from those who listen, who are then included in a liturgy. And we know that she speaks for herself as well when we hear the chorus of the orphans, or of the rescued:

> We, the rescued,
> Out of whose hollowed bones death had already carved his
> Flutes,
> And upon whose sinews death had already stroked his bow –
> Our bodies still lament
> With their mutilated music . . .
>
> We, the rescued,
> Plead with you:
> Show us your sun, but slowly.
> Lead us from star to star, step by step.
> Let us relearn life softly, softly.
> Otherwise, the song of a bird,
> Or a pail being filled at the well,
> Could let our poorly sealed pain break out again
> And wash us away –
> We beg you:
> Do not show us a biting dog, not yet –
> It could be, it could very well be
> That we will fall apart into dust –
> Fall apart into dust before your eyes.[5]

Sun, dust, and stars come together here, surrounded by the same music of death we had heard in Paul Celan's 'Death fugue'. But Celan's Jews were already buried in the sky, while Nelly Sachs addresses us on behalf of the rescued among whom she finds herself. Nelly Sachs speaks 'out of the night of the weeping children' – but it is a strong, clear voice which addresses us.

> O the chimneys
>> And when after my skin this (body) is destroyed
>> Then without my flesh I shall see God.[6]

> O the chimneys
> On the ingeniously thought-out habitations of death
> When Israel's body drifted dissolved as smoke
> Through the air –
> A star, a chimney-sweep, welcomed it,
> A star that turned black
> Or was it a ray of sun?

> O the chimneys!
> Freedomways for Jeremiah and Job's dust –
> Who invited you and built stone upon stone
> The way for refugees of smoke?[7]

Last year, when I visited Buchenwald, I saw a lone chimney stack belching out smoke above the remnants of those buildings. The church bells of the surrounding villages rang nearby. Those church bells rang while the chimneys were sending 'Israel's body as smoke through the air'. There are so many times when past and present coalesce and become one dark pain. If we did not have Nelly Sachs and Paul Celan, the pain would be even worse.

Her choruses of shadows and of stones are always with us. Sadness predominates, and hatred is absent, the hatred which is so often ascribed to the writers who wrote out of the Holocaust and after the Holocaust. Such hatred does exist: the trauma and pain of the events marks the human soul. Yet hatred is not endemic within Jewish life, and is far more often an outer misunderstanding born out of guilt and a lack of knowledge of the Jewish tradition. Nelly Sachs understood the total evil of the Nazi configuration and the evil of those caught up in it as participants. She takes note of the passive onlookers – but without hatred:

Under whose eyes the killing took place.
As one feels a stare at one's back
You feel on your bodies
The looks of the dead.

'You onlookers'

Those onlookers did not raise their hands to commit murder; they simply
stood still and watched. And the core of their being, the yearning which
can reach out to fellow beings and to God, was covered with the dust of
Auschwitz. Nelly Sachs describes, almost with compassion, the fate of those
flawed beings who will be surrounded by dying eyes and unsung cradle
songs. But she spends most of her time in the 'habitations of the dead'
where she picks up the stones and listens to them:

We stones
When someone lifts us
He lifts the time before time –
When someone lifts us
He raises up the Garden of Eden –
When someone lifts us
He lifts up the knowledge found by Adam and Eve
And the serpent's dust-eating seduction.

When someone lifts us
He lifts in his hand billions of memories
Which do not dissolve in blood
Like the evening.
For we are memorial stones
Embracing all dying.

'Chorus of the stones'

The stones bring us back to the beginning of the Creating. Lifting them,
we carry the memories from the beginning to the end of time, into a
continuum where all meshes together into one work, and a stone from any
grave becomes a stone from all graves:

The alphabet's corpse rose from the grave
alphabet angel, ancient crystal . . .

We must not ask what a poem 'intends'. Each poem stands by itself; it is. When all the poems are put together, they become a totality and a design is apparent in this case, a religious design.

The verse just cited is part of a key passage and is linked to Kabbala and Zohar:

> Then wrote the Scribe of the Zohar
> and opened the words' net of veins
> instilling blood from stars
> which circled, invisible, and ignited
> only longing.
>
> The alphabet's corpse rose from the grave,
> alphabet angel, ancient crystal,
> immured in the waterdrops of Creation
> that sang – and through them one saw
> shimmering ruby and hyacinth and lapis
> when stone was still soft
> and sown like flowers.
>
> And the black tiger roared,
> the night; heavily rolled
> bleeding with sparks
> the wound called day.

The Zohar tradition which Nelly Sachs had encountered (relatively late, and not in its fullness) saw the world created by God's use of the alphabet; each letter had its own strength and mystery. The Scribe reached out into the universe so that the forces of creation entered that network of letters which made up the story of Creation in which the letters become interconnected. The stones are sown like flowers, scattered across the world in pain where they address us in their chorus.

Throughout Nelly Sachs' poetry one finds Biblical and post-Biblical words and teachings from the rabbis. It would be odd if they were not present. If, as in Celan, the images of dust and stone constantly recur, these rise out of the accessible traditions of Jewish life where, in the Bible and later, Israel is compared to the dust, ground to the floor and yet surviving even though the image of the human is 'dust to dust'. There is a dichotomy there, since the Jobean outcry of human weakness and futility is joined to the assertion that humanity will yet endure. Eventually, the world will be blessed by the presence of Israel. At the end, the Messiah will come. The tension of Jewish faith rests between these polarities, and Nelly Sachs asserts it. The dust of the crematoria moves across the landscape of earth as an enduring reality of the Holocaust.

And the stones of every grave visited are part of the memory of Jewish life. 'Even the stones in the wall will cry out, and the beam of the timber shall answer it'. Stones are both symbols and realities of Jewish life. When Jacob – who became Israel – fled from his brother into the desert, he lay down on the ground and made a stone his pillow. He dreamt of the golden ladder between earth and heaven, heard God's promise, and in the morning made an altar of the stones in the place.

The prophets were ethical teachers who challenged their people to fulfil their tasks. Nelly Sachs was such a teacher, even if the first task to which she called her people and humanity was the duty to mourn and to lament, to heal and to rebuild. We hear her meditate on the role of the prophets:

> If the prophets broke in
> Through doors of the night
> And searched for an ear like a homeland –
>
> Ear of mankind,
> You, overgrown with nettles,
> Would you hear?
> If the voice of the prophets
> Would blow
> Upon the flutes made of murdered children's bones
> And would breathe out air burnt with
> Martyr's cries –
> If they would build a bridge out of the sighs
> Of dying old men
> Ear of mankind,
> You, occupied with petty listening,
> Would you hear?

This was part of the enduring anguish which she shared with all survivors, whether they had been in the camps or lived outside them: no one listens, no one hears, no one mourns. Dust dances in the air around her; butterflies move across her vision (she wrote of a Theresienstadt child: 'I never saw another butterfly'); and humanity forgets the darkness out of which it has emerged.

*Erich Fried*

Erich Fried was an Austrian author. Born in Vienna, in 1921, he grew up within a comfortable middle-class family, but in a Vienna already charac-terized as the 'red' city. A Social Democrat was in office, and the social legislation for the poorer members of society was a challenged reality. The 6-year-old Erich had no recollections of 'Bloody Friday' but he has written of the burning 'Palace of Justice' and saw the bodies of dead and wounded carried past him. Workers were rebelling against police brutality, and young Erich Fried saw the posters throughout Vienna in which Karl Kraus demanded the resignation of the police president. Erich Fried changed a great deal in the course of time – at one time he republished an edition of his earlier poems and wrote 'counter poems' on the other side of the page; he had moved from support for Israel in its period of suffering to an attack upon Israel in defence of Arab sufferers. This does not mean that he was inconsistent, that he had abandoned his earlier ideals.

The young Fried did not want to be a poet; he wanted to be an inventor. But his father fell into the hands of the Nazis after the *Anschluss*. Hugo Fried, the father, was tortured for a month and died in a hospital the day after his 'release' from the Gestapo-dominated prison. Erich writes about this phase of his life when, as a 17-year-old, he finally left for Great Britain:

> After the Germans marched into Vienna, in 1938, which changed me from an Austrian sixth-former into a persecuted Jew; and after the mur-der of my (unpolitical) father by Gestapo agents, I made a decision. If I would escape alive, I would be that which my father had vainly attempted to be during the last twelve years of his life: I would become a writer. I wanted to write and battle against fascism, racism, and the expulsion of innocent people.

Fried wrote this thirty-six years after the event. Back in 1938, he had founded a 'self-help' group among the other refugees. Before the war started in 1939, they managed to rescue seventy Austrian Jews who found a haven in England – his mother among them. And he became a member of one of the Communist organized refugee groups fighting against fascism. He left them in 1944, recognizing that the Communist structure and its aims were incompatible with his ideals and his need to be a free individual. By this time he had started to write poetry, sustaining himself, his mother and young family (he married for the first time in 1944) as a factory worker and chemist.

He remained connected to left wing politics in the years that followed, years in which his style matured and developed. He began to write one of the important postwar novels *Ein soldat und ein mädchen*. It was a book directed against the death penalty, against 'easy hatred', against stereotyping and setting up barriers within society. And it tried to show that humanity and decency can even be found in the SS soldier or the Communist police agent.

Erich told me of one event in his life which clarified his attitudes. He had been asked to talk on a Hamburg radio programme, in dialogue with a young neo-Nazi, and he had agreed. When the general public heard about this plan, the station was flooded with complaints. The dialogue was cancelled and Fried was asked to broadcast on his own. But, in his talk, Fried kept addressing the young man and went afterwards to the young man's home in order to talk with him directly. Erich said that they spent many hours together in conversation, and parted as friends.

Life and writing were always woven together with Erich Fried. He taught in many ways: poems and epigrams, satire, black humour, and the quick movement from one to the other – this was true of his life as much as of his published works.

Erich Fried could not bring himself to visit Germany until 1953; but then he brought all of himself to that confrontation. He was now the great translator, BBC commentator, poet and engaged political writer who could and did criticize Communism and its political cruelties on many occasions. At the same time, he remained resolutely left wing. The numerous prizes he received did not make him more popular with the government; his writings were banned in Bavaria for a while (1978).

As far as his own personal identity was concerned, he knew exactly who and what he was. Though he accepted the Austrian citizenship offered to him shortly before he received the Literature Prize of the city of Vienna, he maintained his British citizenship and considered himself affiliated to the British Labour Party. He did not cease to be a proud Jew. Let us turn to his poetry with its clear yet cryptic expression of moral issues, whether addressed to Israel or to modern Germans who live in the post-Auschwitz world. In 'Talk with a survivor' he wrote:

> What did you do then,
> which you should not have done?
> 'Nothing'

What did you *not* do,
which you should have done?
'this and that
these and those;
some things'

Why didn't you do it?
'because I was afraid'
Why were you afraid?
'because I didn't want to die'

Did others die
because you didn't want to die?
'I think
so'

Do you have to add any more
to that which you did not do?
'Yes: to ask you
what would you have done in my place?'

That I do not know
and I cannot judge you.
But I know one thing:
tomorrow, none of us
will be alive
if, today,
we once again do nothing

It was typical and right for Erich Fried to move from past to present, to remind the world around him that inaction remains evil. Fried demanded changes in us, just as he demanded them from himself.

In his 'counter poems', Erich Fried challenged his earlier Biblical poems with their image of Jews dying in the wilderness with Egyptian soldiers during the Six Day War who threw away their boots and died of thirst in the Sinai desert. It is not surprising that a besieged Jewish community felt itself attacked by one of their own. Yet Fried's great anger was directed against all who use force, who to his mind practised the old ways which now had to be abandoned. This comes out clearly in his Bremen Prize acceptance speech of 1983, where he could attack the postwar trials at

Nuremberg as bad (because post-facto legislation, and any death penalty, was abhorrent to Fried), but where he could go on to attack the Nazi mentality still prevalent in the world:

> Particularly today, during these sad hours commemorating the fiftieth anniversary of Hitler's coming to power, the burning of the Reichstag, and the burning of the books, we must never forget that one can recall the old misdeeds only in one way: one must fight new misdeeds and their systematic programming even, and particularly if one is a writer. If we do not fight against this, we need not bother to talk about an 'aesthetics of resistance'.

For Erich Fried, being a writer and poet was not, in the first instance, a literary occupation; the writer however was to know how to capture events and feelings, thoughts and fantasies within words. But writers, he believed, had to recognize that their task was a political one, and that only by keeping the past alive could we have a future:

> The crimes of yesterday took
> the memorial days
> for the crimes of day before yesterday
> and cancelled them
>
> Viewing the crimes of today
> we occupy ourselves
> with the memorial days
> for the crimes of yesterday
>
> Tomorrow's crimes
> will take us of today
> and will cancel us
> without memorial days
> if we do not
> prevent them.
>
> 'Ca ira (for Peter Weiss)'

NOTES

1. Translation by Michael Hamburger.
2. Translation by Michael Hamburger.
3. Translation by Michael Hamburger.
4. Translation by Albert Friedlander, printed in various reform liturgies.
5. Translation by Albert Friedlander.
6. Job 19:26.
7. Translation by Albert Friedlander.

PART 5

# [1]

# FIRST LIGHT

'CAN one forget the Holocaust? Can one forgive the Holocaust? Can there be vengeance?' These questions return continually. In a world searching for moral certainties, they are surely answered by religion or by common sense. What is there to debate? But, in the decades after the Holocaust, there has only been controversy and even confrontation among religions, survivors and onlookers.

Even in the camps, there had been different answers. For many of the victims, the questions did not exist. How could one forgive? But to look beyond that, towards vengeance, required first that one would survive. Letting one's mind dwell upon vengeance was a luxury – perhaps a necessary luxury when one was totally helpless and abandoned – but it had to take second place to the grim struggle to stay alive. Day dreams concentrated more upon food, upon reunion with loved ones, upon resuming some sort of normal life. The perpetrators, on the other hand, tried to suppress their thoughts about what they were doing, what lay ahead. Those with a conscience rationalized themselves into a position of helplessness, where they were 'only following orders'. They drew away from the consequences of their actions, distanced themselves from the reality of the camps as a tour of duty in hell, or let their prejudices revel in the knowledge that the evil was now the norm, and that they were right in 'executing vermin', particularly since the distinction had been made between human jailers and the subhuman specimens to be exterminated. Yet the questions, like the facts, could not be totally suppressed. From the very beginning, as little as possible was put on paper. Records were destroyed or forged: when the euthanasia programme was operating, the families of the victims would receive letters giving the cause of death as 'contagious disease', 'heart attack', 'pneumonia', all ending with the information that for health reasons the victim had to be cremated. And at the end, an orgy of destruction of records took place as the perpetrators awaited the vengeance of the world and tried to avoid the consequence of their actions.

Much later, Christian thinkers began to examine the fading memory of the Holocaust as a moral issue, and asked questions of the survivors and their families. The next generation of Jews also began to ask questions. The answers tended to differ in different countries: in Israel, America, England and Germany. Israel, as we have seen, had the particular stance of the survivor nation still living under that trauma, with the concept of *sh'lilat ha-galut* – rejecting the exile or Diaspora life – firmly engrained in the thinking of its people. Wagner's music is still rejected, despite the growing acceptance of Germans visiting Israel, and Israel views itself as speaking for world Jewry in this and other matters related to the Holocaust. The Eichmann trial in particular raises the issue of 'justice versus vengeance', as does the work of Simon Wiesenthal, whom many see only as the grim, vengeful Nazi-hunter, but who is in fact a Rider Towards the Dawn in his quest for justice rather than vengeance. In a way, Wiesenthal's is also an American response since his California Institute builds upon the reactions of an American Jewry which has its own blend of guilt – for not having been there in the centre of the attack upon Jewish life – and which is swallowed up in various patterns of thought based upon post-rational disillusionment, where the American dream and its self-certainties have been replaced by inner doubt and a partial withdrawal from Europe.

Specific situations bring a hidden agenda of confrontation between Jews and Christians to the foreground. In the 1980s, the visit of Ronald Reagan to the Bitburg cemetery with its SS graves in May 1985 brought much of this conflict into the open. In 1990, the case of the Carmelite convent at Auschwitz showed a new development within those battle positions, but also the resurgence of older, darker trends which are discouraging.

We cannot cover more than three millennia of Jewish thought on the nature of sin and of forgiving sin. We must therefore discuss guilt before dealing with forgiving it. There are many kinds of guilt-pardoning and forgiving is affected by this. What is the German guilt which Jews should forgive? Tillich was the first Christian scholar driven out of Germany in 1933 – not least because he defended the Jews. When he returned to Berlin in 1953, it was to give a series of lectures, 'The Jewish question – a Christian and German problem'.

Tillich spoke of five types of guilt. First, there was the absolute guilt of the murderers, of certain groups and individuals who could be viewed separately from the other Germans. Second, he spoke of the guilt that no German could evade: the moral responsibility that was not accepted, the voices that remained silent, the individuals who made not one move to save their fellow human beings. Next, he looked at the audience surrounding him and spoke of the guilt of repressed knowledge, of hiding from oneself, of encapsulating past trauma deeply within one's self in the hope that it would never break into the new life that did not want to know what happened in the past. This could only lead to the fourth type of guilt: that one would really forget the past! More tragedy resided in that fact than in the earlier patterns of self-deceit. Finally, he warned the Germans not to take these moral questions into the area of bookkeeping, not to calculate carefully that the hurt they had suffered wiped out their own guilt of involvement with the concentration camps or wanton murder.

Let us accept this Christian appraisal. We can link it with Karl Rahner's definition of sin as an act estranging humans from God. But how can we respond to it? Is the same process of forgiving to be applied to the crippled conscience of the onlooker and to the murderer? And what is accomplished if we forgive those who forget? What, in the end, is required of us by others? By ourselves? By God?

In the Jewish tradition, we begin by asking, what does God require of the sinner? How can the sinner achieve forgiveness? 'Let him bring a sin offering, and his guilt will be atoned!' Obviously, the road to forgiveness begins with the sinner: 'Wash you, cleanse you – purify yourselves!' Sin is an uncleanness which adheres to the malefactor: the vocabulary of forgiveness is replete with such verbs as *tiher*=purify; *machah*=wipe; *kibbes*=wash; *kipper*=purge, as God removes that sin (*nose avon va pesha*) from the guilty party. Since we are dealing with the contrasts rather than the similarities between Judaism and Christianity (fully aware that it is often a matter of emphasis and that neither faith is monolithic), it might be noted that one idea of humanity confronts another one at this point. Basically, Judaism is opposed to original sin. Man/woman is good. We stumble off the right path, but we can return to it. If we seriously accepted original sin, if we had to live with the fact that all humans are tainted and that they cannot remove guilt from themselves, we might well be pushed into a position more often encountered in Christianity. All have been washed clean by the blood of the lamb, who have accepted the Christ – dare we set ourselves against the Lord who has forgiven them? Must we not accept our brother and sister in Christ who have been forgiven by God?

The simple answer is 'no'. It may well be that we should and will forgive those who have wronged us: not because of a religious belief they profess, but by the actions we have observed in their lives, by their repentance in word and deed which has created a new bridge between us enabling reconciliation to take place. Part of that bridge may well be ritual and religious ceremony. But the Bible (the Torah) is quite clear on the point that the ritual itself, even when conducted properly by the priest, does not guarantee forgiveness for the sinner: Leviticus 4:26, 'The Priest shall make atonement for him for his sin and he shall be forgiven', still clearly indicates that forgiveness itself comes from God and is not guaranteed by proper ritual. Indeed, the ritual itself is that text is related to sins (*bi'sh'gaga* – inadvertent errors). Conscious sins against God are not expiated by sacrifice.[1] And the prophets stress that God hates and despises sacrifices which do not emerge out of true contrition and repentance.

The stress is clear: the winning of forgiveness depends upon the actions of the sinner; the wrong done must be acknowledged and confessed; it must have become abhorrent to the sinner. The sinner must change before receiving forgiveness, and public acts of fasting and self-abasement must be followed by actions demonstrating a change of heart and a new way of life. Considering the different types of German guilt listed by Paul Tillich, one can see that this biblical approach to the nature of forgiving cannot operate within any of the categories enumerated by him until the work of regeneration has commenced within the sinner. More: we cannot be judges; God must judge.

In our first discussion, we had already turned to some of the rabbinic interpretations of *teshuvah*, that of turning back from the path of evil and returning to God and to the right way. Our Ten Days of Penitence, of *teshuvah*, see a pattern effecting reconciliation between man/woman and God, and between all human creatures. It is quite true that in the task of reconciliation one may find a valid role for the mediator. Abraham standing before Sodom and Gomorrah pleads for sinners and God, as it were, lets himself be entreated to open the matter again and to make concessions. The prophets intercede for the sinner – Amos reports on visions, intercession and prevention of evil decrees until the cup is full and there is no more forgiving. Moses himself rejects the opportunity to start again without the People Israel and prays that God forgive that stubborn people. Even more, there is that dimension of ultimate hope, based upon the Covenant and the promise of the future, which contains an assured pardon to the sinner whenever he comes to repent and to return. What happens on high must also happen in the world. If God's forgiving love prevails – can we do less? That is the teaching of Hosea; the story of love between husband and wife reaches out beyond all formulae of guilt, of reconciliation in the human realm, and is as valid as any law of the Torah. But here, too, there is the condition that the sinner and the one who has suffered from the sin cannot come back to each other until the sinner has turned in repentance, has taken the first step in total sincerity. And there must be not certainty, but the strong belief that the repentance is sincere, that more than ritual or empty form is being paraded.

We have a healthy scepticism here; we need to be convinced. The ritual itself is not enough! Sins – *bein adam v'chavero* – need restitution and proper atonement before forgiveness becomes a reality. In a court of law, damages may be paid, there will be redress for the wrong done. It is doubtful whether many plaintiffs leave the court arm-in-arm once the judgement has been given. We might like to see this, nevertheless, in the synagogue. But, unless the injured party is convinced of the sincerity of the wrongdoer's repentance, reconciliation does not really take place. Open wounds remain in both participants of the conflict. Freud has taught us enough to understand what damage buried resentments can do to our psyche. Nevertheless, it seems that an empty formula of forgiveness represses resentment just as much as open rejection of the unrepentant sinner – and the rejection gives the sinner another opportunity to change his way, where the formula of an official pardon can leave him in a never-never land of hypocrisy.

God's forgiving the sins committed by humans against God (*bein adam v'Makom*) is another matter. Biblical and rabbinic teachings both portray his infinite mercy and his willingness to forgive. Hag. 5a states: 'He who sins and repents is at once forgiven'. And it is often argued that the act of *imitatio dei* should make us most ready to forgive on all occasions. In the Talmud[2] we find this sentiment: 'All who act forgivingly (mercifully) toward their fellow creatures will be treated mercifully by Heaven, and all who do not act mercifully towards their fellow creatures will not be treated mercifully by Heaven'. And so Rabbi Nachman says: 'Imitate God by being compassionate and forgiving. He will in turn have compassion on you, and pardon your offences.'

We believe and celebrate the goodness and compassion of God, his infinite capacity to forgive. We cannot arrogate his judgement to ourselves. All humans have the capacity to sin, and all have the capacity to return. One of the great teachers in the Jewish tradition, Beruriah, reminds her husband Rabbi Meir that he must not hate sinners, but rather sin itself. We can have compassion for the damaged, tainted human beings who have come to personify evil in the world. We can hope that they will return and repent. We can and do recommend them to the judgement and compassion of God. But, here in this world, we also have to defend standards of justice and must fight against evil. Blithe words of forgiveness mean nothing. They do not change the individuals caught in a situation of guilt and of suffering. And it can be argued that the pursuit of justice is the best way of helping those caught in their web of evil action. 'The sword comes into the world because justice is delayed . . .'

There are so many types of guilt in the world, and each imprisons those who have done evil. But can the Jews – as a collective – forgive the Germans – as a collective – for the sins committed by the Germans during the dark period we call the Holocaust? Who forgives whom and for what?

The law courts should have dealt with these criminals, the first category in Tillich's list of various types of guilt. But, out of 90,000 cases investigated by the authorities, only 6,478 persons were judged guilty; 82,467 cases terminated without punishment of any sort. Hundreds of cases are still in the files . . . justice is not only blind, but very slow indeed.

We have already determined that children are not responsible for the sin of their parents and that there is no reason for us to set up some sort of sanhedrin to forgive the Germans of today. And, if there are 100,000 Nazi criminals still alive in the world today, there is no way in which a blanket pardon issued by a 'collective Jewish community' could help them or us. We who are here – and the Jewish world we may seem to represent – are not consumed by hate and feelings of revenge against those 'eternal Germans' around the world, far afield in the jungles of Paraguay or near us in Europe. But we – those who are here and those who are not here – are still maimed sufferers with injuries that will not heal. We have lost members of our families. We have lost the great community of Eastern Jewry. We have lost the most special warmth and gaiety of Sephardic Jewry along the Mediterranean Sea. We have lost our scholars and our simple people. And we hate the evil in this world which overwhelmed us, the *Sinti-Roma*, the homosexuals and the anti-Nazis who were wiped out by that evil in the camps. We mourn the million children and we wonder what the world would be like if their lives had been permitted to flower. The actions needed to secure pardon for these crimes must initially come from the perpetrators – and they must be placed before the altar of God. Then, and only then, and as individuals rather than one collective, might we begin to say words of comfort to our neighbours.

There is a sense in which theology divides Christianity and Judaism, with the knowledge that revelation is love, and that our shared work of redemption sends us into the world and 'into life' as one. There is a thought here which I must place before you, even if I am a theologian. The Christian concept of forgiving, and the Jewish concept of forgiving, remains a concept – a frozen thought. Every human being has the capacity to be compassionate, has the ability to forgive. And that human quality must be asserted as a universal reality; it must be common to all. Religious traditions vary and different aspects of human capacities may be nurtured within various faiths. Our capacity to love is the same: *v'ahavta l'rey-acha camocha* – love they neighbour as thyself. We are left with the individual's capacity to love and forgive.

What is an individual's reaction to the request for forgiveness? Simon Wiesenthal's story *The sunflower* has become the almost definitive text for us. In it Wiesenthal comes to ask those questions about guilt and punishment, about forgiving and not forgiving, about forgetting and remembering, which remain crucial for any confrontation with the Holocaust. A young Jew is taken from a death camp to a hospital, to the bed of a Nazi soldier about to die. The Nazi, head and eyes completely wrapped in bandages, reaches out to the Jew and asks him to forgive. He confesses to his crimes: a village burned with its women and children . . . other memories . . . and his need to be forgiven. The Jew feels compassion and horror, but finally walks out of the room without speaking to the Nazi.

What should we have done? Wiesenthal sent his story to many Jews and non-Jews; and they gave their answers. Through them, he reached out to his readers. The moral authority which this deceptively calm story exercised upon those addressed brought many of them to give revealing answers. Rene Cassin, Nobel Prize laureate for peace (1968), principal author of the 'Universal Declaration of the Rights of Man' for the UN, could only reply out of his own experience:

> One must grant to individuals who belong to the victim collectivities complete and freedom of judgment . . . I was brought subsequently to wonder if it was not my duty to overcome my personal grudges as a French Jew in order to contribute to the effort together with such well intentioned German teachers . . . to share in a task which would have bearing on the future, I accomplished it to the full. Far from forgetting [the barbarous way in which my family perished] . . . I stressed this . . . in order to then stress to what extent the French were anxious to live in a state of lasting peace with the German people . . .[3]

Kurt von Schuschnigg was the Austrian Chancellor in 1938, when he was arrested by the Nazis and imprisoned until after the war. His was a straightforward answer:

> One thing was certain, he could not, he should not, forgive. And had he forgiven it would have been a completely meaningless and thoroughly dishonest action. One can only pardon an offence which has been directly inflicted upon oneself ... *The sunflower* casts sombre, but in the last resort, reconciliatory shadows.[4]

Gustav Heinemann, President of Germany after the war, spoke out of his deep Christian convictions:

> The conflict between Justice (in the form of Law) and Forgiveness, is the thread that runs through your story. Justice and Law, however essential they are, cannot exist without Forgiveness. That is the quality that Jesus Christ added to Justice and with which He gave it life.[5]

David Daiches, a leading British academic, is both literary critic and moral philosopher. His own answer is also straightforward:

> In so far as someone who has committed such a crime or series of crimes asks an individual other than a representative of God to forgive him, the request is a device for obtaining psychological comfort, and it may be that we have an obligation to give such psychological comfort to a dying man ...
> But I don't think that this is forgiveness ... I don't see how in any genuinely meaningful sense one individual can offer forgiveness for crimes that were not committed against him ... I would solve the problem by drawing a distinction between understanding and forgiving.[6]

Finally I want to cite some of the poet/prophets. Theirs are the standard answers of religion reinforced by the lives they have led. Abraham Heschel marched from Selma towards Montgomery alongside Martin Luther King:

> No one can forgive crimes committed by other people. It is therefore preposterous to assume that anyone alive can extend forgiveness for the suffering of any one of the six million people who perished.[7]

Primo Levi said:

> When an act of violence or an offence has been committed it is for ever
> irreparable: it is quite probable that public opinion will cry out for sanc-
> tion, a punishment, a 'price' for pain . . . but the offence remains and
> the price is always (even if it is 'just') a new offence and a new source
> of pain. This having been said, I think I can affirm that you did well, in
> this situation, to refuse your pardon to the dying man. You did well
> because it was the lesser evil: you could only have forgiven him by lying
> or by inflicting upon yourself a terrible moral violence . . . but it is always
> impossible to decide categorically between the answers 'yes' and 'no';
> there always remains something to be said for the other side.[8]

We encounter Martin Niemoeller, speaking as a Christian who fights the
evil of his own time, and who was also a prisoner in a concentration camp.
Niemoeller answered Wiesenthal in a similar fashion to Primo Levi:

> Injustice which was done directly to us – we can forgive; but the 'evil'
> done against other human beings, particularly those who are close to us,
> we cannot 'forgive' fundamentally. Only the person who has suffered
> that evil has the authority to do so. As a Christian, which I am or at least
> would like to be, I could only say to a fellow human being who opens
> his tortured conscience to me, 'The evil you did to me, which you now
> regret – I forgive it to you. My own personal freedom which is my
> existence is also only granted to me by forgiveness. As to what you did
> to others and to those who are near to me whose suffering also touches
> me, that has to be forgiven by those whom you injured.'[9]

Simon Wiesenthal is one of the 'compassionate people'. Those who still
view him as a revengeful hunter searching the world for Nazi criminals do
not understand the mixture of justice and compassion found in his life and
writings; he is a teacher and prophet for our time. His 'sunflower' writings
served to evoke responses from the intellectual and religious leaders of
Europe; and his function as a catalyst in the area of guilt and forgiveness
cannot be ignored. The same should be said about his work – in Vienna,
Los Angeles, Argentina, and all over the world. Disagreement can also be
a form of reconciliation.

I have drawn one structure of forgiveness and repentance within Judaism
for you, an expression of an aspect of the thinking of the Jewish people.
This way of thought is a given reality accessible to all. The Jewish people

is a paradigm of humanity: it contains all the faults and evil found in others, it contains the compassion and love which predominate in its texts. It has been called, and it must again be called, an *am b'nei rachamim*: 'a compassionate people, God's children'.

NOTES

1. Numbers 15:30.31.
2. Rosh Hash 17a and elsewhere.
3. From *The sunflower* (Paris, 1970; New York, Schocken Books, 1976), pp. 105–106.
4. Ibid., pp. 201–202.
5. Ibid., pp. 129–130.
6. Ibid., p. 108.
7. Ibid., p. 131.
8. Ibid., p. 190.
9. Ibid., p. 144.

# [ 2 ]

# AN ODYSSEY

## MY OWN JOURNEY TOWARDS THE DAWN

I started my own journey sixty-five years ago, when I was born. The relationship between mother and child is the seal upon our identity, confirming it at that moment, and it continued for more than four decades. In establishing our own identity, we come to that first and ultimate relationship which was recognized in ancient times and which still provides a shield, or at least a skin, between the individual and that outer world which strives to reduce the individual person to nothingness.

There were other support systems, of course: a sister, twin brother, and father – the nuclear family at its best. But it was the relationship with the mother which mattered. In my case, I could see the confidence of my father eroding under the pressure of the Nazi society in Berlin; it surrounded us by the time I was six. Whenever the door-bell rang, my father put on his overcoat and stood at the back door, ready to run away. But my mother's serenity and courage, her protecting, fierce love for her children, and the confidence she projected gave me a foundation for life which could hold the darkness at bay. I listened to a Jungian analyst the other day, who told us of three patients, nuns, who felt helpless and overwhelmed by the total nothingness they sensed around their lives. When the analyst talked of a dark tunnel, they said that a tunnel already had more shape to it than they could visualize. The analyst probed each life – and all of them had lost their mothers at childbirth or within the first three years of their lives. That skin between themselves and nothingness had been peeled away. For a while, the religious institutions into which they had fled had sustained them. Now, suddenly, they were filled with an ontological despair of the individual left in the darkness with no sense of where and why she stood there.

This is not intended as an attack upon a religious institution; after all, I live within the synagogue and find my reasons for existence, and the support of my identity, within a Judaism I celebrate daily, and with a faith in God that falters only occasionally. It is more the grateful recognition that the evil and darkness which surrounded my childhood did not emerge out of me, but out of a world which I had not made. With the reality of my mother's faith and courage surrounding me, I could see that I did not have to stand alone, that I was not one individual against the universe. There were people in the world, good and bad. And I met enough good people, even in Hitler's Germany, to realize that I could not do without them. The Dawn-Riders, poets and analysts, rabbis and philosophers, dreamers and fighters – they all came later; and I am grateful to all the company which we have gathered in these pages. A Maimonides or a Karl Barth could probably draw together all of their teachings and create an edifice of faith in which almost anyone might feel at home. A hopeful pattern could be achieved where entrophy would give way to anthropology, and where the human being would stand in the world and proclaim: 'I am meant to be here!' But religion, or theology, is not an enclosed system for me in which I could finally give up my identity and become a cherished and needed cog in the machine. Long ago, in the days of Hobbes' *Leviathan*, the individual was defined by the state; and it took centuries for the individual to emerge fully out of that machine and to achieve a separate identity. Even today, when at least some of the totalitarian states have crashed to the ground, we are hesitant to emerge out of that cocoon. Too many of us still want to be other-directed, and to be assigned not only our roles, but also our beliefs. That, of course, is our problem. We have met a number of dynamic, charismatic teachers who offer us systems which do not conflict with the reality as we understand it. Why can't I at least point to one teacher as providing the solution for our problems, and gain adherents for that theology or philosophy?

The simple answer which I must give is that it cannot be done. To some extent I have provided strong indications regarding my personal position. Going back to the beginning, discriminating between the Dawn-Riders, I have said that Leo Baeck was my rabbi; Elie Wiesel my *rebbe*; George Steiner my teacher in contemporary culture – and any number of friends have been companions with whom I have ridden gladly. *It does not mean that I could accept their systems.* My Judaism is a broad stream with many tributaries. One day, I can travel with Emil Fackenheim; the next, with

Richard Rubenstein. These are contradictory directions, but when you journey towards infinity, all roads are equal.

Certainly, we can and should define the malaises of our time. We have travelled with the best of doctors, particularly with the poets. And one can even go for a general prescription. Psychiatrists have done this brilliantly, drawing upon Freud, Jung, or Adler. And there were systems developed in the very darkness of the concentration camps in which we rediscover the unquenchable spirit of humanity: Victor Frankl and logotherapy; Eugene Heimler and the recognition of the human quality which seeks meaning in all that one does; Bruno Bettelheim and his awareness of how the human spirit could be crushed in Dachau and elsewhere. I also want to list some of the analyses of the human condition which came to us out of this assembly of human beings who could leave the darkness of the camps and move towards the new dawn of the twenty-first century. But I would still maintain that this was a general prescription for us damaged human beings who find ourselves utterly alone at times because the interrelationship between ourselves and God, between ourselves and our neighbours, has come to an end.

Analysts and rabbis are case-workers. It is quite true that we prescribe for the world, that we outline the directions which our communities should take. But when people come to us, they come to us as individuals. Each one is unique. And whether we diagnose despair, *anomie*, depression, or even over-self-confidence we have to work with each person as a unique individual whose like we will never see again. We can, of course, write self-help books which can be bought by the general public and used as they desire: a DIY course in religion or psychotherapy. There are enough books in this field, some of them to be highly recommended. It is just that I cannot go along with the philosophy of a limited God, even when it is built upon the Utilitarian philosophers. I find Hans Jonas far more complex and convincing, even when I stop short of his conclusions. But who reads Jonas? Not the general public; and that is a great pity. Here is why I keep pleading for individuals to turn to individuals, to be eclectic; to pick out of each teaching what applies to your own situation. The traditionalists call this heresy or Reform Judaism. But Reform Judaism makes much greater demands upon the person, as one can see when one looks at the representatives we have encountered here.

Rabbis, I have suggested, can prescribe for institutions. Eugene Borowitz, one example, probably has the most practical paradigm offered to the searching Reform Jew; and I would suggest that you accept it. The only problem is that you must already be inside that system, wear the same carapace, march along with the turtles or tortoises. The logic is there; and so is the passion, when you consider his dedicated Zionism and celebration of the Jewish people. I don't know why I am tempted to walk along with Stephen Schwarzschild for a while, and at least think about the Messiah as a possible inspiration for myself. But then, I make my own choice and opt for the teacher who inspires me most as rabbi, leader, fighter against the darkness, and person of absolute integrity: Leo Baeck, the teacher of Theresienstadt. I think that Baeck's polarities of faith are of such subtlety and clarity that I find all of myself giving assent to them. 'Mystery' and 'commandment' are at the centre of religious experience, as Leo Baeck is in the centre of contemporary religious life, with his unsurpassed knowledge of mysticism and of the rabbinic teachings which emerged after the destruction of the Temple.

The travellers we have followed across the landscape of our time have gone beyond the darkness of the Holocaust; but its shadow reached out after them, and the light of dawn has not yet reached the far horizon. The present conditions of the religious life, and of the non-religious as well, are totally those of the polarities which we encounter in the universe. We look at a social structure which has disintegrated; at the former empires of power which do not exist any longer; a frail economic security within the West which does not meet its obligations towards the rest of the world; and at the religious institutions which are beginning to crumble. Somewhere in the middle of that dark plain, humanity has charted a course which asserts the continuity of human life upon the surface of a threatened planet.

The Jewish community is still caught within the polarities of a geography which can be seen in the form of an ellipse, with two focal points: Israel as the one centre, with Jerusalem as the lighthouse of faith; and the Diaspora, with the United States as its centre. The dynamic tension within these polarities still gives vitality and new development to each. Nevertheless, the Jewish people, in some ways also representative of humanity, are caught within all the polarities which make up the total human condition. In terms of religious faith, we encounter both the near and the far God; but, in our time, God seems to be very far away, still hiding his face from us as he did at Auschwitz. Jungian analysts can speak of the 'shadow which resides within us'. Those aspects of ourselves we prefer to occlude from consciousness. We are holding opposites in creative tension: distance and intimacy, the near and the far God.

Outside that area, we come to the other polarities which we have tried to explore: the relationship between the victim and the opppressor, this dialectic which has to be solved again and again. How are we to deal with the new oppressors, how to come to terms with the old ones? In East Germany, now absorbed in the larger Germany, we saw that not only the victims are caught in this situation, but also those who were either guilty bystanders, or the oppressors themselves. How could they deal with their past? And how can we cope with it? It is impossible to ignore the situation, since it reaches out and touches us in a Europe which in parts, at least, has become more of a village, as the world itself becomes a global village.

In some ways, our own situation is impossible: all of us are touched by the depression which is endemic in our environment, but also in the human soul. It has been argued that this depression is necessary to life. Any religious insight relevant to our time knows that it has to confront the evil of our time and our inability to resolve the malady of human imperfection. Depression, our analysts teach, touches the parts of our soul other emotions can't reach: this is a sickness unto death. We think again of our Holocaust writers: Piotr Rawicz; Jean Amery; Paul Celan; Terence Des Pres; Uriel Tal; and Primo Levi – all of them suicides. Friends of Primo Levi explain that, suddenly, the dreams and nightmares of the concentration camp came back to him. He had fought his way out of that darkness once; this time, it was too much. And while one can make a 'theology of depression', can assert its necessity for the examined life, it is still an aspect of the human condition which we see as a dark hole in the universe of our soul.

The Dawn-Riders know depression, and generally recognize that they have to fight against it. Depression can lead to an even greater sickness: apathy. So much of the evil in our time is the result of apathy rather than enthusiastic evil. The Nazis in Germany did not depend upon total support for their actions; all they needed was apathy – and there was an abundance of it. Depression can be a variant of enthusiasm, of joy and exaltation; but apathy – indifference – stands somewhere between the polarities of life and does not permit itself any real movement. The Hasidim know that if one of their opponents treated them with cold indifference, he would remain their enemy forever. If he hated them with a great passion, that passion could, some time, be transformed into love – the other side of hatred.

And what of the Hasidic *bitul ha-yesh* – 'annihilation of the self'? Is this suicide of some sort – or transcendence? In the end, self-knowledge leads to transcendence. There is a difference between 'melancholy' and 'bitter-ness' in the Hasidic tradition. The melancholy person is remote from God and Man; his condition resembles death. But the bitter person is at least stirred into vitality. He fights. And in that fight the bitterness may be resolved as he reaches a higher plane of life. Is hatred itself helpful? I do not think so. But, if hatred is a type of frozen anger that must be resolved, it is at least a surface symptom which can be treated within the religious and its structures, or by the analyst.

The issue of powerlessness is significant today. It is central to the theology of liberation and to the feminist theologians in America, where the changing position of woman in religious and secular law has created a totally new pattern of thought and action. What has to change here is the religious law and the dogmas which try to keep woman in a situation of powerlessness. But should a therapist criticize and attack older religious teachings where they cause damage? Religion also has its own duty to challenge psychiatry and analysis in those areas where the world had clearly moved on, and where old-fashioned ideas and practices seemed to prevail. For myself, I can only affirm the necessary partnership between religion and psychiatry, so long delayed.

We can never even review all the questions, let alone the answers. And, where I state my own approach, I must always point out that it is not prescriptive. Thus, in the debate on joint prayers and liturgies with our Christian neighbours, I find myself in the minority, in relation to the more liberal branches of the Jewish community. There is a difference in attitude to a community or an individual. I cannot see the many dogmas of Christianity as being the central aspect of the divine revelation to humanity, and, when I enter a Christian house of worship, I am rarely there as the representative of the Jewish community. When that is so, I try to be circumspect – why upset my community? My encounter with the divine presence at Christian services has been through individuals, rather than through the Church in all its glory. To put it in a simple, old-fashioned way, I am a believer in God. When I meet others who believe, I can worship with them without worrying much about the liturgy, although I will be careful not to say in a Church what I could not say in a synagogue. But I often meet Christians who shine like incandescent candles and light up the world for me with their faith. That is why I can participate in inter-faith services, to the sorrow of my Orthodox colleagues and the slight unhappiness of colleagues and members of my synagogue.

There are other areas of disagreement. The most respected scholars have dealt with the traditional response of Judaism to the Holocaust, among them Rav Hutner. Yet I cannot go along with their premise that 'the Jews were fooled into believing they could trust their neighbours'. The whole rejection of the outer world as a type of 'enticement' for which Jews must first repent is alien to me. Nor can I set a Torah-view history against secular history. As I indicated, a Jew has the right to withdraw from society. I honour Rav Hutner for affirming humanity, but I could not live in his enclave.

It is hard for me to be at odds with Michael Wyschogrod. He is a wonderful human being, open to Germany – he often lectures in that country and joins those Jews who, like myself, disagree with him. In terms of Orthodoxy, I find him perhaps clearer and more profound than most of his colleagues. I have learned much from Wyschogrod, who respects my actions in life, but rejects my way of thinking. I can live with that; and I do accept Wyschogrod's challenge against those who would see the Holocaust as a revelation from God. 'The Holocaust was totally evil, and to draw (moral) lessons from that evil is a suicidal pacifism', he said to me. But here as in all cases, I come back to my contention that this is one of the many ways of coming to terms with the Holocaust.

I cannot accept the notion that God gave moral imperatives through the Holocaust. I do accept the reality of an event filled with so much evil that it assumes mythic proportions. I must deal with it through my own experience and my personal faith, and I can also turn to those who emerged out of that darkness and moved towards the light. As I follow them, I come to see that there are new discoveries to be made upon the way – and I will not deny what I will find tomorrow.

The traditional thinkers, as I have said, operate out of a system which does not function properly for me. But British traditionalists have been able to open themselves to the questions of Reform colleagues. And it is a pleasure to watch many of them plunge into these topics and persist until they or someone else have learned from this encounter. When one moves into the actual Halacha of the death camps, I can only be silent. But in that silence, especially when it reaches out through survivors like Hugo Gryn and we listen to the voices which came out of the darkness, we come to learn that the road from darkness to light commences here; and that it must not be forgotten.

I would name myself among the Progressive and radical rabbis and thinkers who have tried to cope with the Holocaust. I have been shaped by my teachers. And I have been shaped by the lands which we have examined: life in Germany, in the United States, and in Great Britain, had its own paradigms which touched my thinking. The advantage in that was the encounter with friends and teachers. The disadvantage: that I stand somewhere in the middle of the Atlantic, unable to go along with my Americans, not totally in tune with Great Britain, and in some ways very close to my Christian friends in Germany. Is it any wonder that I shy away from all possible systems? But I do want to share with my individual readers, and somehow to engage in a one-to-one discussion with each one. I do not offer a system or demand special privileges for myself. I am a believer, an espouser of Progressive Judaism, a worshipper. I do not subscribe to the limited theology of a God who can be fitted into one's vest pocket and produced whenever needed, nor would I ever strip worship and rituals from the word 'God'. My own experience, from my childhood in Nazi Germany to my many travels in the free world of the West which I continue to celebrate, is the assertion of the encounter with the divine, confirmed in my dialogue with Jews and non-Jews, believers and unbelievers, through whom I find myself in the presence of God.

Non-believers may well be annoyed by this assertion; for it would seem that the invincible ignorance of the believer refuses to be touched by the dark denial of the atheist. It is bad enough being rejected, without being used as proof for the opposite contention! But my own faith structure has been strengthened by meetings with the questing minds of scientists, with their challenge to the traditional paradigms of faith which still build on medieval models. If nothing else, they have made me desist using design within the universe – the watchmaker and the watch – as an absolute proof of God's existence. I still have some sympathy for the ontological proof; but my faith does not depend upon this. The universe, as a unique phenomenon, might as easily have a design of chaos as of order; and our faith in the divine Creator is based less on the orderly movement of the stars through their courses than upon the unexpected beauty and uniqueness of every human being which can be encountered in its surpassing goodness or in the raw pain which strikes out in a destructive fashion.

Creation and destruction belong to the same paradigm. The Kabbalists sift through each letter of the story of Creation, in a Torah where the letters are black fire written upon white fire. And I find, with Baeck, that I cannot encounter the Commandments of God without the mystery, and that the mystery has to lead to the commandment.

Original myths are myths because they point to what cannot otherwise be spoken of, what happened in the beginning when the categories of intelligibility which come after do not yet exist. To this extent they must necessarily be resistant to even the most ingenious attempts to get behind them.

The Kabbalist and Karl Barth would look at this same text, and one would speak of the *en sof*, the other of *das Nichtige*, the 'Nothingness' which is part of the Creation; and both assert their faith in God. Despite my admiration for Karl Barth, he cannot be my guide since he puts God too far beyond human reach, beyond the questing mind. And the Kabbalist also rejects human reason and wants me to be overwhelmed by my emotions, wants my surrender. I know that Jewish mysticism strives more for communion with God than for union, for total absorption. But here again I find my refuge in the calm serenity of Leo Baeck, who begins with reason but does not permit it the ultimate rule. He stands in the middle; and so do I.

Paul Johannes Tillich was my teacher in New York. He correlated theology and philosophy, making it a rational enterprise in quest of the ground of being which is God. For many Christians, he seemed to be too open to the outer culture; he was a liberal when the times were against the open mind. His involvement with civil rights, with a fight against the Nazis which made him the first university professor to give up his post for his ideals made him my hero. In the realm of philosophy I happily acknowledge the influence of Christian thinkers and teachers upon my mind. Perhaps that is why I chose to stand between systems, and to see the quest for meaning not confined to one faith or house of prayer. And I do know that wherever I encounter the ethical dimension in a human being, as in Paul Johannes Tillich, that I am also close to God. This is more than a rational perception of the righteous action; it is also the intimation of the divine mystery where the human being strives towards those attributes of God which the Torah ascribes to God, that doing of *chesed* (loving kindness, justice) which comes to be revealed within the basic structure of the universe. Here, religion and science do enter into a partnership. The story of Creation is not an attempt to clarify how the world came into being, but why we exist and are stamped with the divine imprint for good. Science tries to explain natural phenomena within the frame of mathematics, but religion is often less than generous in assessing its own role in relation to the sciences. A mature religion is one where our sense of beauty and feelings of duty cause us to see, beyond our perceptions of the universe, that personal force to which we refer when we talk about God.

The concept of 'miracles' is rather remote to me, particularly when it is claimed in terms of interventions of natural laws, as a proof for the existence of God (which Tillich might have viewed as an atheistic notion, anyway). I could sympathize with Eugene Borowitz when he saw God intervening on behalf of Israel in the Six Day War. I could see it as an aspect of Borowitz's sense of solidarity with the Jewish people, and as his own expression of faith. It caused me far more worry about the future. Of course,

Eugene was a navy chaplain, and it is partly the function of the priests to have God fight on the right side. But, 'miracles'?

A number of years ago, I visited a rabbi friend, Michael Goulston, whom I loved very much, and who was dying of one of those rare diseases which might kill a dozen people in the course of a year. The poet Dannie Abse, who was also a friend of Michael's came along with me. In the course of our visit, we began to discuss miracles, and Dannie was somewhat surprised at the attitude his 'religious' friends took in this matter. Dannie is a secularist. In due course, he wrote a poem about that afternoon's visit, although he changed the rabbi into a priest. It was a justified change, as I think about it. Somehow, it opened the situation more to the average reader. After all, it is no longer thought surprising that a rabbi should reject the notion of miracles which contradict natural laws. But a priest! This was Dannie Abse's poem:

> Last night, the priest dreamed he quit his church
> at midnight, and then saw vividly
> a rainbow in the black sky.
> I said, every day, you can see
> conjunctions equally odd – awake and sane, that is –
> a tangerine on the snow, say.
> Such things, said the priest, do not destroy a man,
> but seeing a rainbow in the night sky
> – awake and sane, that is – why, doctor,
> like a gunshot that could destroy a man.
> That would not allow him to believe in anything,
> neither to praise or to blame. A doctor must believe
> in miracles, but I, a priest, dare not.
>
> Then my incurable cancer patient,
> the priest, sat up in bed, looked to the window,
> and peeled his tangerine, silently.

'Miracles'

I think a lot about my scientist-doctor-poet friend, Dannie Abse. In one of his poems about medicine, an unconscious patient during a brain operation cries out because he claims the lancet touched his soul. In another poem, my secular friend sits in his garden and sees the procession of believers move towards the synagogue on a Saturday, towards the church on Sunday – and he adopts Heine's attitude, a cynical one, watching the religious mob in action. And I still find I can learn much from him, particularly in the field of religion.

The secularist, and the scientist – the two terms are only sometimes congruent – are in some ways better prepared to come out of the darkness and to move towards the dawn. They can be more optimistic because they operate out of an intellectual climate where the capacities of the human being are either viewed in a geological age-span, where humanity has barely begun to exist and has done surprisingly well to stay alive, or out of the context of human limitations where the failures which have taken place are not surprising. The religious traditions which take themselves seriously demand so much of us that the necessary failures must then be judged or dealt with in the next world. Some cling to the belief of the Messiah or the *t'chiat ha-metim*, the physical resurrection after death, as the religious option to which one should return, perhaps the one way to move out from the darkness and to give an adequate answer to the problems the Holocaust sets for us. But I can only live one world at a time. If I accept the neo-Kantian notion that the infinite tasks set for humanity require an infinite time to complete them, this is an intellectual assent which does not enter daily life as the assurance I need in time of pain. I will meet the next world when it comes; but I prefer to keep that event as far possible in the future. Meanwhile, I want as much solved as possible in this world, and I understand the world of today better when I explore the notion of a suffering God, of the *Shechina*, whom I encounter in the dark valleys of human endeavours. The Christian formulation of that aspect of God stays far from me. How can I accept my relative Jesus as God? But I can and do hear God speaking out through my Christian friends who walk a parallel way to mine. And I refuse to join my colleagues who worry away at the flaws they see in the Dawn-Riders who enriched the religious traditions of the Christian world by their courage and self-sacrifice. Bonhoeffer, Niemoeller, Kolbe – they are too often attacked by Jews and Christians who feel that the times were too dark to permit any figures to emit an aura of saintliness. The *advocatus diabolus* works far harder in our time than those who would enshrine noble lives with a mythology which transmits truth in other ways. I do object to the political saints who appear on the horizon from time to time, to political concessions by the Church which obscure the divine image we can find within life, shining through humanity itself.

We cannot fashion God in our image. But I believe that we were fashioned in the image of God and I still believe in the Torah as the place where our ancestors discovered divine revelation and teaching. Torah is another word for revelation. God is revealed in the Torah. Each religion is based upon sacred texts, and these texts are given the authority of the revelation. In Judaism, that involves all of Jewish life, since the Halachah, the walk-way of law which we are supposed to accept, is as sacred at the end as at the beginning. If the Pentateuch is seen as the written law given by God, all of the exposition which went through the proper rabbinical channels is also revelation, the oral law.

On one level, I can simply side here with my Reform theologians, who will fight bravely against the divine infallibility of the Orthodox rabbinate. All of the subtle differences between revelation and divine inspiration as this applies to the Biblical texts can be left to them. For the average reader, or the laity (whichever term applies), one can just point out that the Bible is like no other book. It has an authority over me which rises partly out of the fact that this is what I have inherited, the religious house in which I have grown up, and in which I found so many alternatives that I may well have shaped it after myself even more than it has shaped me. I also respect the tradition of other faiths, and concede that revelation takes place outside of Israel. They have their 'Torah', and we have ours.

The problems which arise here are curious. First, there are times when Christianity tries to take our Torah away from us. These attempts to disinherit the Jew have gone on for two thousand years, and I will not deal with it; it is, after all, more of a Christian problem than a Jewish one. Luther for instance, to distance the reformer from the Nazi mob who claimed him as their patron saint, believed in the New Testament more than in the old one, and set revelation against revelation. If the Hebrew text in Isaiah did indeed say alma – a young woman who could be married – he stoutly asserted that the Gospels had revealed a different truth: the word should have been bethula, a virgin. One had to ignore the flawed Isaiah text and use the new vision from the New Testament. This was not good logic, or good theology.

Until Christianity has rid itself of its burden of 'pre-figuration', of Messianic prophecies which were not prophecies and had nothing to say about the Messiah, there will remain flaws in their faith which are impairments. I can only regret this and trust in the Christian scholars and thinkers whom I have met who try to rebuild a more authentic Christian faith which is built upon historic and theological truth and accurate history.

But all of this is ancillary to our understanding that the religions of the Book (a term coined by Mohammad, whose Islam is also a religion of the Book, the Quoran) have to come to terms with these texts which are their revelation, and which are then explored through centuries in which the new insight is brought into the old text to give it legitimacy. This can also happen within secularism, of course, which can develop its own saints and texts. That these can topple is the current recognition in Europe, where the Communist Manifesto and its saints have literally been smashed to bits, although one cannot rule out a revival in various guises. The world of science too has its 'Torah'. Right now revelations in the field of quantum theory, and the reverberations of the Big Bang have shaken apart many of the scientific theories which were almost considered 'gospel truths'. The 'failure of nerve', so often ascribed to religion, is paralleled when doctors begin to wonder whether their own researchers have helped create the latest plague attacking the human body, and whether the scientific advances of our time, directed towards the consumer market, have torn the ozone layer apart. One need not feel *schadenfreude* – malicious glee at the discomfiture of an opponent. None of us have done too well, and all of us have to reassess our guiding texts.

What is truth? What is revelation? It is not a Pilate question, but an anguished outcry of humanity betrayed by its own intellect. If I posit a possible answer in religion, and assert the religious enterprise with its ethical imperatives and sense of mystery as a partner to science, this must not be seen as a triumphalist stance. We are all scared and scarred. Yet the tempered optimism of a future must be asserted by those who believe, and who want to believe in a future of humanity in a world where the economic separations are lessened, and where mutuality moves to the foreground of human existence. The partnership which is required here moves beyond religious differences and nationalistic divisions. It requires a new openness to the Torah of our neighbours, and an understanding of our own tradition which makes moral demands upon us. These demands are not suggestions on how to get along in the world, on how to be nice to others because it pays. 'Love thy neighbour like yourself. I am the Lord', is an ethical imperative in the Torah which carries divine authority. It is revelation, the commandment combined with the mystery. What is Torah? What is revelation? As the human enterprise moves along its way, all of the Dawn-Riders whom we have followed seem to be carrying some aspect of revelation along with them, pieces of a mosaic which will only be put together at the end of time. The Kohinoor stone was carved out of a much larger precious stone, faceted and brought into greater brilliance, before it was placed into the royal crown of England. Yet any piece of the revelation is a light to follow, and often it is the way, rather than the goal, which matters most. Without the Torah, without the revelation, the journey of the Jew through time and space would have ended a long time ago. And still, the journey itself enlarged that stone of truth, added new layers of insight to it. Rightly understood within the field of religion, we come to see that transmission itself is revelation, because the uniqueness of each human being along the way is added to the revelation. In Judaism, the word Kabbala means 'reception', 'transmission'. It is also the secret, as it is the known truth. The first phrase in the 'Sayings of the Fathers' is: *Moshe kibel Torah*: 'Moses received and transmitted the Revelation.' Each generation carried and advanced the truth, which continued to grow. In Ecclesiastes we read: 'One generation goes, and another one comes; but the earth abides forever'. Leo Baeck pointed out that this could also be read: 'One world comes, and one world goes; but the generations abide forever.' There is a trust here in humanity which must be acknowledged. The command goes out to those who are ready to be commanded. We are in a covenantal relationship to God; and there is a point where agreement from us is necessary. If this is not placed into the book of the Covenant, where it is actually implicit, it must be put into the book of life which is the continual commentary upon the text.

We are that commentary, that text, and Israel is part of the revelation from God. If this seems arrogant, surpassing the claim that the Jews are the Chosen People, the assertion that the Jews are a revelation from God is no more than a restatement of the meaning of Torah. We are the commentary to the text, and the commentary and the text are cut from the same cloth. If I affirm that word, it is more an affirmation of humanity than a chauvinistic proclamation of a fancied superiority. *Every* people is a revelation, has a special purpose in the world, moves towards the dawn in its own way. Jehudah Halevi saw a special quality in his people, the gift of prophecy. Among our Dawn-Riders, we have seen George Steiner proclaim the Jews as the troublers, the conscience of the world. We have seen the special relationship between the people and the land. These assertions can create problems, placed in a political context, made to war with conflicting claims, but this should not obscure the particular truth of the meaning of Israel which others have also tried to claim for themselves. The reception of a revelation can and should transform a people, should give special meaning to that community.

Any community, moving towards universal goals, should be more than the sum of its parts. One cannot attain universalism except through particularism. Just as any individual is unique and special, but moves towards union with other human beings, so a people must move along the same way. Israel is a totality, which, through the centuries, has come to mean the Jewish people within the elliptic pattern of history: in the Holy Land, and in the Diaspora. Together with almost all of the Jewish Dawn-Riders,

I have to accept and to celebrate the oneness of a people who are *arevim zeh lazeh* – bondsmen, guarantors for one another, who ignore their communal responsibilities. Often, this loyalty is misunderstood. It is assumed that it will change our understanding of truth, of obligations towards others; that it will rob us of the function of self-criticism. Sometimes, more often than I would like, this happens. The State of Israel (or rather, some of its leaders) demand unquestioning support of any action by that state. Even if they are wrong, it is suggested, we must not join the hosts of critics arrayed against them; we would be doing common cause with the enemy! That, of course, is nonsense. Part of the support that the Diaspora has to give the beleaguered land is the criticism which can give a better perspective. It can and should be joined with the appreciation and active support of the achievements which, in less than fifty years of an existence always threatened by extinction, has brought a Jewish presence in the world where the attainments far outweigh the wrongs which have arisen out of the political situation of our time.

The Palestinians are also a people. They, too, have an identity. Uri Avneri, a Dawn-Rider who moves against the current of the society in which he lives, gives us a perception of necessary action to be taken for the alleviation of some of the Palestinian suffering. In this, too, Jews and Arabs can and should find a common bond: the exposure to particular suffering has shaped and changed both people. For political reasons, the Palestinians cannot acknowledge, even to themselves, that much of their suffering has come upon them through their Arab brethren. One cannot turn back history, or redress ancient wrongs when they have been incised into that landscape with iron tools, but there can always be a new beginning.

Peoplehood. In a world of burning nationalist conflicts, one might think that we should get away from that term. But how can we? We are a people, even with a religious dimension: 'This people that I have formed for myself, that they may tell My praise' are the prophetic words. If, in a more secular age, the emphasis has shifted away from religion, it has not shifted away from the People Israel who lives in the secular as well as in the religious world.

How far have you travelled with the Dawn-Riders? I want to ask you. Where did you leave them? And which one have you followed to the end? These days, some children's textbooks offer alternative endings – as does the new Holocaust Museum in Washington. As you enter, a computer matches you with one life, and you follow it through to the end, not knowing whether you will reach the dawn. Sometimes, this project worries me: it is too much simulation, a vicarious experience which might deceive the visitor into thinking that the actual Holocaust has been experienced. On the other hand, it does instruct our emotions. In the meantime, this book may enable you to follow certain patterns of action, to enter into contemporary paradigms which can sustain you. I cannot offer the one pathway which leads towards the dawn. There are so many parallel ways. But I can tell you of the way-stations of my own way which was no *via dolorosa*, which was also a Jewish way, but one of the positive walk-ways of Judaism.

I was born during the dusk of the Holocaust, shortly before the darkness came upon the earth. We were all seared by that darkness, but not destroyed by it. Our family fled at the last moment, and the decency and compassion of America enfolded us. And yet, from childhood on, I lived with the knowledge of the Holocaust, and felt the need to share that knowledge. Most of my books have dealt with it, but out of the context of a living Judaism which did not provide all the answers, but certainly pointed towards the dawn which follows the night.

I met the Dawn-Riders. They had gone into the night and, after that, into a deeper night. I cannot divorce my thoughts from that reality, and it returns to me again and again. I see them sitting at my table: Paul Celan, shrouded in deep melancholy; Piotr Rawicz, with his desperate gaiety; Uriel Tal with his profound intelligence which unravelled the Romantic roots of Nazi terror but could not assuage the hurt in his own soul. They could not emerge out of that darkness, even though they travelled towards the dawn. Paul, although he had not been in Auschwitz, could describe all of its aspect so vividly in the 'Death fugue'. I have wept many times. I think that everyone who really strives to know something about the Holocaust will weep with the realization that all of us have something of that darkness within us as we move through life, regardless of our personal history. That is the first lesson of our encounter with that group of men and women I have called the Dawn-Riders.

We awaken in the middle of the night. All is pitch-black around us. And, for one desperate moment, we do not know where we are and *why* we are. Recently, I read an interview with a man who was caring for his father suffering from Alzheimer's syndrome. 'We are the real victims,' he said. 'We, the family. He just walks about in blissful ignorance, but we have to create and recreate his life all the time, without an end to it. The family suffers more than the victim!' I could sympathize with the family in its desperate plight, and honour them for not abandoning their loved one, but I still think the father's plight was worse: to lose one's memory is to lose an aspect of human life which Judaism, in particular, has always placed on the highest level. What would a Jew, the People Israel itself be, if it lost its memory, could no longer say *secher litziat mizraim* ('in memory of the Exodus from Egypt') as part of its prayers? And what would *we* be, as individuals living after the Holocaust, if we did not have memory which links us with the others – the *Sinti-Roma*, homosexuals, all those considered 'less than human' by the Nazis – and if we divorced ourselves from that suffering?

As Jews, we view ourselves as the people of history. 'History', for us, means the generations which have preceded us, as shown in the Hebrew word for history, *toldot*. We are linked with the past as with the present, with all the generations of humanity in their anguish as in their triumphs: we celebrate Creation. And how could we do this without the gift of memory? When, in our prayers, we ask God to remember the merits of our ancestors, up to Abraham, up to his 'sacrifice' of Isaac, there is no concept in our liturgy that God does not remember – we only assert that *we* have not forgotten our past. In the world of today, when we have been diminished by the Holocaust, we express a great sense of loss when we encounter Jews who have forgotten that they are Jews. Even when we recognize their right to leave us we cannot help but feel that they have been maimed in their humanity. All over the world, we see the Jewish community shrinking through intermarriage and through assimilation. There are those who say that it is *because* they remember the Holocaust that they would leave the Jewish community; but that is a loss of faith in humanity and a total mistrust of a world in which they expect another Holocaust. The answer to that fear must be a self-assertion of Jewish identity, a proclamation of trust in God and divine creation.

We are linked to one another through memory, and the moments of 'ontological anxiety' which we encounter must not destroy our identity. That is why Alzheimer's disease is such a dark mirror of the human soul linked to the frailty of our body. And I recognize the anguish of the children linked to the suffering parent – the loss of the parent's memory also destroys the next generation who need that memory. Elie Wiesel's new novel *The forgotten* (1992) describes the close relationship between father and son caught in this darkness. Without once mentioning the name of the disease, he describes it fully:

> Thus did Elhanan helplessly witness his own destruction. Forgetfulness was for him the death not only of knowledge but also of imagination, hence of expectation. Mentally torn, struggling vainly to control his actions, to transform time into consciousness, he submitted himself to constant examinations: What was the name of the man who . . . What

happened on the day when ... His reason, still clear, watched over a shrinking, progressively impoverished memory. In his brain a huge black sponge scrambled words and images. Time no longer flowed, but toppled over the edge of a yawning precipice. Overcome by a sense of inevitability, Elhanan decided that the end was approaching. He was losing sight of his landmarks. Forgetfulness was a worse scourge than madness; the sick man is not somewhere else; he is nowhere. He is not another, he is no-one.[1]

As long as we remain *someone*, as long as there is memory, we remain linked to humanity: and we remember the suffering of others.

The Dawn-Riders taught us that their experience is our experience, and that we will always be part of their company. They transformed their anguish and sorrow into the poetry and theology which permitted them to journey forwards. We cannot accept their gifts unless we take all of that heritage, the sorrow together with the joy. The Dawn-Riders teach us to know ourselves, and not to hide from the demons which lurk within us. We carry our shadows with us. The German author Adalbert von Chamisso created the character of Peter Schlemiel (certainly related to the Jewish line of schlemiels) who sold his shadow to the devil and came to regret it bitterly. Many in post-war Germany did just that in their efforts to evade the past; and we try to do it every day. Again, that is why the Jewish emphasis upon memory is so vital to our identity. *Yizkor*: the liturgical action of remembering the loved ones who have died – is an indispensable part of our tradition. And our individual quest for identity begins with that inner journey towards our origins.

Let us stay with that thought for a moment. In a fractured, uncertain world of shifting boundaries, the search for roots has become the continuing enterprise of communities and of individuals. We resent the ready-made identity which society tries to stamp upon us, the relegation to a set place within the organized structure of corporate business. More than anything else, there is the rejection of dictatorial state structures which robbed so many individuals within Eastern Europe of their private identities. And so, ethnic communities have tried to re-establish themselves on the basis of past history. This had led to gruesome excesses as old enmities are re-kindled – Central Europe bids fair to become a battleground for the next decade as the various minority groups seek their independence. This is not unrelated to our own selves. Having lost ourselves, we must now find ourselves as human beings. (But this does not justify the events in Bosnia!)

The Dawn-Riders, on the whole, had attempted this self-discovery through the choice of a religious option. Having established their identity, against all the odds, they then sought out those aspects of their tradition which could support them in an age of unbelief and amorphous identity. I think of Nelly Sachs here, slowly weaving together a life-line towards the past, turning to the mystic texts which were unknown to her family, creating a space within herself in the Elysian fields of poetry where she could find a fragile security. Few of us can live so completely in the world of letters; but it has become an acceptable road for many whose predilections and temperament keep them more isolated from the community. Abba Kovner, on the other hand, turned towards his people and linked his life with theirs through an active service where he was a communal rather than a private person. It was, again, one way of many. The path can lead through religion, in both ways: a resolve to accept a particular paradigm of religious faith tested in the Holocaust; or self-submission into the group discipline of a communal life where one can have all the assurance of a shared Jewish fate. There, a secular faith can live alongside deep traditional beliefs, and both share in the triumphs and achievement of the community – and suffer the pain of a shared past and present.

There is also the way of doubt.

And there is the way of total unbelief which wants to learn how to live in darkness, since it sees no escape from the night.

The Dawn-Riders have ridden along all these roads, ever pressing towards the light. At times, we may see riders coming back towards us. Are these Kafka's riders, booted and spurred, messengers of the king, ever criss-crossing the shadowed kingdom? Or have they found a new way which first demands a return through the ultimate darkness? Unless we follow them, we will not discover the truth. The others are journeying along a different road. Whom should we follow?

The choice is always ours.

All of us start at the same place: self-knowledge, acceptance of the darkness into which we were born. Job cursed the day on which he was born, 'the night in which it was said "there is a man-child conceived"'. Still alive after all that had befallen him, he then had to decide what course he should follow. For a week he had sat in total silence, outwardly the picture of apathy and defeat, which seemed to the onlookers a natural path to follow. Within Job, an enormous bitterness built up, directed against the religious tradition which his friends represented. In the discussion which followed, they pointed out that they knew the truth, having learned it from the theology books of their time. Suffering was God's punishment for sinners, and Job was suffering. Therefore, he was a sinner. Let him return to the tradition, confess his sins, and the suffering might come to an end. For a mediating alternative, he was offered the advice that suffering purifies; if he did not accept the truth of his sinfulness, he might at least accept the purifying pain of his ordeal, and become a better person who would understand the suffering of others.

Job had made his own choice. He would stand within his own experience, and challenge all of the counsels he was offered. The Book of Job is an existentialist presentation within the field of religion. Anyone, everyman, can approach God directly: and so Job challenged God. Apathy would have buried him in the shell of his body; anger burst through the bonds which had imprisoned him, and he moved into that area where the human being feels the right to challenge God directly, to receive a direct answer. That was a forward move, an outward journey. And God answered Job, which was the justification against the friends who had counselled submission. Job heard the morning stars sing, and he discovered that there is meaning and fulfilment in life even after ultimate darkness has touched body and soul. Job, as we know from the text, was not a Jew, could not subsume his suffering under the doctrine of the 'Suffering Servant' which makes the Jewish people and its prophets liable to carry the burden of vicarious atonement for the sins of humanity. Job was himself. He was a partner in the Covenant of Creation where humanity accepts the tasks to fashion a better world as God's partner. But a partner can ask questions. Job asked, and God answered him.

*Va-yomer Elohim* – 'And God said . . .'. They tell the story of a Hasidic *rebbe* who could not be entrusted with the task of reading the Torah at public services to the congregation. Whenever he came to that most frequent of all phrases in the Pentateuch 'and God said . . .', he would go into ecstasy. 'God said'! 'He really said . . .'; 'He addressed us'; 'God spoke to humans . . .' – he would go on and on without stopping. And why not? This is the central surmise and truth of the religious life. More than the philosophic conclusion that reason can establish the Creator of the universe, it is the assertion of faith that God does not withdraw from the universe, or the countless universes he may have fashioned in time – that God cares, that he enters our world and cares for us – that he speaks to us. 'And God said . . .'.

What did God say to Job, and what does he say to us after the Holocaust? The Biblical answer to Job, which does not appeal that much to the modern temperament, is that the full divine plan is beyond human comprehension, and that Job must take God on trust. The conventional interpretation of the book sees this as a brow-beating of humanity which dismisses the human mind and simply demands obedience from us. Conventional belief and unbelief both view God's speaking out of the whirlwind to Job as that assertion of the unbridgeable difference between God and humans which one either accepts or rejects. But the Book of Job becomes an existential text in which Job is justified because God brushed aside the protestations of the friends and speaks to Job directly. Job's silence at the end of that encounter was different from the silence which preceded his outbreak. At the beginning, he wanted to understand. In the end, he understood. And that is a testimony which we can take into our lives.

Job is not the answer to the Holocaust. The Book of Job is not even the book towards which we turn for instruction in our time. The book is there for an individual who has gone through the darkness. We, who have not suffered in that fashion, are not entitled to make his answer our own. Of course we can see Job as a Dawn-Rider – but then we must first follow him through the darkness. The answer given by Job cannot be transferred easily; we cannot pretend to be the children of Job.

Perhaps we are the children of Ezekiel, the prophet who lived after the Holocaust of his time, and tried to bind up the wounds of the Jewish people. He taught them how to live in exile, how to pray in foreign lands and be part of a new place in which Jewish life could flourish. And he taught the Jewish people, in the teaching of the 'Valley of Dry Bones', that the People Israel would live again, and that they would come to live in their land, since the land – that land – was part of Jewish existence. Job and Ezekiel shared the basic truth of *homo religiousus*: God entered into dialogue with them, and the life of the individual and of the people thus acquired the religious dimension which we posit as the heart of Jewish life: the knowledge of God. In our own assertions, at the end of a long quest, I here return to the traditional exposition of a person who has faith, and talk about God, Torah, and Israel as they are part of my own stance in this world where I can travel with absolute despair to a kind of tempered optimism.

In my mind's eye there arises the vision of Israel as depicted in the first chapter of the Book of Numbers, with each tribe following its flag and led by its leaders; the Jews outside Israel who have established their place within the People Israel through their many contributions and through their support of the Jewish community in Israel.

Peoplehood. It is not based upon race, but upon adherence to the totality, by a proud claim of Jewish identity which need not necessarily conform to the traditional Halachah. There are limits: you follow your own flag, not another standard. The 'Messianic Jew', the 'Jew for Christ', has joined another company, which may well find a way towards the dawn, which is

linked with other communities, but parallel to ours. The Messianic Jew
has rejected the basic structure of Jewish peoplehood, and I can pity the
lonely road which often finds rejection from Christianity as well as from
Judaism. Peoplehood is defined by God, not only by the individual. My
traditionalist friends are unhappy about my ideology, but see me as a Jew
not just by ancestry but also by my faith: an errant faith, but one which
still gives them hope that I may 'repent'. I won't; but I am still part of the
Jewish people.

This, then, is the journey which I go on towards the dawn. I follow many
of the Dawn-Riders, but only those which lead me in the general direction
indicated to me by my very special companions. Elie Wiesel, my *rebbe*,
understood that my pattern of life differs from his, that the paradigm of
belief which I have come to acquire draws from different lands and situations than his own. But Elie looks at the heart, at the intention; and he
approves of me. How can I convey what I have learned on the way? Make
your own choice. Choose a Dawn-Rider whom you can follow. Do not stay
with one person alone: we need many friends along the way. There are the
poets who suddenly confront you with burning beauty that is more than a
vision of the night – it is Job hearing the morning stars singing. There is
the philosopher who weans you from the notion of your original sin, who
makes you accept the fact of human weakness and a life of exile: 'We are
cut out of warped wood (to use Kant's metaphor) and do not deserve to
live a carefree, happy, and idle life'. Don't think that advice is absurd. It
comes from a great contemporary thinker, Leszek Kolakowski. He also
showed me, once, that it is easier to believe in the devil than to believe in
God – but I did not want any easy belief. In any event, read Kolakowski's
*Religion* and explore new options.

I have tried to present you with my personal odyssey. It started with
despair. Unlike so many others, it did not go through the concentration
camp, although the forecourts of hell are bad enough. And I was surrounded
and protected from infancy through the link with my mother (I *still* dislike
jokes about the Jewish mother – even when I tell them). I must also confess
that I have always found support in the outside world, and that has wreaked
havoc with the creation of philosophic pattern for a dark time such as this.
I have moved from the necessary despair of a spark escaped out of the fire
into a tempered optimism which hopes in the world and believes in the
neighbour.

We have lost our way. Why, then, do I claim that the dawn is just beyond
the horizon? The simple answer is to say that I am Jewish. There is a joy
of life within us which rises out of our community, built upon our knowledge

that we are survivors, and that we can trust each other. Of course we will be disappointed – but not always. And one cannot live in distrust. There is the knowledge that we live within a Covenant, and that we can trust our partner – God. And, of course, we will be disappointed. In ourselves, in the situations in which we find ourselves, in the grief which we will encounter. Partly, that is because we do not fully understand ourselves, and demand joy without achievements, something which Bonhoeffer called 'easy grace'.

And I will find fulfilment in the journey, even when it does not reach the goal. So much is happening along the way, so many encounters are waiting for us. Many of the Dawn-Riders who instruct us did not get to this part of the road, but sent their messages ahead of them, out of the darkness, towards the light. They depend upon being heard. We, the remembrancers, will carry their lives along and mourn the darkness which destroyed them, to celebrate the goodness which endures.

NOTES

1. E. Wiesel, *The forgotten* (New York, 1992), pp. 197–198.

# GLOSSARY OF HEBREW TERMS

*Akedah* 'The Testing'. Refers to the story of God testing Abraham's ability to sacrifice Isaiah to Him.

*Aliyah* 'Going up'. Refers to the call-up to the reading of the Torah, which is given as an honour. The term can also be used to mean the 'going up' to settle in the promised land.

*Alma* 'Young woman' (Biblical term).

*Amida* 'Standing prayer'. The central part of Jewish liturgy.

*Apikoros* 'Questioner' and 'challenger of faith'.

*Baale teshuvah* 'Repenters'. A term used nowadays to describe assimilated Jews who have been born again by 'returning' to strict Orthodox practice.

*Barmitzvah* (fem. *Batmitzvah*) 'Son of the commandment' ('daughter of the commandment'). The definition of a Jew after the age of 13, when he (or she) can be called to the reading of the Torah in the synagogue. The term also describes the ceremony itself.

*Battai* 'Daughters'.

*Bethulah* 'Virgin'.

*Bi'sh'gaga* 'By mistake'.

*B'nei rachamim* 'Sons of loving kindness'. A description of those who follow the basic Jewish teaching of showing compassion to all of humanity.

*Chassidei umot ha-olam* 'The righteous among the nations of the world' – those who saved Jews and others during the Holocaust.

*Chesed* 'Compassion' or 'loving kindness'.

*Chevlei hamasiach* 'The suffering of the Messiah'. Refers to the idea of suffering being part of a Messiah's task.

*Churban* 'Destruction'. In religious literature, this term can refer to the Holocaust, and also to the destruction of the first and second Temples.

*Dayanim* 'Judges'. Nowadays, this refers to the scholars forming the rabbinic courts of Orthodoxy.

*Din toirah* 'Legal dispute' before a rabbinical court. The term is sometimes used to mean an argument with God.

*Dybbuk* 'Evil spirit'. In the traditional teaching of the transmigration of souls, this is the spirit of a dead person which enters a living body.

*El Mistater* 'The hiding God' in mystic teaching – one who has turned away from humanity for a time at a particular point in history.

*El mole rachamim* The opening words of prayer in funeral liturgy, which stress the idea of the soul being given eternal life by a compassionate God.

*Emunah* 'Faith'.

*En sof* 'The unending one'. A basic teaching of the Transcendent God.

*Galut* 'Exile'. A term that can be applied to Jews living outside Israel. It can mean 'living far from God'.

*Ge'ula* 'Redemption'.

*Golem* A mythical figure. The 'golem of Prague' were fashioned out of clay by Rabbi Loew and given life to serve the people. The term can be applied derisively to a clumsy person.

*Haggadah* The book recited at a home Passover Seder, when the story of the Exodus is told in great detail.

*Haim* 'Life'. *L'hai* means 'to life'.

*Halachah* 'The way of the law' according to the tradition as observed by rabbis, which arises out of halachic discussions in the Talmudic and post-Talmudic texts.

*Hamasiach* 'The anointed one'. The Messiah from the royal family of David. David.

*Harachamim* 'The merciful one'. A term for God.

*Hasidism* (adj. *Hasidic*) A movement which started among the Jews in eighteenth century Eastern Europe, and stresses piety and learning.

*Ha-tzur tamim* 'The rock he is perfect'. Part of funeral liturgy.

*Hurban* See *churban*.

*Illui* 'Illuminated one'. Young genius, often Talmudist.

*Kabbala* 'That which has been received'. A technical term for the Jewish mystic tradition.

*Kahal* Assembly governing community.

*Kal v'chomer* 'From light to heavy'. Rabbinic argument in the field of hermeneutics.

*Kehillah* 'Community', 'Congregation'.

*K'llal Yisrael* 'All of Israel' – the totality of Jewish communal life.

*L'rey-acha* 'Your neighbour'.

*Mathmid* 'Student'. Often one immersed in deep Talmudic study with great fervour.

*Midat* 'Attribute' (of God). For example, *midat harchamim*, God's attribute of mercy.

*Midrash* 'Exegesis'. The genre of rabbinic literature of homilies, legends and other interpretations of Biblical texts.

*Mipne chattaenu* 'Because of our sins'.

*Mishnah* 'Teaching'. The collective name of the 63 tractates, divided into six main sections, compiled c. 200 CE as a source of Jewish Law.

*Palmach* The 'striking force' of the Israeli army.

*Rabbi* 'My teacher'. The technical term used to describe the religious leader of a congregation of Jews. The title can only be bestowed by other rabbis after a thorough examination of the candidate's knowledge of all aspects of Jewish tradition.

*Rebbe* Diminuitive form of 'Rabbi', honorary title used in Eastern Europe, particularly for Hasidic teachers.

*Shechina* Term for the divine presence, with special reference to God's presence in the world.

*Seder* Ceremonial meal on the first night of the Passover.

*Shabbat* The Sabbath, the seventh day of the week, the day of rest.

*Shakla v'tarya* 'Rabbinic argumentation' used in the Talmud.

*Sh'lilat ha-galut, sh'lilat had-golah* 'Negation of exile, of the Diaspora'.

*Shoah* Technical term for Holocaust.

*Sinti-Roma* Two major tribes of the group often called 'gypsies'.

*Statlanut* 'Representation'.

*Tallit* The traditional Jewish prayer shawl.

*Talmud* After the conclusion of the *Mishnah*, schools in Babylonia and Palestine continued to discuss its content and harmonize it with other sources. The record of these discussions, together with the text of the *Mishnah*, is known as the Talmud. The Babylonian (and more authoritative) version was completed in the sixth century; the Palestinian some 150 years earlier.

*T'chiat ha-metim* 'The resurrection of the dead'. An ancient Jewish belief.

*Tenach* The entire Hebrew bible, with its three divisions: Torah (Pentateuch), N'vi-im (Prophets), Kh'tuvim (Writings).

*Teshuvah* 'Repentance', and also, a 'turning'.

*Tisha B'Av* The ninth of Av, the day of mourning when the Temple in Jerusalem was destroyed (by the Babylonians in 586 BCE, and the Romans in 70 CE).

*Tochacha* 'Admonition', usually divine.

*Toldot* 'History'.

*Torah* 'Instruction'. The Hebrew word for Pentateuch. It can also be used to mean the entire transmitted Jewish tradition (where the Pentateuch is called the 'written Torah' and the Talmud, 'oral Torah').

*Tremendum* A theological term. The *Mysterium tremendum* describes the inexpressible which is encountered in revelation. The Holocaust is often referred to as a *tremendum* of evil, which cannot be fully understood or expressed.

*Tzadikim* 'Righteous ones'. This can apply to Hasidic leaders.

*Tzimtzum* The Hasidic teaching of God withdrawing to make room for His creation.

*Va-yidom* 'And he was silent' (Aaron). Short scripture verse which describes the silence of Aaron on the death of his sons.

*Va-yomer Elohim* 'And God said'. The most frequently occuring phrase in the Pentateuch.

*Yemach sh'mo* 'May his name be blotted out'. An expletive.

*Yeshiva* 'Place of study' in Jewish life. Can mean a training school for rabbis.

*Yetzer* 'Inclination'. *Yetzer ha-tov* means the inclination towards good; *yetzer ha-ra*, the inclination towards evil.

*Yisrael Mensch* Image of the devout Jew, used by the German teacher S. R. Hirsch.

*Yizkor* Memorial prayer for the dead.

*Yom Ha-Shoah* Memorial day for the Holocaust, which occurs in April.

*Yom Kippur* Day of Atonement. The holiest day in the Jewish calendar, a 25-hour fast.

# INDEX

Haganah (Jewish defence force), 227, 241
Haggadah, 21, 22, 24
Haigh, Field-Marshal Douglas, 196
Halachah (Jewish law), 41, 51, 54, 59, 77,
   118, 202, 205, 206, 299, 304, 313; of
   the Holocaust, 45, 66, 67–77
Halevi, Yehuda (Judah/Jehudah), 12, 19,
   52, 129, 132, 226, 306
Al Halladsch, 12
Hamburger, Michael, 261
Haolam Hazeh ('This World'), 241
Harries, Bishop Richard, 198–9
Harris, Air Marshal 'Bomber', 198
Hebrew language, 229, 230, 233, 234,
   236, 238, 255
Hebrew Theological College, Stokie, 59,
   155
Hebrew Union College, Cincinnati, 127,
   129, 131, 134, 135, 136, 137, 150–1,
   152, 153, 155, 156, 163
Hecht, Ben, 150
Hegel, Friedrich, 47
Heidegger, Martin, 193
Heidelberg, University of, 134, 151, 176
Heimler, Eugene ('John'), 82–3, 85,
   90–4, 295; 'Memories without hate',
   91; Night of the mist, 90, 91
Heimler Method, 91–2
Heine, Heinrich, 167, 227, 303
Heinemann, Gustav, 108, 290
Hersey, John, The wall, 162
Herzl, Theodor, 246
Herzog, Chaim, President of Israel,
   224–5
Heschel, Abraham, 151, 290
Heschel, Joshua, 18
Hess, Moses, 246
Himmler, Heinrich, 61
Hiroshima and Nagasaki, 18, 37, 156
Hirsch, Rabbi, 75
Hirsch, Samson Raphael, 133
Hitler, Adolf, 13, 43, 44, 47, 79, 80, 86,
   95, 100, 101, 102, 105, 106, 107, 108,
   109, 116, 117, 119, 120, 123, 134,
   147, 209, 210
Hobbes, Thomas, Leviathan, 294
Hochhuth, Rolf, 98; The representative,
   98–9
Holocaust Museum, Washington, 307–8
homosexuals, 96, 108, 110, 288
Honecker, Erich, 171, 173, 180; show
   trial of, 170–1, 180

el-Hosseini, Amin, Grand Mufti of
   Jerusalem, 44, 47
Hranich, Ukrainian poet, 23–4
Huizinga, Johan, 178
Hume, Cardinal Basil, 199–200
Hume, David, 125
Husserl, Edmund, 193
Hutner, Rav, 42–5, 46, 57, 298–9

Immer, Karl, 100
'In the gardens of the Finzi-Cortini', 222
Irgun Zvai Leumi, 238, 241
Islam/Muslims, 14, 44, 118–19, 120,
   121, 193, 304
Israel, 14, 19–20, 34, 42, 43, 44, 47, 53,
   54, 59–60, 62, 65, 68–9, 70, 80,
   117–18, 120, 121, 122–3, 128–9,
   130, 141, 142, 143, 157, 164, 165,
   202, 223–53, 275, 296; and the
   Diaspora, 68, 204, 225, 226, 240,
   245, 247–8, 250, 251–2, 284, 296,
   306–7; Eichmann trial (1961), 248,
   284; and Germany, 173, 174, 182,
   184, 246–7; Lochamei Hagetaot,
   243–4; Munich Massacre of Olympic
   team, 249; Museum of the Diaspora,
   246; Six Day War (1967), 80, 127,
   165, 171, 277, 301; and USA, 148,
   165, 224, 252; writers in, 225–42;
   Yad VaShem, 42, 142, 187, 244–6;
   Yom Kippur War (1973), 165, 249
Israeli Symphony Orchestra, 224
Italy, 14, 209–22

Jakobovits, Lord Immanuel, Chief Rabbi
   of Britain, 53–8, 200, 201, 202
Jerusalem, 42, 60, 117, 118, 121, 223,
   233, 235, 252–3, 296; Hebrew
   University, 226, 230; Jewish World
   Congress (1986), 171; Old Testament
   Congress (1986), 171; Wailing Wall,
   252; Yad VaShem, 42, 142, 187, 244,
   245–6
Jewish Agency, 243
Jewish Brigade, 233
Jewish Theological Seminary, New York,
   18, 131, 151, 155, 157, 163
Jewish World Congress, Jerusalem
   (1986), 171
Jonas, Hans, 295
Josephus, 220–1
Joshua, Rabbi, 72–3, 74